Praise for Raquel Cepeda's
"honest, passionate, and moving"* memoir

"Snappy, jazzy. . . . Asserts that constructing one's identity requires expressing and celebrating its makeup. . . . A spirited memoir deeply committed to personal self-worth."

—*Kirkus Reviews*

"Revealing."

—*Ms.* magazine

"What will stay with the reader is Cepeda's tale of how a girl becomes a woman, and how a child who grew up in the least promising of circumstances grew up to become an artist. . . . Just as Junot Díaz uses New York City as a character in his work, so that enormous and demanding city comes alive in *Bird of Paradise*."

—*Ebony**

"At a time when Latinas of any age struggle with owning our voice and our identity and dealing with the mixed messages we get from this country—'We love you, we hate you! Stay! Go!'—Raquel Cepeda opens her heart and shows us all a new and real path toward the *futuro*, the future. I believe this book is transformational and will not only change lives, but save them too."

—Maria Hinojosa, award-winning journalist and NPR and PBS anchor

"I'm so appreciative of the book. It's the science of the DNA. It's the personal narrative of the finding of the finding of the self. It's a little bit of hip-hop thrown in there. It's all those different things. It is really a lovely book."

—Melissa Harris-Perry, host of MSNBC's *Melissa Harris-Perry*

"Cepeda's complex family history is both uniquely Latino—the book is peppered with Spanish idiom—and paradoxically universal in this nation of immigrants. It will appeal to those who watch *Who Do You Think You Are?* and wonder about themselves."

—*Library Journal*

"Cepeda writes of her troubled upbringing with divorced Dominican parents, then delves energetically into DNA testing for a deeper search into her African roots. . . . Her intrepid journey . . . will surely be useful for her readers."

—*Publishers Weekly*

"There's something about Cepeda's storytelling—laced with poetry and profanity in the best way possible—that conjures up Junot Díaz. Still, this story, the heartbreaking memoir, and the investigation into the racial and ethnic makeup of the Dominican people, is totally original. Trust me, you'll love it."

—*My American Meltingpot*

"Cepeda's family, her culture, and her childhood experiences all spur her quest to learn just what it means to be of Dominican heritage."

—*International Society of Genetic Genealogy*

"In *Bird of Paradise*, Raquel Cepeda takes on, with cultural flair and brutal honesty, what it means to be the living embodiment of a global society. What she finds is a revelation not just for her or for Latino Americans, but for anyone who cares about the way the past connects us to the future."

—Farai Chideya, author of *Kiss the Sky*

"A thrilling and impassioned quest into the heart of the race question and the Latino—a label as we've come to understand it. With meticulous research and refreshing honesty, Cepeda breaks the code not only of her own origins, but those of an entire people. *Bird of Paradise* is a necessary and important book for our time."

—Patricia Engel, author of *Vida*

"I applaud Raquel Cepeda's courage and brilliance. This is an important book, shedding light on questions that many us ask ourselves, but seldom speak about out loud."

—Marcus Samuelsson,
New York Times bestselling author of *Yes, Chef*

"Raquel Cepeda has long been one of the hip-hop community's most passionate and visionary writers and filmmakers; now, with this stunning blend of memoir and reportage, mythos and Logos, we will have to share her with the world. An elegant, electric mash-up, *Bird of Paradise* offers resonant snapshots of a bygone New York City, family portraits saturated with beauty, honesty, and pain, captivating travelogues, and a fascinating, wide-angled look at ethnicity and identity. Cepeda's story is wrought with care and insight—and ought to increase the sale of DNA testing kits by about twelve thousand percent."

—Adam Mansbach,
#1 *New York Times* bestselling author of *Go the F**k to Sleep*

"Unflinching and immediate as the hip-hop pulsing through its pages, *Bird of Paradise* is all about straddling fences: Santo Domingo and Washington Heights, Cepeda's complicated father and her capricious mother, and finally—grandly, bravely—she explores the complex genetics that make her Latina."

—Ayana Mathis, nationally bestselling author of
The Twelve Tribes of Hattie

"An impressive story of self-understanding and redemption. Cepeda's mix of New York's hip-hop slang and Latino ghetto language with an extremely rich and sophisticated style has produced a rare piece of high-level American contemporary literature."

—Frank Moya Pons, author and foremost historian of
Dominican and Caribbean history

"An amazing book that deals in-depth with DNA, identity, and how it can all tie into your perception of yourself."

—rookiemag.com

"A tale of self-discovery through the many racial, ethnic, and linguistic conflicting forces that lie at the heart of US Latino identity, as well as the story of a personal struggle against a supposed *fukú*, or ancestral curse, that has haunted the author's families for generations."

—Claudio Remeseira, NBC Latino

Also by Raquel Cepeda

*And It Don't Stop: The Best American Hip-Hop
Journalism of the Last 25 Years*

Bird of Paradise

HOW I BECAME LATINA

Raquel Cepeda

ATRIA PAPERBACK
NEW YORK   LONDON   TORONTO   SYDNEY   NEW DELHI

ATRIA PAPERBACK
A Division of Simon & Schuster, Inc.
1230 Avenue of the Americas
New York, NY 10020

First Atria Paperback edition February 2014

ATRIA PAPERBACK and colophon are trademarks of Simon & Schuster, Inc.

For information about special discounts for bulk purchases, please
contact Simon & Schuster Special Sales at 1-866-506-1949 or
business@simonandschuster.com.

The Simon & Schuster Speakers Bureau can bring authors to
your live event. For more information or to book an event, contact
the Simon & Schuster Speakers Bureau at 1-866-248-3049 or
visit our website at www.simonspeakers.com.

Designed by Kyoko Watanabe

10 9 8 7 6 5 4 3 2 1

The Library of Congress has cataloged the hardcover edition as follows:

Cepeda, Raquel.
    Bird of paradise : how I became Latina / Raquel Cepeda.—1st Atria Books hardcover ed.
    p. cm.
    Includes index.
    1. Cepeda, Raquel. 2. Cepeda, Raquel—Family. 3. Hispanic American women—
Biography. 4. Hispanic American women—Ethnic identity. 5. Hispanic Americans—
Biography. 6. Hispanic Americans—Ethnic identity. 7. Genetic genealogy. I. Title.
CT275.C383A3 2013
    305.48'868073—dc23   2012034482

ISBN 978-1-4516-3586-7
ISBN 978-1-4516-3587-4 (pbk)
ISBN 978-1-4516-3588-1 (ebook)

Because of Djali and Marceau . . .

For my little sisters at Life is Precious: you are loved.

Always in your stomach and skin there was a sort of protest, a feeling that you had been cheated of something that you had a right to. It was true that he had no memories of anything greatly different. . . . Why should one feel it to be intolerable unless one had some kind of ancestral memory that things had once been different?

—GEORGE ORWELL, *1984*

As all historians know, the past is a great darkness, and filled with echoes. Voices may reach us from it; but what they say to us is imbued with the obscurity of the matrix out of which they come; and try as we may, we cannot always decipher them precisely in the clearer light of our day.

—MARGARET ATWOOD, *THE HANDMAID'S TALE*

CONTENTS

Part I

Part II

AUTHOR'S NOTE

The events in this book are all true. My word is bond. The story of the car wreck that was my parents' relationship was constructed by interviewing the two of them and other family members. The story about the Indian couple in Chapter 1 was one of the few incidents that both of my parents recounted with no bias or variation. Some of the sequences have been rearranged, and in most cases, I changed the names and certain identifying details to protect the innocent and the guilty. Doña Amparo is a composite of a few elderly women in the 'hood.

On another note, I capitalized the word "Black"—as I would, say, African-American—throughout the book. I believe that "Black" is used interchangeably, like "Hispanic" and "Latino/a" are, as an identifier for a larger ethnic group bound by their shared transatlantic experience with slavery. I don't think the same is true when it comes to whiteness. I also use the term Native and Indigenous American interchangeably, preferring the latter but using the former sometimes so as not to confuse readers.

Last, I prefer to use "Latino" and "Latina" over "Hispanic," although I don't find the latter offensive. I personally identify as a Latina when I'm in the company of other Americans, a Dominican-American when I'm in the Dominican Republic or here, in the company of other folks whose parentage hails from Latin America. And sometimes I identify as a *pura dominicana* when I'm in my 'hood.

PREFACE

> Who in the world am I? Ah, *that's* the great puzzle.
>
> —LEWIS CARROLL, *ALICE IN WONDERLAND*

AS I WRITE THIS, MY THREE-MONTH-OLD SON IS STARING AT ME intensely from his bouncy seat. He's cooing loudly, like he's trying to tell me something important, something he'll forget by the time he utters his first word. Marceau has been here before. Of this, I am sure.

The left half of our brains, programmed to think that seeing is believing, would dismiss this kind of thinking as esoteric new age bullshit. However, there's the other half that can't dismiss the idea that there just might be something to it. Many of us have recognized old souls in babies and children. We've felt the presence of some force, be it a spiritual guide or God, intervening in our lives at some point. When I look over at my son in his bouncer, I'm reminded of what a rabbi in Brooklyn, a seer in Fez, and a santero in Queens told me with slight variation when I was writing this book. We travel with the same clan over and over again, from one life into the next, until some ultimate purpose is fulfilled and we no longer need to return. When we illuminate the road back to our ancestors, they have a way of reaching out, of manifesting themselves . . . sometimes even physically.

Last year I embarked on an archaeological dig of sorts, using the science of ancestral DNA testing to excavate as many parts of my genetic history as I could in the span of twelve months. The DNA kits I collected were processed by Family Tree DNA, a Houston-based commercial genetic genealogy company. The company's founder and CEO, Bennett Greenspan, provided further analysis. I tested myself, my father, a paternal great-uncle I hadn't met until the beginning of my project, and a maternal cousin I found on Facebook. I wanted to learn as much as I could about my ancestors' origins *before* we became Latino.

I've always been intrigued by the concept of race, especially in my own community and immediate family, where it's been a source of contention for as long as I can remember. The United States has the second highest Latino population in the world, second only to Mexico. And still, the media—they lump us all together into one generic clod—doesn't get us, either. Are Latino-Americans white? Black? Other? Illegal aliens from Mars? Or are we the very face of America?

Some see Latinos as the embodiment of this young country's cultural melting pot. And though Mexicans have been residing here since before the arrival of the first Europeans, many of our fellow Americans view Latinos as public enemies. What our parents see isn't necessarily what we first- and second-generation American-born Latinos see when looking at ourselves in the mirror. According to the 2010 census, over half of all Latinos here identified as being solely white, and about a third checked "Some Other Race." I was one of the three million, or 6 percent, who reported being of multiple races. I guess it all depends on whom you ask and when you ask. Race, I've learned, is in the eye of the beholder.

I don't look all the way white or all the way Black; I look like someone who's a bit of both and then some—an *Other.* In Europe, people have mistaken me for Andalusian, Turkish, Brazilian, and North African. In North and West Africa, I've been asked if I'm of Arabic or Amazigh descent. In New York, Los Angeles, and Miami, it varies: Israeli or Sephardic, Palestinian, Moroccan, biracial Black and white American, Brazilian, and so on. I've been mistaken for being everything except what I am: Dominican. My own racial ambiguity has been a topic of conversation since I was a teenager. Blending in has filled the pages in my book of life with misadventures and the kind of culturally enriching experiences that make me feel, truly, like a world citizen.

In more recent times, I found the idea that we live in a so-called post-racial society downright fascinating. I suspect someone at the White House or Disney created that catchphrase after the election of President Barack Obama, to fool us into thinking we're now living in a parallel universe where race is suddenly a nonfactor. The term "post-racial" is an epic failure. More than four years after the fact, our first Black president's skin tone is still getting people punch-drunk with hate. It has fueled the dramatic rise in hate groups and the revival of the so-called Patriot movement. Sure, our sucky-ass economy factors in to the foaming-at-the-mouth vitriol against President Obama, but there's something else contributing to the mainstream's arrogant contempt for him. As intangible and trivial as our differences are, we cannot pretend that race doesn't matter anymore.

The exploration of and how we choose to identify ourselves is something else that compelled me to set upon this journey. Our identities are as fluid as our personal experiences are diverse. How I arrived at my own is one of 50.5 million possibilities. While Latino-Americans share enough cultural traditions to relate with one another and whatnot, we are also crazy different. One size doesn't fit all. That's why Part I of this book is a memoir. I grew up in a household where I was discouraged from celebrating, much less expressing, the Dominican half of my hyphenated identity. I was, quite frankly, sweated hard to mask it. In the first part of the book, I detail how I resisted the pressure to bend and how I constructed my own identity. My parents' Dominican roots, my father's apparent low self-esteem and hatred, '80s hip-hop culture, and growing up in my beloved New York City are all significant.

The results of our ancestral DNA tests are outlined in Part II.

Both of my parents were born close to the site of the first European settlement in the Americas, Santo Domingo, on the island of

Hispaniola. The Indigenous people we now refer to as Taínos—they stumbled upon and were subsequently duped by Columbus and his crew—originally inhabited the island. Our eastern part of the island is also the wellspring of blackness in the New World (and the site of the first slave rebellion on record). Modern-day Dominican Republic is also where English pirates, Europeans, crypto-Jews and Muslims, Arabs, Asians, our Haitian counterparts, and people from all over the world contributed to the cultural and racial tapestry of her people. With this in mind, I had absolutely no idea what I would find in my own DNA.

I'll share one of the results here. What I didn't expect to find, other than in spirit, was a direct link to the Indigenous peoples of the island. I've been taught over the years that the Spanish, through disease and genocide via slavery, killed off virtually all Taíno people throughout the Caribbean; they basically do not exist and are figments of our self-loathing imagination. When I saw an episode in Henry Louis Gates, Jr.'s series *Black in Latin America* focusing on the Dominican Republic and Haiti, I heard it again.

The documentary opened with Gates mistakenly calling a Cuban *guaguancó* a Dominican merengue (the mistake was later corrected). While I tried not to see that musical snafu as an omen of things to come, I couldn't help but brace myself. I was certain that Gates, a man who's become famous for connecting celebrities with their ancestral past, would shed some light on the complexities of identity and race in the Dominican Republic. I thought he would wax poetic on how racially diverse we are and how, thanks to ancestral DNA studies being done on the island, we are finding that significant numbers of people carry indigenous mitochondrial DNA. *Indios* have, alas, found ways to survive, like everything else on the island—in fragments.

As Gates strolled down *Calle Conde* with an employee from the Ministry of Culture named Juan Rodriguez, he asked the man how he'd be identified or racially categorized on the island. Rodriguez, a dark-caramel-complected man, replied, "*indio.*" Rodriguez went on to state that by the nineteenth century, there were no more Indigenous people left on the island like there were in South America, so

Dominicans used the term to negate their blackness. Yeah, I know many *dominicanos* and other Latinos who deny their blackness, but the conversation could have been pushed further by exploring the reasons *why*, adding to the complex narrative about race and identity in our community. It would have been less archaic. A conversation with younger Dominicans and transnational Dominican-Americans about how and why these ideals are shifting would have been less archaic. That cipher never went down.

At the time of this writing, the Dominican government has passed a bill called the Dominican Republic Electoral Law Reform, eradicating the term *indio* on its citizens' ID cards. The categories mulatto, black, and white will be the only ones people will have to choose from. I find it troubling that if I wish to officially recognize the Indigenous fragment of myself, it won't be legal. Foisting an identity on people rather than allowing them the freedom and space to create their own is shady.

Henry Miller, in his book *Big Sur and the Oranges of Hieronymus Bosch*, wrote: "One's destination is never a place but rather a new way of looking at things." This journey—as the most unforgettable ones often do—led me to places I hadn't expected to go. The skeleton of this book is my exploration of the concept of race, identity, and ancestral DNA among Latinos, using my own story as one example. Race and identity have been a source of bitterness between my father and me since before I can remember. How I arrived at some sort of understanding and peace with Dad, something that never would have happened had I not invited him to take this trip with me, is the proverbial meat on the bones. I look over at Marceau, thankful that this illuminating ride has stopped here, in a place where *logos* and *mythos* exist in tandem, guiding me from one place to another with purpose.

PART I

~

CHAPTER ONE

Love, American-Style

> Every wo/man is the architect of her own fortune.
>
> —*Appius Claudius Caecus*, REMIXED

MY STORY BEGINS BEFORE I WAS BORN, SOMEWHERE IN BETWEEN my parents' memories of when they met and how, with the quickness, they fell in and out of love.

Rocío stares out a window of the new apartment she shares with her husband, Eduardo, in Washington Heights. Looking to her right, she can see that the slabs of concrete lining Broadway are littered with trees in full bloom. On her left, a groundswell of people moving about in tribes of four and five women, with as many children, are bustling toward 181st Street, the shopping district for folks who rarely leave the relative comfort of their neighborhood.

"Everybody's always in a rush in this city," Rocío says to her husband. "People rarely make eye contact with each other here, like my *vecinos* did back home in Santo Domingo."

Eduardo shrugs, only half listening.

Everything here is foreign to Rocío. The streets are dirty, and the trains are full of *jodedores* who look you up and down like they're planning to stick your ass up or worse. But here, lounging across from her *papi chulo*, the teenager feels impervious to the dangers lurking in the strange new city. She is full of hope, with me growing in her impossibly large belly.

Rocío looks over at her *bonbón*, Eduardo, sitting cross-legged on the couch, reading a newspaper. She spends most of her days thinking of their kismet meeting back home, how it all happened so fast. Reliving the fairy tale helps Rocío get through the hours she spends cleaning other people's apartments and working at the *fábrica*. Today she wouldn't recognize her life back in the Dominican Republic if it played before her on a screen.

It was all Paloma's fault, the meeting. Although she was less than a year younger than Rocío, the two sisters were nothing alike. Paloma was the wild child to Rocío's *santa* in training. A crazy-popular teenager in their *barrio* of Paraíso and at the local country club, Paloma was more interested in being the neighborhood census taker—she made it her business to know everybody, and everybody knew her—than a good or even fair student. Sometimes opposites attract, or so they say, but Paloma and Rocío were like *arroz* and *mangú*: they didn't really mix well.

Mother Nature had been much kinder to Paloma than to Rocío. Paloma developed into a bottom-heavy human hourglass with golden skin like fried ripe *maduros*, skipping that awkward phase that vexed most of her peers, aside from being bucktoothed, which was sort of sexy in a weird way. Her laugh was a contagious roar erupting deep from within like lava, complementing the girl's joie de vivre. What Paloma did have in common with her older sister and their baby brother, Antonio, were those amazing eyes. When any of them grinned or laughed, their eyes moored into a slant that evoked an alleged maternal ancestor who made the impossible trip to the island from a place called Indochina, *di'que*.

Right before she met Eduardo, Rocío had been slowly recovering from an onset of acne that left faint scars in its wake. Her hair was *un poco duro,* but lusciously thick, like Paloma's *culo,* another gift bestowed upon her by Mother Nature, which came with a perfect set of *tetas.* A spitting image of her father and hero, the esteemed and dapper Don Manuel Mancebo, Rocío was much prettier in person than in photos. Don Manuel had an unforgettable and unusual face, with a complexion that made one crave a *taza* of *café con leche* with a little extra milk. His rather coarse hair was shellacked with pomade into a style that never moved. Ever. They say his father's half-Haitian mother, *apellido* Durán, was the ancestor who made her mark on his head. Don Manuel didn't look like too many other Dominicans lighter or darker than he. And neither did Rocío.

Rocío's gift was the left side of her brain. She started reading Socrates by the time she was twelve. Later, Rocío got into Jean-Paul Sartre and decided she wanted to be a poet or a nun and retreat into a life of solitude and reflection. Rather than hanging out with the girls from her school or going to Club Paraíso with Paloma and Antonio on the weekends, she chose to spend hours in her bedroom alone. When Rocío did go out, she preferred the company of her elders, particularly her mentor, the recently published psychiatrist Dr. Antonio Zaglul, for whom she worked part time as an administrative assistant.

Unlike Paloma and Antonio, Rocío rarely got in trouble with her parents, but her peculiar antisocial behavior did cause them to freak out on occasion. As punishment for refusing to act like a normal girl her age, Rocío was regularly banned from her room and forced to tag along with her siblings to the neighborhood country club. This was torture for Rocío, who hated pools and having fun.

So it came out of nowhere, like a lightning bolt on a sunny day. This is what I was told years later. Not even the barrio's most prolific santera could have divined how Rocío came completely undone at fifteen. It happened on the day Eduardo Cepeda dropped into town from Nueva York and into her life like Chango himself, with a drum in one hand and his dick in the other.

On that day Paloma insisted that Rocío stop acting bizarre and accompany her to visit Perla's neighbor on the outskirts of their 'hood. Everybody knew that Perla, an acquaintance, was expecting her only brother—the one she hadn't seen since they were kids—to drop in that day for a visit. If the girls were lucky, Paloma thought, they'd catch a glimpse of him on her block that afternoon. That was where they met, walking up the stairs to another teen's house. Paloma introduced herself and her sister to Eduardo. And from that moment, it was on.

Eduardo had a twofold mission in Santo Domingo that spring in 1971. He flew in to make an appearance on a popular TV variety show that promised to catapult him from being a singer with decent street credibility to full-fledged Desi Arnaz baller status. He was also in town to reunite with his mother, Ercilia, and his sisters. Eduardo hadn't seen them since before his paternal grandmother, acting on a strong hunch, sent him to live with his father in Nueva York.

From that afternoon on, Rocío and Eduardo, a man twelve years her senior, started to see each other on the low for as long as they could keep it a secret. Out of nowhere, she started listening to boleros. At first her younger siblings couldn't wrap their heads around their fifteen-year-old sister's sudden obsession with old folks' music, especially when Héctor Lavoe and the *santiagero* Johnny Pacheco were killing it. Soon, however, they started to suspect that it was a certain *bizco*, a cross-eyed masked singer, who inspired her fanaticism. It didn't matter to Rocío. "Boleros are for mature people," she said. "You two wouldn't understand." The more they stole away with each other, the more Rocío realized Eduardo had been sent to her by God Himself. Nobody, she felt, understood her—not her mother, not her father, not her sister or brother, none of the girls or boys at school, *nadie*—except her man.

Rocío nearly swooned the first time she saw him onstage in Santo Domingo, ritualistically wresting off his mask to reveal a thin chiseled face and slanted eyes. When he gyrated his stiff hips—he didn't even try to catch the beat—his slicked-back hair took on a life of its own. Eduardo's stage name, *El Cantante Enmascarado*, struck her as genius. He must have been illustrating the complex duality of man, she thought. In reality, Eduardo hoped the mask would make him appear vulnerable and self-conscious, like a wounded animal these stupid women would fight each other over to mend. Eduardo was a broken man willing—*coño,* hell-bent—to play patient with any chick willing to take his temperature with her mouth or any other available orifice. And then he met Rocío, his *reina,* the one girl whose curves fucked his head up. On the afternoon they met, Eduardo told her as much. "*Mujer,*" he said, "you make my world come to a complete standstill."

Rocío is a born stubborn Capricorn and fixed in her beliefs, the way she loved, the way she hated. Her resolve back home paid off, she thinks, watching the gringos coming and going on the street below her. She now sat triumphantly across from this beautiful man whom so many other women loved but who loved only her. "*Nosotros estamos felices,*" she whispers to herself over and over again, *we are so happy.*

"Rocío, we have to buy a few things for my sister's baby," Eduardo says, reaching for a tennis magazine.

Rocío doesn't respond, pretending not hear him go on about Esperanza, who's married and apparently capable of providing for her own son.

Esperanza's a leech in Rocío's eyes, a jealous sister-in-law who too frequently drops in from Newport, Rhode Island, unannounced, and almost always with her *comadre* Sara in tow. A handsome Puerto Rican brunette, she runs to New York City at every chance in order to get away from a husband she desperately wants to leave. Sara is just as bad as Esperanza, if not worse. There is something about Sara that Rocío doesn't trust, and it isn't only her association with Esperanza. Plus, she has the weirdest fucking accent. She pronounces the double R in words like *arroz* and *carro* like she's going to spit up a wad of *mocos* right in your face. Rocío prefers Ecuadorian and Mexican Spanish because they sing their words.

Today Rocío is going to ignore any talk about Esperanza to avoid another argument, choosing instead to remember the soft timbre in Eduardo's voice back when he was courting her, singing to her, writing to her from New York. He was so passionate in those days. She tries not to dwell on how much more excited Eduardo seems to be about Esperanza's son than me, their baby.

"Did you hear me, Rocío?" Eduardo barks. "What are you looking at down there on the street?"

"*Ay*, Eduardo, *nada*. This is the first day I've had off in many. I'm just relaxing—are you letting your hair grow out?"

Eduardo's dark hair and sideburns are, in fact, longer. His hair looks as disheveled as it did on their honeymoon night, when he first, like a vampire, accepted his bride's most sacred gift.

Before Eduardo, Rocío hadn't allowed anyone to touch her. At almost sixteen and a half, she was barely halfway through high school and more interested in her books than getting laid. And she didn't need her mother, Doña Dolores, to remind her what was common knowledge across the island. Everybody knew Dominican men were a bunch of *rubirosas*, players. Regardless of class, color, and creed, they turned savage over fresh meat. And after feasting on the finest cuts and, shit, even their *compai's* leftovers, gristle and all, the bones were spat out before these horny men headed back out to the human *viveros* on El Malecón and here on the pewter streets of Nueva York. Eduardo convinced the girl that he was the exception.

Rocío imagines that the baby she's carrying will look just like him and inherit his perfectly straight white teeth and tall stature. She fantasizes looking after a houseful of his children, at least six of them. Rocío is certain Eduardo will make good on his promise to her and her family and finally leave the music bullshit alone and focus on becoming a dental technician. She'll go back to school and devote herself to raising children and learning how to cook something other than rice and beans. *They are all wrong*, Rocío thinks, looking out at nothing in particular. Her family said Eduardo wouldn't take care of her in the long run, but she is convinced things will only get better. They have to.

Rocío has resolved to create her own *paraíso* here. Paradise is a state of being, more than just the name of a suburb or a home. If she works harder cleaning the homes of the rich Americans and Europeans living in Lincoln Towers and, in between classes, pulls in more shifts at the factory to help Eduardo pay for school, paradise will be her reward. Someday Rocío will assume the same position here that she had back home in respectable dominiyorkian society. Wadsworth Terrace is only the first step.

Eduardo sits on the couch, thinking about the future, his future, and, more important, his miserable present. *How did I get here?* he thinks. Eduardo retraces every moment of the last several months that led him to this couch. Then he thinks about which one of his girlfriends he'll go out with tonight, comparing each one to Rocío. His *reina*, with her thick long wavy hair and *ojos de almendra*. She isn't the girl he met in Santo Domingo. She doesn't look as sexy pregnant. And worse, Rocío has turned into a bossy nag.

"*¿A quien estas mirando,* Eduardo?" she barks almost every time they go to a restaurant, host one of their get-togethers, even on line at the *supermercado,* every-fucking-where.

"I'm not looking at *no* one. What you *talking* about, Rocío?"

"*Bueno,* I think I saw you looking over at her."

"Rocío, come on, you're listening to those *tontos* you work with again, they—"

"Stand over here next to me right now, Eduardo," she demands, before he has a chance to make his case. "*¡Ahora!*"

Coño, qué lío, he thinks. Eduardo sits, taking stock. Theirs was an intense, mostly long-distance affair consisting of stolen moments after gigs in Santo Domingo and letters that definitely would have been plagiarized by Shakespeare himself had the man laid eyes on each scalding word. *Te lo juro,* Eduardo thinks, *I swear.* The other women keeping him company at the nightclubs and speakeasies he performed in, whether in New York, South America, or *La República Dominicana,* were only good for providing evanescent relief for the physical pain he felt when his *reina* wasn't by his side.

Eduardo swore to himself on the day he met her that he'd make a woman out of Rocío. He didn't understand why, but he spent more time thinking about her than any other woman he'd met. And it most definitely didn't hurt that Rocío was the mother he never had.

Rocío was the ideal girl back then, without life experience or a past, like these *putas* in the city. Regardless of what her family thought of him and his family, they would be together. Rocío became Eduardo's muse. She was good to him and for him, an unexplored *cueva* he could mold into his own personal *puta* in between the sheets and lady on the streets. But now Eduardo, who fancied himself the Romeo to Rocío's Juliet, sits on the couch utterly underwhelmed.

Eduardo feels duped, as if Shakespeare had the last laugh. Maybe he wrote the ending that way for a reason. Had Romeo and Juliet awakened from their slumber, fucked until their bodies were nearly gripped by atrophy, and Romeo become totally pussy-whipped, any real man could have foreseen that he would eventually get over it. *I don't think he would have been stupid enough to go through with it,* he thinks, sitting there pretending to read the paper. *Man, I did a shitty thing. How did I get here?*

Back in Santo Domingo, Eduardo took Rocío any way he could have her. It didn't matter that the wedding went on without the sincere blessings of his bride's family and the two hundred and fifty witnesses made up of Santo Domingo's finest. Only two people from Eduardo's side were in attendance: his perpetually sad mother Ercilia, dressed like a church lady in shit brown, and the stunning *india* Perla. An opera singer serenaded the newlyweds during the civil ceremony. *What a fucking freak show,* Antonio thought as he bore witness to the entire spectacle.

For months, Paraíso had turned into everything but paradise for the family. It was no longer a safe haven for Don Manuel and Doña Dolores's children but, rather, the scene where, in a formal dining room the family grimaced through dinners with their blushing daughter and *that man*. Paraíso became the site where an upper-middle-class family gave their favorite daughter and eccentric sibling away to an undesirable.

"Rocío, *mi hija,* that man is running around with other women," Doña Dolores pleaded. "We hear his father is an even bigger *mujeriego*."

"He loves me more than life itself," she responded. "I don't care what his father has done or does. He didn't even raise him. Eduardo is different."

"That man doesn't love you, he conquers women, and I hear he has a stable of them in Nueva York," Don Manuel interjected.

"Nothing will come in between me and my Samson, my Romeo. We're going to be married one day and have many children," she yelled. Rocío was becoming a raving teenager. Nobody in Paraíso recognized her anymore.

The beatings once reserved for her siblings were now directed at Rocío. Every whipping made her all the more determined to be with Eduardo. She locked herself in her bedroom for hours, in protest, screaming, "We. Will. Be. Married."

Don Manuel was dressed as if attending a funeral in a somber yet impeccably tailored black suit and tie and starched white dress shirt. Rocío wore an exquisite yet conservative white gown and veil that looked like it had been designed for a woman twice her age. Her train was long, dragging dirt from the large front lawn into the house. The irony wasn't lost on her quick-witted mother.

Rocío looked like a child—hair coiffed in loose curls not quite touching her shoulders, sparkling white gloves, fantasy-blue eyelids— playing dress-up in a life-size dollhouse. The child bride cheesed throughout the entire ceremony. She was the only one. The next day, on their honeymoon, the couple was still infatuated, though Eduardo was a little less so.

"*Nosotros estamos felices, nosotros estamos felices,*" Rocío assured Dolores and Antonio back in the Dominican Republic while on the honeymoon, almost a hundred miles away from home in the dreamy town of Jarabacoa. Eduardo sat quietly. He didn't care much for water-falls and long nature walks, like his new bride did. "We are *sooo* happy, so very happy," she said, hobbling around like an injured puppy.

Less than a whirlwind year after Rocío and Eduardo started fooling around, Antonio sat in a restaurant watching his eldest sister limp in his direction. He wondered whether all the threats to commit suicide if the family forbade the wedding and the intervention of Dr. Zaglul on her behalf would pay off. *El doctor* had convinced Don Manuel and his wife to allow Rocío to stay with Eduardo. She was a determined girl, so much so that Zaglul felt she was capable of running away with Eduardo, or worse, killing herself, if they didn't let Rocío have her way.

Antonio sat, watching his eldest sister labor through each step, imagining her, a sainted virgin, getting banged by this reputed *desvergonzado* nymphomaniac. Eduardo had been around the block in more ways than one. This was a fact everybody seemed hip to except Rocío.

It was bad enough that Rocío's parents had to swallow becoming in-laws with Eduardo's father, Ismael, a *tigere* whom Don Manuel had investigated. He reportedly fucked every woman in sight and without discretion. And worse, they found out that Ercilia was a *recogida*, a street child picked up by the *prieta* Doña Francisca Prandis and Don Pedro Rabassa. Was leaving a big house, her family, and a comfortable life in Santo Domingo to be with this man from a broken family and no history all worth this one fuck? To Rocío, it was.

Rocío may have been a bookish nerd, but she was also kind of a social retard, a person incapable of sympathizing with anyone who didn't share her conservative views, including Doña Dolores. Rocío felt like a victim of her mother's circumstances. She believed that *la doña* had warped priorities and cared more about being a revolutionary and activist than a mother and wife. However, it was Rocío who had it twisted.

Dolores was a woman ahead of her time, a proud *cibaeña* and outspoken critic of the tyrant Rafael Trujillo. When she was a teenager, Dolores and her father, Don Felipe Valdez—a well-known civil judge and *padrino* to almost every child born in their *barrio*—were labeled *communistas* by the regime. Don Valdez was too popular in the 'hood to kill, so the dictator waged a devastating economic war against the family's deep pockets they would never recover from. Being branded an enemy of the state by Trujillo's *monos* only made Dolores more fierce and resistant to shit most other men and women would have cowered before.

Dolores's political convictions gave her a sense of purpose, something she sorely lacked at home. If not for the striking resemblance she bore to her father, she might have started believing that she was, like her siblings declared, adopted. Most of them favored their mother, Rosario: They were tall for girls, and thin, with *pelo lacio* in dark blond and bright reddish tones. Dolores's sisters taunted her for being physically *astrasado*, like their father. She struggled with her weight, had thick brown skin, a wide nose, and almond-shaped eyes *como una africana*. "*Tú eres una recogida, negra haitiana*," they'd mock her, "you're adopted, you black Haitian street child." Rosario said nothing as Dolores bled inside from the emotional wounds her sisters dealt her.

Dolores started believing that her lighter-skinned sisters, with their pretty thin noses and fine hair, were not only more beautiful but also better, more human. She became convinced at a young age that she belonged to some other, less developed species. After years of jabs to her ego and self-esteem from the mouths of her own family, Dolores learned to deliver blows and absorb them with the grace of a boxer.

Today Dolores didn't want to stay quiet, like her own mother did when she was being publicly humiliated. She wanted to protest the wedding, to scream and shake her daughter until Rocío awoke from the lovesick stupor she was in, but alas, she didn't. Despite her eldest daughter's devastating stupidity and her own husband's marital shortcomings, Doña Dolores kept a cool head throughout the ordeal, hoping things would somehow correct themselves.

From the moment she landed in Nueva York, Rocío started missing her father terribly. And Don Manuel was grief-stricken in those first few months without his favorite child. Don Manuel loved her so much that he often chose to spend time with Rocío over his harem of prostitutes on Avenida Nicolas de Ovando, a sleazy artery of the capital littered with pawnshops and whorehouses. Now that Rocío had broken out to New York City, Don Manuel shifted all his attention to his least favorite child, Antonio. He spent the next several months trying to convince the boy that he wasn't gay.

Don Manuel had been stung, his world rocked to the core, when Antonio broke the news. *¿Un maricón dominicano?* Not in this family. After a few long moments thinking about his son's unfortunate affliction, he countered, "What makes you so sure that you are gay? You know, most teenagers have confusion."

"Because I don't recall ever being sexually turned on by girls," Antonio responded.

"I have an idea," Don Manuel said. "I think you should consider having sex with a prostitute who can teach you what a woman is." Surely this would cure Antonio of his bout with insanity.

"Well, the whole idea repulses me a great deal, but I'll think about it."

"Oh, I'll *remind* you," Don Manuel said. And he did a couple of weeks later.

Together, the distressed father and bewildered son ventured into the seedy *avenida,* far away from Paraíso.

Doña Dolores waited at home, ambivalent about the whole thing. She wanted to straighten out her little boy, but not if it meant Manuel would be tempted to play her dirty yet again.

The ride to Nicolas de Ovando was silent. The voices of the city's poorest children screaming, *"¡Maní! ¡Maní! ¡Maní!"* could be heard along El Malecón, making Antonio hungry. The boy thought about what his friends might have been doing: drinking at the underground gay bar, smoking marijuana, jerking off to straight porn at the movie theater. Antonio tried not to think about all the pussy he'd be faced with that night. Vaginas reminded him of papayas, which nauseated him.

Boîte el Criollo was a tiny bordello run by Ligiah, a tall fat *mulata áspera* with gold teeth and a huge-ass wig. She roared at the sight of Don Manuel. *"¡Ay, Dios mío, hombre, cuanto tiempo!* Where have you *been*? I haven't seen you in so long." Madame Ligiah turned away from the cash register and welcomed Antonio with her deep rasp. "We love your dad here, you know? And I have some great-looking *muchachitas* for you." Antonio's knees almost gave out under him. A mama's boy, he was repulsed by how warmly his father was received in this shit hole. He had wished many times that his mother would leave Don Manuel.

The first girl Antonio was offered was about thirteen, fourteen. *This doesn't feel right*, was his first thought. Sensing his discomfort, Ligiah offered him a different girl. "She's helping at the register, but I could send her up with you."

"No, I prefer someone a little older."

Janet was a fat, juicy *morena* in her mid- to late thirties. Horrified and amused, Antonio followed the woman to a filthy room down the hall. "Oh, lie down and relax on the bed while I get ready," she said, taking off her clothes.

Janet squatted down atop a *ponchera* in the corner of the tiny room. Maintaining eye contact with the boy, she grabbed a wet bar of *jabón de cuaba* and began to scrub her vagina and *culo* with a mixture of dark soapy water and cum from previous customers. The boy struggled to keep down whatever he'd eaten that day as her dirty *chocha* dripped even dirtier water back into the basin.

"Okay," she said, patting her legs and feet dry, "*now* I'm ready for you."

Janet lay down next to Antonio, who was still fully dressed, and unzipped his jeans before taking his dick into her huge experienced mouth. Antonio closed his eyes and imagined Janet as a man until he started to get hard. But just as he began to relax, he was startled by a cacophony of slapping and moaning, crying and yelling from the room next door. Antonio went limp.

"Oh, that's Maria. She's very tough on men, but they all seem to like it that way," Janet whispered, stroking Antonio's face gently with her rough hand. "Don't give it a thought."

"*¡Yo te voy a enseñar hacer hombre coño!*" Maria screeched, slapping her customer so hard it sounded like rounds of firecrackers going off on *Noche Buena*. He squealed, begging for more punishment, and she complied. "*Desgraciado maricón*, who's the real bitch here!"

Antonio had enough. He paid *la vieja* Janet in full and went downstairs to meet his father.

"How did it go, *mi hijo*?"

"Actually, nothing went, and I want to get the fuck out of here, and I don't really want to do this."

"Ah. This may not be the right place," Don Manuel said, "let's go to Nancy's."

As he left Ligiah's brothel, Antonio was even more convinced that he was gay.

Several places over from Boîte was a larger, well-known establishment with a curiously ordinary name: Nancy's Nightclub. The brothel's namesake was a popular and straightforward madam, Don Manuel said. Antonio could barely make out what she looked like because of the flurry of whores who rushed out like a wave, dancing around him as soon as he sat down on the bar stool.

"*Papi, Papi, Papi, Papi, vamo' a sing'a,*" they sang, competing for his attention.

"Oh my God, this is worse than that other place," Antonio said to his father.

"Okay, let's go to the last one, and I promise—"

Herminia's Nightclub was a massive whorehouse, the largest in the *barrio,* originally erected to cater to invading U.S. troops in the market for *chocha.* The joint was so large that no one recognized Don Manuel among the *chulos* and tourists on the massive dance floor. Tons of *putas* of all ages and shapes in the variant shades of brown present on the island—from *leche condensada* to espresso—danced like lactating mothers around their young.

Don Manuel and Antonio sat at the bar. Soon the women flocked around them, swaying their hips suggestively to the live music. Antonio found Herminia's whores less aggressive than Nancy's and certainly more attractive and charming than those at Boîte.

"Oh, do you like the way I dance, *chulo?*" asked a blonde with a large *pajon.* Her hair was thick and curly, her eyes piercing blue. Her face evoked a time when African women bore their masters' children.

"*Mira, mira, mira, mira* . . . do you like, do you like?" she asked Antonio.

Antonio looked over at his father and said, "I'm enjoying this, but for all the wrong reasons."

"Excuse me? What do you mean?" Don Manuel shouted over the music.

"I think these women are actually funny. They're comedians, all of them."

"Oh God, there's no hope for this guy," Don Manuel said, staring up at the high ceiling. "He's really not going to fuck anybody after all."

Father and son finished their drinks and went home.

That night Antonio thought about his sister Rocío on the ride back home. He wondered if she was coping better than he was in the love department.

CHAPTER TWO

Mean Streets

Mete la mano en el bolsillo
Saca y abre tu cuchillo y ten cuida'o.

Put your hand in your pockets
Take out and fling your knife open and be careful.

—Héctor Lavoe, "Calle Luna, Calle Sol"

Rocío followed Eduardo to New York City in 1972 with a knot of cash gifted to her by Don Manuel. Eduardo promised to move her into a sprawling apartment, but the couple made a detour. They began their life together in a room at Germosa and Raul Cepeda's prewar apartment on 145th Street and Broadway, where a few thousand newcomers from the island found themselves feeling a little unsettled.

The fact that Eduardo didn't make good on his first promise didn't matter much to Rocío. The girl was finally free to be *la reina* in Eduardo's kingdom: a tiny rented bedroom down a seemingly endless hallway in the elderly couple's fairly large apartment. Every week they paid a little extra cash for the right to use the bathroom. The kitchen was off limits.

The king and queen spent hours in their room, planning a future full of children and riches. Eduardo didn't understand when Rocío started going off about existentialism and Jean-Paul Sartre and someday visiting Paris, where the philosopher had been born. For some reason, not knowing turned him on. Rocío was the smartest woman he'd ever met. "I'm going to take you on my next tour all over South America," Eduardo promised his child bride. "They love my show over there. They love *me*." When the couple got tired of talking, they took breaks to make love and, when Eduardo could get Rocío in the right mood, fuck each other to sleep. They couldn't afford to do much else.

Months later, just in time for my arrival, Rocío has her own kitchen in a decent two-bedroom apartment. She can come home after work and fetch something to drink from *her* refrigerator in *her* kitchen. She can use the bathroom without worrying that someone will walk in on her. Rocío is free to be the doting mother she feels she never had, as well as a loving maternal figure to her husband.

She glances over at Eduardo, dozing off on the couch, then back out the window.

A Hindu couple exits a building from across the street, screaming at each other in a language Rocío doesn't understand. The commotion startles her back from daydreaming to reality.

A boy—he can't be over two years old—is at the woman's side. *He's probably their son,* she thinks. The boy is crying and holding on to the hem of his mother's skirt. The white noise coming from the couple is deafening even from Rocío's window. The boy looks terrified. Perhaps he's not used to seeing his parents fight. Or maybe the impending feeling of doom, like Rocío's own, is what's scaring the shit out of him, causing the child to sob uncontrollably.

"*Ay Dios, por favor* call the *policía,* call," she begs Eduardo. Rocío is picking up English with relative ease by reading everything she can get her hands on and watching the news. Eduardo's English isn't much better, but it's easier to understand than hers. "I said call the *policía,* Eduardo, *por favor, hombre.*"

"Stay away from the window," Eduardo responds. His voice is flat and almost unaffected by the shouting outside.

"But I think *algo malo sucederá* if you don't call—"

"Get *out* of the window right now, Rocío, you're not supposed to be watching them."

Rocío doesn't move. The woman and child disappear into the building. The man leans quietly against the rear of a double-parked moving van in front of the building. The sun is shining down on the silver ramp the man had been walking up and down all morning, moving pieces of furniture and boxes he neatly stacked from back to front.

Rocío can clearly make out the beads of sweat racing down the creases of his forehead into his red eyes. He is thinking, waiting, it seems—but for what?

"You see? *Nada pasó.* It's nothing. Now get away from the window," Eduardo says.

The feeling of dread doesn't abandon Rocío. The weight is even heavier than when she first boarded the airplane bound for New York City. She had never left her country before that trip and wondered how the huge chunk of steel would make its way from the familiar world to a distant one without falling apart.

Rocío continues to stare at the Hindu man, hoping he won't become aggressive again when his wife and child reappear, for the child's sake.

The creases disappear from the man's forehead. His expression is almost subdued when he starts tracing the building with his eyes, forcing his head up despite the unforgiving sun, looking up until he spots his wife and son, holding on to his mother's hem, on the roof.

Rocío follows the man's gaze, brick by brick, up to the roof where his wife, yelling again, is looking down at him. Her son stands next to her, his eyes swollen almost completely shut from crying. The man's eyes are fixed on his family standing on the roof. He doesn't respond to her.

"¡Eduardo, *Dios,* call *la policía, hombre!* She is going to do something crazy," Rocío screams. She braces herself, praying to *La Virgen de la Altagracia* that the woman doesn't jump from the roof and traumatize her child for life.

"I *said*, it's none of our business."

The Hindu man doesn't yell. Doesn't move. The woman picks up the boy, now silent, over her head and tosses him off the roof.

The boy's father doesn't move.

Rocío, a sheltered teenager from Santo Domingo, hasn't witnessed this kind of violence before, not even during the civil war in 1965. She becomes distraught, wailing for the child who has been reduced to pieces of skin, brain tissue, and all kinds of unrecognizable matter splattered on the ground and on his father.

Rocío looks at me through her protruding belly. She believes in omens.

Eduardo is sad for the child, but the sadness is fleeting. He quickly goes back to thinking about the mess he's gotten himself into, and about other women.

Too soon afterward, everything goes back to normal.

Rocío immediately returns to cleaning houses and working at the factory, back to signing over all her checks to Eduardo, back to defending Eduardo to her bosses and coworkers.

"Rocío, how can you give that man all of your money when he's spending it on other women, *no seas tonta,*" people would say.

"You don't understand how much Eduardo loves me. He would never do that," Rocío would respond.

"You're a brilliant girl but with no common sense," was the usual response. "Go back to Santo Domingo, back to school."

"I don't expect anyone to understand our love."

I'm born at the end of that spring, not long after the woman tossed her son off the roof. My father finally makes good on one of his many promises and abandons his singing career to get a real job as a dental technician. And my mother, still cleaning rich people's apartments downtown, has stopped daydreaming about a life of literature and philosophy. Rocío dropped out of Lehman College to help my father finish his degree, hoping he'd someday return the favor. She begins to doubt he will.

My mother has trouble taking care of me. She can barely take care of herself.

My earliest memories are adrenaline-fueled vignettes set in Inwood and Santo Domingo. I star in each; my father, hardly ever; my mother, more so, and never without those *tacónes* raising her five-foot frame high off the ground as she sped to and from our apartment on Seaman Avenue.

I call Rocío "Mami," even though I'm not sure she's mine or that I'm hers. There's no real bond. I haven't spent much time with her or Eduardo. I call him "Papi," though I don't remember a single instant between him and Mami that illustrates their connection or where I fit in. The only proof of parentage I possess is a black-and-white photograph of us all together, taken shortly after I was born.

When I turn six months old, Mami drops me off in Paraíso on the first of many round-trips to the island that I'll take before my sixth birthday. There, I'm sent to live with her parents, Don Manuel and Doña Dolores, whom I call Papa and Mama. I meet my *tíos*, Antonio and Paloma, and a gray bipolar poodle named Oliver. A Donald Duck mobile becomes the thing I cherish most, next to Mama's company and Papa's grilled cheese sandwiches.

I fall in love with Paraíso. It's like a giant playground where I'm never scolded for running around recklessly, where I'm almost overwhelmed with the amount of attention and love I receive from Mami's family. In New York, I'm invisible. I hate going back to live with Mami, especially during the winter.

Mami walks fast, gliding over the snow in her high heels like an ice skater; my tiny legs can't keep up with hers. My sides hurt real bad from walking so fast, but I don't want to lose her, so I start running, barely holding on to her cold wet hand.

"Camina, muchacha," she scolds me. "Come on, girl, walk faster."

I can't answer her. I'm out of breath. The cold air stings the back of my sweaty neck. My knees give out, and I slip on the sheet of ice. Mami lifts me up by the elbow. She rolls her eyes at me, disgusted. I am slowing her down. Tears stream down my face because I can't part my lips to say "I'm sorry, Mami" for letting her down. I miss Paraíso terribly.

Mami's always heading somewhere, dropping me off with people I don't know, running late to work before picking me up and running back home to cook dinner. I think Mami prefers the chaos. I'm afraid that if she stands still even for a moment, she'll realize that she is completely alone. I can tell she doesn't want to be quiet with her thoughts and all the bullshit promises Papi made back home in Santo Domingo. She tries not to allow her mind to race back to what could have been had she stayed working for Dr. Zaglul. Regretting her present would mean regretting I existed, and she doesn't feel free enough to admit that, at least not out loud. Mami does not have to say it. I can almost hear her curse the day I was born and ruined any chance of her plotting to leave Papi and start over in Santo Domingo as if none of this happened. I can feel her sadness.

The gaping hole in her heart is amplified when she catches a glimpse of the strands of silver hair framing her once young face in the mirror. "I look like a woman twice my age," I hear her mumble under her breath. And to think she isn't even twenty-one.

To me, Mami looks like a fashion model (though shorter), an exhausted version of the stylish women who go to the Latin Quarter and the Palladium to dance salsa. I bet they can't walk across the ice in *tacónes* like her. She is pretty to me, though her teeth are slightly too big for her small face. And even if there are strands of gray hair crowning her young head, the dark waves cascading down her back make her impossibly small waist look even smaller. Everything she wears looks pretty on her.

At home, I sometimes climb up on her bed when she's sleeping and stare at her face, a kaleidoscope. I see someone different every time I look at her, depending on the angle. One day Mami looks like the funny Indian lady on TV who sings about being something called a "half-breed." On other days she looks like a *china,* especially when she smiles. Lately, Mami's eyes have been so dark, I don't like looking into them because I'm afraid I'll fall in. When she awakens, I try to play with her, but she never has time.

Ever since Rocío arrived in Nueva York, the city has been really mean to her. As much as she wanted to believe otherwise, the truth is, Eduardo hasn't been much kinder.

On one of those rare evenings off, Rocío and Eduardo decide to throw an impromptu party at their apartment. Their friend Miguel drops in with his violin. Eduardo invites his sister, Esperanza, who happens to be in the city with Sara. Rocío squirms when she opens the door to find her sister-in-law and Sara with an acoustic guitar standing in the doorway.

"Esperanza, you have to spend the night. I can't le' you go back all the way back to Newport," Eduardo says without Rocío's consent. "And Sara *se puede quedar,* too."

The family and friends spend the evening singing popular boleros and religious songs. Sara strums her guitar throughout and sings a couple of duets with Eduardo. At some point in the night, Miguel overhears Sara talking to Eduardo—sitting next to her like an obedient dog—about a divorce. Esperanza makes herself scarce and ventures into the kitchen to help herself to a plate of food.

Though Rocío is the queen of Eduardo's kingdom, she doesn't get the respect due to her from Esperanza and Sara. They ignore her while Sara openly flirts with Eduardo, leaning a little too close to him when they sing. But Rocío, the obedient wife and naive woman-child who wants nothing more than to make Eduardo as happy as they were when they first met, does nothing. Despite her own reservations and Miguel's warning, Rocío offers Sara one of her negligees to sleep in. *Eduardo may be immature,* she thinks, *but he can't be that stupid.* "*Carajo* Rocío, I guess it's true what they say," Miguel says, "the more bookish a person, the more she lacks common sense, *mi hija.*"

The following morning, Rocío is running late for work yet again. She leaves early, tiptoeing over Esperanza and Sara, sleeping in the living room. She's almost at the 1 train bound for Lincoln Center when she realizes she forgot the keys to one of the apartments, that of a French filmmaker currently out of the country on location back home. Though Rocío could leave that one apartment for tomorrow, she goes back to her *paraíso*, carefully unlocking the front door and taking off her *tacónes* by the entrance in order not to wake anybody.

Rocío is so careful not to disturb anyone as she walks toward the kitchen that she doesn't realize Sara isn't where she left her minutes earlier, next to Esperanza on the couch.

The muffled groans coming from the bedroom paralyze her. Rocío's world is imploding. With every step she takes in that direction, she feels, sickened by her self, by her own stupidity. The warnings from friends and coworkers, from her parents, are like a hurricane spinning around in her mind. Rage is shooting through her body.

When she reaches the door, Rocío thinks of turning around and walking away. If she leaves the door closed and goes about her day, perhaps she'll find an excuse in her mental file to justify what sounded like heavy sex coming from her bedroom. Rocío braces herself.

Shakespeare had it right all along: Love will kill you in the end. And if your so-called love manages to survive the city's blackouts, the *jolopeos*, the nadir of her financial and moral history, it won't do shit to strengthen your bond to each other. It'll just draw out the end and make it really fucking agonizing.

Rocío pushes herself down the hallway and opens the bedroom door as quietly as she entered the apartment. Eduardo and Sara don't notice. The *puta* is too busy riding him in the white negligee Rocío lent her.

This is what I know about my parents. They spent the next several years trying to forget each other, and me.

Rocío set off to find herself soon after catching Sara riding her king like a stallion. She divorced Papi. Eduardo, now free to walk around with Sara *como un sinvergüenza* in public, inherited half of the furniture from their apartment after the split, along with money Rocío gave him in hopes that he'd move as far away as possible. As a gift to the new *puta* in his life—Rocío was generous—she rolled up the published divorce papers like a diploma and awarded them to Esperanza. "Here, you can have him," she said.

Eduardo moved into a small one-bedroom apartment two buildings down from Rocío. He was within walking distance of his favorite place on earth next to a woman—the tennis courts.

I went to live with Mama and Papa in Santo Domingo so Mami could get back on her feet. My poodle, Oliver, tired of my erratic trips to and from the island, ignored me in the beginning, and in protest of my last jaunt back into his life, he stole all my dolls and decapitated them, strewing them about the backyard and leaving the heads underneath all of our beds. Just as he got used to me, comfortable with the notion that I, his best girl, wouldn't abandon him again, I returned to New York City. He'd had enough. I never saw him again. Oliver died shortly afterward of an epileptic seizure.

Soon after I return to New York, life falls back into a routine, a familiar rhythm. I become invisible once again. Mami's days and nights are like they've always been, a seamless grind. She spends her life working, running to job number two, then three, paying bills, going back to work the following morning. Sometimes I tag along and pretend to help her clean toilets and dishes, anything I can do to be with her.

It's on one of these routine outings that Rocío's life is interrupted once more. We're waiting to be seen for my yearly checkup at Sydenham Hospital in Harlem. In the waiting room full of mothers and their children, Pascal Baptiste, a social worker at the hospital, spots Mami. He circles around her like a vulture, waiting patiently. He must smell the musk of rejection Mami has worn since leaving Papi less than a year earlier. The wound is still fresh.

Suddenly, Pascal is standing before Mami, an impeccably dressed *caramelito* of a man with a small yet solid build, not quite like Bruce

Lee's but close. His eyes are light and alert, his smile wide. Pascal's clothes are so hip, he looks more like a disco dancer than a hospital bureaucrat.

"Hi," he says with a slight accent familiar to Rocío. "You know, I have a little girl named Sable. You two resemble her. Where are you from?"

"The capital city of the Dominican Republic," replies Rocío, speaking English that's a little less broken than it was a few years ago.

"Oh, we are relatives!"

"How so?" she asks.

"I am from the other side of the island, from the capital of Haiti."

"That's nice. Nice to meet you," Mami says, extending her hand.

"May I have your number?" he asks. She shakes her head no, but that doesn't matter to Pascal. He finds our number by looking through the hospital records and calls Mami anyway. She's creeped out at first, but Pascal's game is tight and persistent, and he says all the right things. In no time, the calls start coming in more frequently, and by the time Doña Dolores deposits me back into Rocío's life from yet another trip to Santo Domingo, the calls sound like a barrage of bullets spraying from an AK-47.

"Rocío, *coño hombre,* this guy calls way too many times," Dolores says. "Who the hell is he?

"*Nadie,* Mama, just a friend," Rocío responds, irritated by her mother's prying. Everything about Dolores bothers her.

"It's not good. You have to be careful."

"But we don't have anything going—not really."

"I hope you're not thinking of bringing this *loco* into Raquelita's life."

"Please, Mama, relax. I'm twenty-one and allowed to have friends."

Rocío is impressed with Pascal's Ivy League education and drive. She resented having to drop out of college to take care of Eduardo and me whenever I was in town. Pascal appreciates Mami's beauty and youth. The fact that she's impressionable and easy to control is a bonus.

Papi finds Pascal charming and well spoken, especially for *un haitiano.* The man is always honest and forthright when talking about his relationship with Rocío. "I have to hit her sometimes when she steps out of line," he once told Eduardo, who understood that his ex-wife was capable of driving a man to this threshold. He voiced no objection to Pascal's *modus disciplina*.

Pascal may have mastered the science of manipulating the mind at prestigious institutions like Yale and Harvard, but that was nothing compared to the fieldwork he conducted on Mami. In under a year, he convinces her to relocate to San Francisco by promising to put her through law school, going as far as buying her books to prep for the exam. Mama smelled the bullshit all the way from Santo Domingo, but Mami wasn't having it.

Shortly before we move to San Francisco, Mami insists that I start referring to her rebound as "Papito." I oblige without putting up much of a fight. Pascal demanded the affectionate nom de guerre regardless of whether or not it was genuine. At this point "Mami" and "Papi" are names that lack meaning. And Papito is just another person on the growing list of people who don't fucking matter.

CHAPTER THREE

Journey into the Heart of Darkness

> Being a woman is a terribly difficult task, since it
> consists principally in dealing with men.
>
> —Joseph Conrad

WE LIVE IN SEVERAL RENTED HOUSES BEFORE SETTLING ON EDDY Street. It's close enough to the Mission, where Papito's new shop, The Smoke House, is located. It's right next to the old theater crowded with tourists and weirdos. I guess he makes enough money at the hospital—although he's hardly ever there—to afford a side hustle. It doesn't take long for Papito to become a popular fixture in the area and at the discotheques he and Mami frequent almost every night. A magnetic and larger-than-life character, Papito is showered with attention everywhere he goes. People often tell Mami how lucky she is to have him. At home—his home and our prison—it's another story altogether.

I'm five years old when we move into the two-story three-bedroom avocado-green house on the corner, with avocado-green carpeting and an ecru kitchen that matches the tiles in the bathroom. The extra room is for hosting Papito's relatives when they fly in from New York City and Port-au-Prince, and for storing his massive collection of vinyl: disco, funkadelic, salsa, afrobeat, soul, Motown, rock, country, and some reggae. With all that wax at his disposal, I wonder why he pumps Journey and Fela nonstop when he's not practicing disco routines with Mami in the basement.

Papito is even more of a dandy now than when we lived in New York City. He maintains a tightly cropped 'fro and well-manicured hands painted with clear polish. He makes Mami iron everything down to his socks. And he coordinates his outfits and jewelry with Mami's, even when he's at the hospital and she's at The Smoke House.

Papito now calls Mami Rosie. He says the name feels more suited to our new lives here. I barely recognize Mami anymore. She works every single day at the shop, selling tobacco, incense, and San Francisco souvenirs, never seeing a dollar. I join her after school during the week and with Lady, my Doberman pinscher, on the weekends. Papito pops in and out the store to count and pick up money, sometimes yelling at Mami in front of customers and other times waiting until they leave.

"Rosie, why did you smile at him like that?" he asks one day after a man leaves the shop. Papito walks over to the front door and hangs up the SORRY, WE'RE CLOSED sign. I wrap my arms around Lady's neck.

"What do you mean, Pascal?" she asks. "I, I was just being nice to the—"

"Are you fucking him, Rosie? Are you cheating on me?" Papito shouts.

I walk over to Mami and hold on to the hem of her dress. I can feel her trembling.

"I promise you, Pascal, I, I was just trying to sell—"

Pascal flicks me on the wrist. I am not allowed to cry, although it hurts. He grabs Mami and goes to the back room, leaving Lady and me alone behind the counter. Mami starts screaming, begging him to stop whatever he's doing to her.

SMACK! SMACK! SMACK! Mami sobs, "Please, Pascal, Raquel is outside, please—"

SMACK! "I fucking love you, Rosie," he yells. "Why are you forcing me to do this?" I think I hear the sound of a belt hitting flesh. Mami is screaming her head off.

I wrap my arms around Lady's strong black neck and begin to cry. She starts barking toward the door. The louder Mami yells, the louder Lady barks. Minutes later, Mami walks out of the back room. Her face and arms are bleeding, and her eyes are black and swollen. Papito is calm, almost jovial. He bends over and smiles at me. I want to scratch his eyes out, but I'm too scared. "Here," he says, giving me a dollar bill, "go buy some candy."

I go to the bathroom and clutch the dollar bill close to my chest and start praying to *la india*. I first saw her, a tall handsome woman with long black hair, sitting at the edge of my bed weeks before we left Seaman Avenue. She told me she belonged to me and promised to appear whenever I was scared or in danger. "I pray Mami takes out the tiny gun she keeps in the kitchen drawer, the one with the pretty white handle, and shoots Papito in the brains, like they do on *Tom and Jerry*."

Later that evening they go dancing, like they do most nights. Mami is wearing a ton of makeup to hide the marks Papito left on her body as a token of his love. Tonight Dickie McAllister, a flamboyantly gay white guy who adores Papito, is babysitting me. When Dickie isn't available, they leave me with Lady.

In a low, menacing voice, Dickie sends me to my room as soon as Mami and Papito leave for the club. "But I'm not tired, Dickie," I whine.

"Oh, girl, go to your room. And if you don't listen to me, I will tell Pascal you were a very naughty little girl when he gets home," he almost whispers back.

Later that night, I become Wonder Woman, flying in an invisible helicopter. I spent the day staring directly at the sun through the large living room window to charge my powers with its rays. I knew Dickie was coming over later that evening, and was determined to find out why he always sends me to my room as soon as Papito and Mami leave.

I try to look the part, sneaking into Mami's bedroom and climbing on the seat of her vanity in my Wonder Woman panties and tank top. I put on Mami's red lipstick and sweep my hair with her roller brush, trying to re-create the superhero bouffant. The closest I get is a mess of combed-out frizzy curls. It doesn't matter. Dickie won't be able to see me spying on him from my invisible plane.

I peek out of my bedroom and find Dickie watching a movie with naked men rubbing each other. Dickie is sweating, nodding off in front of the TV set with no sound. There's white powder on the glass table in front of the couch and a bottle of wine. He looks up at me, halfway startled but mostly out of it.

"Oh, Raquelita," he whispers in a funny flavorless accent. I hate the way he says my name. "You're going to be in so much trouble when Papito and Rosie get home."

"But I just had to go pee, Dickie," I say, pretending I'm half asleep.

"Oh yeah? Well, when you use the bathroom, be careful, because I think I put too much paper in the toilet. Oh, the water is too high, I'm afraid." He doesn't change the channel or turn off the TV as I walk into the bathroom. I close the door and flush the toilet with the lid still down. Bright yellow stinky water starts pouring out of the sides, spilling all over the floor and my feet. Dickie knocks on the bathroom door.

"Oh, now you really did it, Raquel my *belle,*" Dickie sings in a descending scale. "Oh, you better find a way to clean that up before they get back, girl."

I start panicking. Last time I got Papito angry, he spun me around by my ankles until I couldn't see in front of me and nearly threw up. He let go, and I landed on the couch, where he punched me in the stomach and started laughing. Another time he became annoyed when I wouldn't finish my plate of spinach, and he made Mami serve it to me over the next several days for breakfast, lunch, and dinner. When he wasn't home, I begged Mami for food.

"Please, Mami, I am so hungry. I promise I won't tell him if you give me food."

"I can't, Raquelita, he'll kill me if he finds out."

"But how will he find out?" I whimpered.

"Don't you understand? He has his brother Jean watching us when he's not here." I had forgotten about Jean, sitting in the living room watching *Scooby-Doo.*

If Gerard, Papito's youngest brother, had been here, I would have been able to eat. They shared a mother and father, though Gerard didn't look anything like Papito or Jean. He was very tall and had a pretty face the color of brown sugar, like Papi's nieces in Santo Domingo. His hair was more like mine, big and curly. When Gerard was around, there was peace: He worked at the store with Mami and let me climb up his legs to the top of his soft head as many times as I wanted. Lady loved him, too. When Jean dropped into town, Lady was locked in the basement because she tried to attack him. It was as if Lady could smell Jean from the airport—a couple hours before he arrived, she'd start to bark incessantly. Jean was a darker-skinned version of Papito and way more sinister. I started thinking that what Dominicans said about *haitianos* was true: Their darker skin did make them more evil.

Mami avoided eye contact with me, placing what used to look like cooked greens on the table before me with a glass of milk. I begged her for a slice of the bread she pulled out of the oven minutes earlier, but Mami didn't answer me. The spinach had turned into mush with a layer of white mold coating it. Papito never covered the plate when putting it back in the refrigerator. I scooped up spoonfuls of the greenish mush and swallowed without chewing, washing it down with two glasses of milk.

I can't let anything like that happen again. I take off all my clothes, ball up my Wonder Woman panties and tank top, and begin to mop up Dickie's piss from the floor. I wring it out in the bathtub and go back to mopping. I start to smell like piss, the ammonia is making my skin itch as if I have chicken pox. Dickie pecks in.

"Oh, good. *Gooood.* It's almost clean. Girl, you better go to sleep. They'll be back soon," he says.

"Do I have time to take a quick bath, Dickie?" I ask. My legs are covered in welts from scratching.

"Oh, no, I don't think so. I don't think *soooo,*" he sings softly.
I go to bed. My entire body stings.

When they come back from the club, I can hear Papito screwing Mami in their bedroom, which he does every night whether she wants to or not. If she doesn't scream when he fucks her, Papito accuses her of having an affair. I begin to hate her for allowing him to treat us so badly. Mami is so weak.

The following morning I sit with Mami in the yard while she plants flowers. It is one of those rare days when Papito decides not to open the store. I say nothing, following Mami to her sliver of a garden and then upstairs into her bedroom. She slides open the doors of her large closet that's full of fabulous clothes Papito bought her. She isn't allowed to buy her own gear and jewelry or go to a department store without his permission.

There are shiny hot pants in electric blue and black with matching sequined tube tops; bright white clothes that glow under the ultraviolet lights at the club; designer jeans and fitted T-shirts; flowing silk dresses; and more *tacónes* than she could wear in a lifetime, for all those disco-dancing competitions Papito regularly signs them up for. Diamond rings, big wooden bracelets, and turquoise jewelry are stuffed into large ornate boxes next to the bottles of perfume on her dresser. Mami didn't bother packing the rags she cleaned apartments in when we left New York City, but something tells me she hates all the expensive shit hanging in front of her more than anything she left behind.

Papito makes Mami dress up all the time, even when they practice their disco routines in the basement. Today Mami picks out a sky-blue halter dress and white heels with chunky bracelets that match her shoes. She does her hair and puts on makeup while Papito parks his canary-yellow Porsche in the driveway, leaving the cherry-red motorcycle inside, like they do when he throws house parties. I watch Papito and Mami practice their routine for hours. Mami labors through the Hues Corporation's "Rock the Boat" and anything by Donna Summer, Chic, or the Bee Gees, all with an uneasy smile plastered on her face. They run through the routine over and over until they perfect the combinations Papito choreographed. He takes a break to go to the bathroom, leaving Mami downstairs. She looks like an empty shell of a woman with her soul hovering above her. We believe in spiritual *guías* in Santo Domingo. Hers is her own self. I can see Mami's soul desperately trying to find its way back into her small body.

"Mami, can I get you some water?" I ask. She looks through me and doesn't respond. Papito's obsession with disco is slowly killing Mami. Disco fucking sucks.

Papito's other obsession is karate. He's a black belt. The walls of the house are lined with daggers and swords covered with brightly colored velvet sheaths, Chinese stars, and martial art–inspired art. In Papito and Mami's bedroom, I found a pair of nunchakus in a wicker chest full of black whips and magazines with naked men and women hurting each other. Sometimes, especially when Jean comes to town, they take the weapons off the wall and wildly stab the air like musketeers on coke.

My sister, Giselle, came out of nowhere. I barely noticed Mami's belly expand, like those of the pregnant ladies I've seen at the supermarket and Jack in the Box. I used to think they found her, a gorgeous brown ball of flesh with large eyes and long eyelashes similar to Papito's, at the nightclub.

Giselle's arrival doesn't change things much at home. Mami is still treated like an imprisoned African Grey locked in a twenty-four-karat gold cage. She's expected to give birth, slim down, and fit back into her disco clothes in no time flat. Even after she does, Papito remains more preoccupied with his Rosie's looks than their newborn daughter.

I instantly fall in love with her, my new roommate who occupied Mami's body for months and months, like I did six years earlier. Giselle doesn't cry much. Papito probably trained her to fall in line while she was in the womb.

Stalking Dickie proved to be a tawdry undertaking. I'm now content staying in my room with my baby sister. I climb up and balance myself on the railing of her white crib and watch her sleep for hours, placing my index finger under her nose to make sure she's still breathing.

The noise comes from the guest room next door. It starts with faint groans and quickly escalates into terrible high-pitched shrieks coming from a woman who isn't Mami. Papito pounds on the door, demanding that Jean, who's in town again, open it. Mami, visibly shaken, stands behind Papito. I guard the entrance of our bedroom, virtually unnoticed. Jean, sweating profusely and dressed only in a pair of bright red high-waisted jeans, opens the door.

"This bitch doesn't know how to behave," he yells. His girlfriend for the night, a lanky woman taller and darker than Jean, is prettier than a Virginia Slims model. She's kneeling on the carpet in the background, her tiny *tetas* are out, holding her smooth long arms over her short 'fro. She is trembling.

"Jean, please keep it quiet," Papito says calmly.

Jean, sweat pouring from his hot head down to his bare chest, grabs the model by her 'fro and drags her, wailing, farther into the room. She begs Mami to help her, but from experience, I know that appealing to her will get this poor woman nowhere. Mami is speechless; her eyes are bulging out of her head. I peek in.

"Put your dirty face in *this*, bitch," Jean screams at her. He takes out his ugly thing from his pants and takes a leak on the avocado-green carpet.

"Jean, *stop!*" Papito yells, but Jean doesn't seem to hear him.

"Please stop, *please stop.* Help me!" screams the model between sobs. She lifts her head, guarding her face with her bloody arms. She looks at Mami for help, but Rosie does *nada*. The model notices me standing by the doorway and starts weeping quietly. I can't help her. I don't want Jean to attack Mami, Giselle, or me in her stead.

Jean slams the model to the floor, grabbing her hair once more. He goes on to rub the model's hair and face against the carpet where he pissed, so hard that the model stops crying. She looks like she's surrendering to something, her body goes limp. Mami and I start crying.

"*Please*, Pascal. *Please*, Pascal. Please, my love, do something," she says softly into his ear.

"Jean, that is my carpet, and this is my home. Stop it, now. You *will* leave tomorrow," Papito screams. "My God, brother, we have sisters, a mother." Mami says nothing but is wearing an expression I've never seen. She looks livid, almost determined. She stops crying and helps the model get dressed.

I run back into the room and sit down cross-legged on the floor in front of Giselle's crib.

It happens one morning not long after Jean left. Gerard is in town visiting us from New York. As usual, I'm spending the morning climbing up his lanky body while Giselle sleeps in our room and Mami makes breakfast.

"Rosie, why are you dressed like that?" I hear Papito ask Mami. The familiar sound of Papito scolding and then smacking Mami reverberates down the hallway. Oddly, Mami doesn't cry or beg him to stop, like she usually does. Instead, a deafening silence fills the air. I stop climbing and start walking slowly behind Gerard toward the kitchen. Halfway there, I hear Mami smack Papito so hard it makes me shudder.

"That is enough, Pascal," Mami says.

Mami and Papito are at a standstill in the kitchen. He's rubbing his cheek with his right hand, and Mami's fists are balled up in front of her and she is standing like Muhammad Ali, ready to rumble. Mami is usually dressed up, even in the morning. However, today her hair is pulled back into a tight ponytail, and she's wearing a pair of tight faded Levi's, a fitted blue-and-white-striped T-shirt, and dirty white Chuck Taylors. Her long nails are painted blood red.

"She smacked me. This bitch *smacked* me," Papito says to Gerard, all the while staring at Mami.

"Pascal, let's stop this," Gerard says.

Papito lunges at Mami, striking her in the face. Her head snaps back, but she doesn't scream. She doesn't cry. It's like she doesn't feel a thing.

Mami punches Papito squarely in the face, and the two fall to the floor, punching and scratching each other. Despite his tall stature, Gerard can't separate them. They are rolling around on the tile floor, taking turns on top of each other. Punching. Smacking. Scratching. Jabbing.

After a few long minutes, Mami pushes Papito off. She gets up and leaves him bleeding on the floor. Pieces of his skin are hanging from the tips of her long fingernails.

"That's enough, Pascal," she says, *"no más."*

Mami grabs me by the wrist and drags me down the stairs and out onto the street, leaving Giselle in Gerard's care. We run until we stop at a pay phone, where Mami places a collect call to Santo Domingo.

"Hello, Antonio? *Dios, por favor,* help me. He's going to kill me."

Antonio is standing at our doorstep less than forty-eight hours later.

Those three weeks Antonio stayed with us in 1980 were the first since Papito came into our lives that there was no hitting of any sort. Antonio found Gerard hot and Papito adorable, though bordering on effeminate. In the beginning, Papito came off solemn and charming, underplaying how bad life really was in his beautiful prison. Mami didn't challenge him, wanting to keep the peace until we were safely out of Papito's house and back in Paraíso before she told Antonio the truth.

Papito showed Antonio how to use the bus, gave him a tour of the city, paid for lavish dinners, and introduced him to his friends. He treated Mami with deference, like he did his own mother—that mean witch. It crosses Antonio's mind that things weren't as bad as his sister made them sound when Rocío called him, crying hysterically.

During the second week things become clearer.

"Oh, I'll drop you off at the store so you and Gerard can work a little bit for us," Papito says to Antonio one morning at breakfast. "My Rosie needs a break."

"Who the fuck is Rosie?" Antonio asks.

"Your sister—that's what I call her. Rosie suits her better."

Antonio looks over at Mami, washing dishes in the kitchen. He notices for the first time since his arrival that something is awfully wrong with this picture. He doesn't see the headstrong woman in his sister anymore.

"Before we go to the store, let me show you something," Papito tells Antonio. "I'll be right back." He goes into his bedroom and comes back out smiling and holding a gun in each hand, instructing Antonio and Gerard to follow him to the roof. Antonio reluctantly goes, thinking that nothing too crazy will happen in broad daylight. I hear gunshots and laughter coming from above, none of which sound like Antonio's. Mami looks like she's going to faint and falls onto the couch. I sit next to her. Minutes later, Papito, Gerard, and Antonio come back down, and we go to the shop as if nothing happened.

"It's time to go, to leave this place," I hear Antonio whisper to Mami in the car. She doesn't respond.

Things get tense quickly when Antonio starts making plans to leave and take us with him. Papito is more paranoid than usual, taking time off from the hospital and The Smoke House in order to keep tabs on us at all times.

The negotiation goes down in the living room. Gerard sits next to Papito. I sit between Mami and Antonio.

"You don't understand. I cannot live without Rosie or Raquelita," Pascal says. He doesn't mention Giselle.

"Pascal, if it were Maureen or Marie, you would want the same," Gerard says. "Let them go."

"Pou ki-sa, frem?" Papito asks. "Why, brother?"

"This so-called relationship of yours is toxic," Gerard responds. "It will end wretchedly, with one of you dead and the other in jail."

Mami says nothing. She reaches over and holds my hand, something she rarely does.

"We need to go back to Santo Domingo. I have to go back, and Rocío and the children must come with me," Antonio says. Papito starts to cry. He is losing control.

It's settled. Antonio rents a Toyota, and we try to leave. Our first attempt to escape is thwarted by Papito, who trashes the car the night before we are to depart.

"Okay, Pascal, there are two ways to go about this," Antonio says the next morning.

"You're not man enough to talk to me that way," Pascal responds. He is furious.

"Oh, a guy like you, who wears masks, wants to talk about being a man?" Antonio says. "I don't think you've been treating my sister like a real man would."

"Let's prevent a tragedy here," Pascal says, sitting on the couch, staring through Antonio at one of the swords hanging on the wall.

"To prevent a tragedy, why don't you make sure you don't prevent us from missing the flight this time, because I will report this conversation to the authorities and tell them you crashed the car on purpose."

We wait for the next flight out of San Francisco to Santo Domingo at San Francisco International for what feels like hours.

Tío Antonio risked his life to save ours.

Mama and Papa are furious with Mami.

"God only knows what Raquelita was subjected to over there," is the first thing Mama says to her. "You will never admit it, out of shame."

"*No era cómo ustedes piensan.* It's not what you think," Mami says. She's right. It was much worse.

In the time since I last saw Mama she decided she had taken enough of Papa's playboy shit and divorced him. They sold our house in Paraíso to an ambassador who realized soon after he moved in that he couldn't cope with the iguanas overrunning the place. Maybe it was for the best, because Mama and Papa's split was short-lived, and they wanted to start the next chapter of their life together somewhere new. They moved into a new two-story house in Fernandez. Mami, Giselle, and I moved into the first floor of a spacious colonial apartment on Arzobispo Portes.

It takes only a few weeks for Papa to call Papi and convince him to fly into Santo Domingo to pick me up and take me back to New York City with him and his wife. I eavesdrop on a few of their phone conversations. Papa doesn't feel that Mami is stable enough to take care of both Giselle and me alone. I assume Papi agrees, because Papa tells me that I'm going to soar like an eagle in Nueva York. Now that Papi was remarried—this time to an older woman, a gringa or something close to one—that meant he was stable and presumably paid enough to take care of me.

When Papi comes to Santo Domingo with his wife, Alice, I get excited just hearing him talk about New York City. "We're going to make a snowman in the park this *invierno*," Papi says to me. "I have room for your toys and everything." He showers me with affection and gifts. Alice sits by, watching and smiling, keeping her distance so that I can have Papi to myself. I'm so excited that I start planning how I'm going to decorate my bedroom once we get there. My bed will be big enough to accommodate my *abuelitos*, Paloma and Antonio, when they drop by for a visit. When the time comes to have the conversation with Mami, it's straightforward.

"Mami, I have to go. I'm sorry," I say. "I want to have a better life."

"What do you know about what a better life is?" she asks me.

"I know what it's *not*, Mami," I respond. "You've shown me that much."

"Go to hell. I hope you die and go to hell with your father," she says. "I never want to see you again."

It's April 1981. I'm almost eight.

CHAPTER FOUR

Uptown '81

> DJ's spinning I said my, my
> Flash is fast, Flash is cool.
>
> —BLONDIE, "RAPTURE"

AFTER THAT CONVERSATION ON ARZOBISPO PORTES, MAMI FLEW back to San Francisco with Giselle, back to her perch on Eddy Street.

I board the plane to New York City by myself, leaving behind the only people I feel a connection to. The plane is enormous. Legs are everywhere—thick, skinny, very light, burnt rust, like those of my *primas,* and dark, like those of Jean's Virginia Slims model—racing up and down both aisles. My legs are unspectacular in comparison. They are short and light brown, like *caramelito,* and covered with scabs and welts from scratching. "The mosquitoes love you more than most people," Mama said often.

A gorgeous long pair with nude shimmering pantyhose on stops by my seat every so often to drop crayons, Pan Am 747 coloring books, a bunch of wing pins, bags of pretzels, and ginger ale on my tray. The stewardesses smile but don't say much. I wonder if any of them are Dominican, like me. Or *americana,* like me.

I look at the clouds and imagine life in New York City. I will live in a big and beautiful apartment like those old white women in Lincoln Towers. I will have a room that will look just like my room in Santo Domingo, that will be big enough for my dolls. Papi will treat me better than Papito did and never tell me to go to hell.

I haven't finish coloring an entire page before I'm told to put my things away in preparation for landing. The trip is so short, I'm going to ask Papi if I can come back to visit Papa and Mama on the weekends.

Papi picks me up from John F. Kennedy International Airport with his wife, Alice. Nothing remarkable happens when we meet; he doesn't pick me up and twirl me around, like he did back in Santo Domingo. He and his wife speak to me only in English. Alice is dressed in polyester pants and a pastel blouse with a scarf cinched around her neck. I can make out the blue veins through her blanched face, neck, and hands—the only parts of her that are exposed. Her complexion perfectly matches her blouse.

Papi's tousled hair makes him look younger than thirty-eight. His face is slightly more ashen than when I saw him a couple of months ago in Santo Domingo. He's dressed in almost the same outfit he wore in Papa and Mama's living room: lightweight sweatpants, a polo shirt, a pair of Stan Smiths, and white tube socks hugging his skinny calves.

I don't like Alice. Papi pays too much attention to her, like Mami did Papito, even at the airport, where he should be paying attention to me. Alice's razor-thin blond hair is what people in Santo Domingo call *bueno*, but I don't understand how that kind of hair can be good. It doesn't move at all, or ripple like the water in Boca Chica when I throw shells at it.

I imagine I don't look much better to her. My arms, legs, and neck are covered in mosquito bites, and I'm rail-thin. I haven't fully recovered from living in San Francisco. I wonder if Alice knows how to cook as well as Mama and Papa. She reminds me of the ladies Mami used to clean for who rarely entered their kitchens. Alice looks harmless, like she won't turn into a monster when Papi isn't around or make me eat rotten spinach. More than anything, I hope she doesn't start insisting

I call her "Mamita" or something that will give off the impression that I am her flesh and blood.

Looking at him in the rearview mirror of his gray Chevy Impala, I notice I have Papi's face and lanky body and Mami's sad baggy eyes. I guess we are somehow related, regardless of how disconnected I'm feeling to him right now.

We drive slowly past a road onto the Van Wyck Expressway until we reach the interstate heading north, lined with black shiny bags spilling garbage on either side of the road. There are dead birds, raccoons, and squirrels everywhere and a couple of what look like decomposing dogs in shallow graves of debris and oil from the other Impalas, station wagons, and punch buggies whizzing by. It's as if the dead don't matter.

In only a few hours, the sky has changed colors. Santo Domingo's sky makes her waters turn shades of the brightest blue. The sky in New York City is a sad mixture of rust brown and slate. The airport, the streets, the park, the people—those from the islands included—eventually lose the luster on their skin, like Mami did. I notice the golden brown is already leaving my own hands and face, escaping out the cracked window.

Cars behind and on either side of us are honking at Papi; drivers are pouting, and a few throw their middle fingers up in his direction. "Come on, fuckin' drive, buddy, would ya?" a driver screams at Papi. He makes a funny motion with his hand under his chin, as if he's scratching it, followed by what I think is a bad word in another language: *"BAFANGUL!"*

Papi ignores him, keeping his eyes fixed straight ahead.

"Eduardo, *please.* I think you have to drive a little faster, what? You're going to get a ticket," Alice says from the passenger seat.

"Come *on*, dah'ling. Let me drive!"

We inch onward, driving so slowly I think I may be able to walk faster to wherever it is we're going. The whole world is passing us by, yelling all kinds of "fuck yous" and throwing gestures of what feels like *fukú* in different languages. Papi glances back at me through the rearview mirror. I smile at him. He doesn't smile back.

"Come on, mothafuck*you*," we hear from time to time on the expressway.

"Eduardo, *please*," Alice says.

"*Dah'ling*, keep your mou'se *shut*. I'm *driving*," Papi says.

A lot of time goes by before we arrive on a street I've seen before. We are on Seaman Avenue. Mami's building is on the corner. I can see our old window facing the front. Papi lives two buildings over, down the block. It's the same building Mami helped him move into years earlier, after she caught him in bed with a guitar-strumming Puerto Rican church lady. After Papi and Alice got married, they decided to live here over her place on the Upper East Side because he wanted to stay in walking distance from the tennis courts and his favorite Cuban-Chinese restaurant on Dyckman Street.

We walk up the stairs to the place where Mami left Papi for good before we split to San Francisco. He unlocks the door to an apartment that looks a lot smaller than I remembered it. Dark wooden floors are covered with dusty rugs. The walls are sad, loaded down by kitsch and official-looking plaques that make the place look more like a doctor's office than a home.

From the instant I walk across the threshold into Papi's apartment, cramped with tennis equipment and furniture meant for a much larger place, I start to feel disoriented and dizzy. Mama would not believe that a woman lived here. There is no room for me, no spot where I can extend my hands without knocking something over.

Papi's building is on a block where a lot of white people still live. The white people are super-friendly to each other, clustering in small groups in front of the building. They keep mostly to themselves.

Our building is like a *barrio* within a *barrio*, full of its own *bochinche*. I heard that the little quiet man with the DA haircut down the hall from us—he's been described as being Dominican, Cuban, Puerto Rican, and sometimes Mexican—was recently abandoned by his wife because he had violated their son in a nasty way. There's a *morena* around the corner who I think helps solve other people's problems, a social worker. She looks like Michael Jackson, only darker, with a wide nose and a dry Jheri curl. There are a few enormous neighbors in the building who move like the fishing boats on Samana Bay, slowly and deliberately. One looks exactly like Raj and Dee's mom, Mabel, from *What's Happening!!*, a show I loved watching on Eddy Street. I can hear her breathing heavy as she steers herself toward the mailbox, her door, and up Seaman Avenue. And when she speaks to her daughter, Mini-Mabel, or says hello to us, her words are slow and rhythmic. It takes nothing for beads of sweat to surface around her shiny hairline, even during the winter months.

There's a man in the apartment directly across from us that looks like a real-life Fat Albert who doesn't like to walk. Each and every night he returns home from work in his boat of a car and waits for hours in front of the building for a parking space to free up. Sometimes he reads the paper and eats fried chicken legs to pass the time. He is a patient man.

There's a middle-aged white couple downstairs who are shaped like matching cantaloupes. A man older than Jesus who used to be the super and his elderly sister live upstairs; they always look sad. I heard they are Jewish.

Most of the people on my new block look down or straight ahead and avoid making eye contact. The only exceptions are Fat Albert and his wife, Michael Jackson, Mabel, and Mini-Mabel.

I hear people walking their dogs outside complaining about there being too many Dominicans and other Spanish-speaking people flooding this side of the block. They already made a mess of the building directly across the street from Mami's old place by playing dominoes and music through the night, and talking too loudly for the sensitive ears of the block's white settlers. These new people are invading the area like they do the trains, walls, and parks when night falls. Every morning they leave evidence in the form of elaborate murals that stretch ten feet high and more across, painted on the concrete barricade wrapped around large sections of the park's baseball field.

"They chu'd *take* all of dose Dominicans and *kill* 'em," Papi says one day to Alice when she comes home from work. She gets home too late from the hospital to cook dinner. On the weekends she tries to make food but can only boil potatoes and eggs. I'd rather swallow spoonfuls of rotten spinach than eat the herring she likes straight from the jar with *näkkileipä*, a sour flat bread from her country.

We meet her where we usually do, in front of the shack in the park. From there we walk down to Broadway to eat dinner at the Golden Rule, a Greek diner, or its bland alternative, Capitol.

"Eduardo, *please*," she says.

"Papi, but aren't *we* Dominican?" I ask, tugging at the hem of his polo shirt.

I am confused. Papi wants Mama, Antonio, Paloma, his own relatives killed just because they are Dominican? And Papi's skin looks like dark butter when it snows and only if the sun doesn't come out for weeks—but *white*? Papi looks more like Aladdin than he does the Jewish man upstairs.

"But we don't look anything like the man upstairs. Your mother is very brown, a *trigueña*, and—"

"*Shut* your mou'se," he snaps back, looking at me like I'm one of the Dominicans he wants killed.

"Eduardo, *please*," Alice says. She always says "Eduardo, *please*" and little else.

"If they kill all the Dominicans, what will happen to you and—"

"I say to *shut* your mou'se," he says in my ear so that only I can hear him.

My body feels heavy inside. My eyes are weighted down with water, but I am afraid to cry. Papi is beginning to scare me even more than Papito used to.

We walk down Isham Street in silence. Papi is angry. Alice is still frowning and apparently annoyed with him because she doesn't utter a word during the walk over to the diner. I try to forget what Papi said by pretending I'm Blondie, singing to my fans in that crazy-cool "Rapture" video.

I'm hungry for a pizza burger deluxe and hoping for a cookie with chocolate sprinkles from the bakery next door afterward. Mostly, I want everything to be okay when we get home.

• • •

It only takes a few weeks for Papi to bring Alice and me to the tennis courts. He gives me a wooden racket and says playing tennis will boost my appetite and help me bulk up so I can look less scrawny. Papi walks over to one side of the rectangle, and we stand on the other, close to the service line. Playing tennis is fun until I miss the ball too many times despite his instruction.

"Come on, I say follow *tru*, follow *through*," he yells from the other side of the court. I'm not sure what that means.

"I'm trying, Papi. I'm trying. Please don't get so mad," I yell across the court.

"Eduardo, *please*," Alice says. I look over at her. If she says "please" one more time, I just may punch her in the face.

Papi is flushed and has completely lost his patience. "Less get out o' here," he screams over at us. The guys on the basketball courts to our left are looking at us, so are some of the other tennis players on the courts.

Alice and I trail Papi as he races up Seaman Avenue back to our apartment. My hands are shaking as I think about what I could have done to piss him off this badly. When we arrive at Papi and Alice's gloomy place, I feel like I should find somewhere to hide, but I have no privacy, just a bed where I imagine a couch should go in the dark living room. I sit down on the bed, going over the minutes we were playing tennis, trying to figure out where things went wrong. Alice follows Papi into their bedroom, where he begins screaming something about me.

"She is going to be on welfare like her mother, a *na'thing*."

"Eduardo, *please*. She just moved here, she isn't even—"

"If she can't *lissen* to simple instructions, I guess she is as *lousy* as her moth'a."

I manage to stand up and walk to the bathroom, though my knees feel like giving out. I hook the door shut and splash cold water on my eyes so I won't look like I'm crying. I sit on the toilet lid, cupping my face with my hands, and start to sob. Papi storms out of his bedroom, kicks the bathroom door in, and stands there with his eyes wide open, scowling at me. I can hear my heart pounding so fast that I start feeling faint. If I could hide in the little space between the back of the toilet and the wall, I gladly would.

"Eduardo, *please*," Alice says in the background. Papi doesn't reply. He just stands there panting like an exhausted dog, glaring at me like he hates me more than Lady did Jean. I can't move.

"Please don't kill me," I plead, almost under my breath.

"Stap—*cryin'*," Papi howls.

"Eduardo, *please*," Alice says, now standing behind him.

Papi marches away from the bathroom, then stomps across the living room and out the door.

I walk over to the bed and lie down, crying for Mama and Papa.

When he comes back a couple of hours later, Papi decides I am going to play tennis every day after school. He will make a champion out of me whether I like it or not.

I'm enrolled in a Catholic grammar school called St. Thaddeus, located near the Dyckman Houses. I learn that Thaddeus is the patron saint of desperate cases and lost causes, which is appropriate, considering our surroundings.

I like it much better than I did Mahatma Gandhi in Santo Domingo. The adults there were very mean, smacking our knuckles with rulers for nothing. I guess our *familias* were fooled by the peaceful image of the skinny bald man in round glasses, draped in white fabric, that greeted them each morning they dropped us off at school.

The best thing about St. Thaddeus is the journey there. The colorfully painted trains I pass every morning on my way to school rock my world. The IRT number 1 is the only line on the island to have elevated station stops. The trains are like moving canvases, almost always completely covered with letters and characters in bright colors from tiptop to bottom. They are more engaging to me than school, where I'm an average and mostly ignored student.

The bright purples, greens, pinks, blues, and yellows are a welcome contrast to their pewter backdrop and are more interesting than the dull pocked walls at school. I've heard the grown-ups sitting on the park benches by the tennis courts say that the last couple of mayors paid millions of billions of dollars to erase it. Mayor Koch is promising to get rid of it forever and the people who do it, too. The people on our block believe the tagging and the murals are making people fight, bringing gangs into the neighborhood. It irritates the city and many adults that these vandals—graffiti writers—are catching so much fame in newspapers and on television and even in the movies. I didn't realize it until I saw on TV that there are a lot of white boys getting up, too. Papi ignores me when I ask him if he wants to see all of them rounded up and killed now that white boys, maybe even Jewish ones, are painting the trains.

It's mostly teenagers who are doing it, from all over the city. They write their names and sometimes add their street numbers to their aliases. For the adults at the MTA, the writing and art plastered on the trains and walls are a public nuisance. To me, it's the shit.

Almost every morning I'm greeted by an old lady at the entrance of St. Thaddeus named Sister Frances, who glows like an angel. I'm not sure she's even a nun, because she doesn't wear a habit. Sister Frances looks like a mummy wrapped in skin, almost as skinny as Gandhi and even brighter than Alice. She uses both hands to drop pieces of mint and other candy into our palms every morning and afternoon without fail.

In the beginning, I feel out of place at school. My English is somewhat funny, a bit broken. I'll say something backward, like "Juice is what I want, please" instead of "I want juice, please" to the lunch ladies.

At first everybody laughs and calls me "ass backwards" at several points throughout the day: attendance, lunch, recess, after school, and any time I open my mouth.

"*Yo*, Rachel, you are ass backwards," says Josefa or any number of Marias or Joselitos.

"Yo, my name is Raquel," I insist.

"Na, it ain't, you hick. Why do they say Rachel when they call your name during attendance every morning then?"

"My papi—"

"Where you come from?"

"I was born here, but I was staying with my *abuelos* in D.R. for—"

"Yo, you ain't Dominican. That lady that looks like Sister Frances—she yo' mother?"

"Hell, no. She Papi's wife."

"Are you rich? I heard you live where them rich white folks live, by the good side of the park."

"Na. He works with teeth, he makes sure they are okay and makes fake ones sometimes. He told me he made one for the wife of that guy from the Beatles they shot by Central Park and—"

"Why don't you live with your mother—what the *fuck*, she dead or somethin'?"

"Yeah, she is. Kind of—"

"You the only one I know who has a dead moms. That shit is *ill*, yo."

It was easier to say that Mami was dead than try to explain that I wasn't sure where she was. At some point, I cannot remember when exactly, I stop telling people my name is Raquel. I always loved my name, especially when I was referred to as Raquelita, *un nombre de cariño*, by people like Mama and Paloma, who knew me before now. Maybe, like Mami, I was paralyzed and unable to communicate that I had been somebody before my new masters took ownership of me. Maybe the name Rachel, as unremarkable as it sounds to me, suits me better now.

I turn nine, ten, and eleven with each unchanging day and night running into one another so fluidly, it feels like I'm doing hard time rather than living life. The donning of my butt-ugly blue and green plaid uniform skirt tells me it's daytime. The tennis skirt and racket means it's either stupid early, afternoon, or early evening. Stained silverware and cheap restaurant plates signal that it's dinnertime. Papi's strong arms shaking me and throwing me against a wall, or his tennis shoe digging into my back or wherever it lands, are how the day ends when I don't live up to his standards on the court. When I do please him—I rarely do—shit is sweet.

Speaking of which, what finally does change my routine is something brown and shitty. One day, I come back after tennis to find a used Steinway upright that Papi and Alice bought from the thrift store near Broadway and 204th Street sitting in my living room–makeshift bedroom. *They must have gotten a great deal on it*, I think, *because that thing couldn't possibly be used to decorate any other apartment in the city unless it's a huge bathroom.* The piano looks like a large pile of brown shit, as if it came from an elephant or some extinct creature that left large shits in its wake. Because every inch of our place is used for storage, the top of the piano immediately becomes cluttered with my first- and second-place tennis trophies and medals, photos, and other knickknacks. My bed is now parallel to the kitchen table. I practice piano every night for an hour after tennis and before I do homework, regardless of whether or not I'm exhausted. Sometimes before I start running through my scales, Papi interrupts to share story after story about his days as a nightclub singer and musical composer and arranger. "They loved me so much," Papi says, sometimes breaking into sections of Schubert's "Ave Maria" in Latin. "You will be a good piano player, too."

I take piano classes with Ms. Kaufman, a spinster with thinning wiry hair in the Bronx. Ms. Kaufman scares me because she looks like San Lázaro, with open wet sores covering her body from her forehead down to her feet. There's a rumor that her body erupted when her mother died because she couldn't take the pain of losing her. She had a nervous breakdown and quit being a fairly successful concert pianist, dedicating her life to teaching kids. I cannot imagine caring that much for anybody.

Papi sits, as he often does, on my bed, watching me practice the piano. Alice is in the kitchen making instant coffee. I would rather be anywhere but in front of this shit-brown piano with Papi burning holes in my back with his savage eyes.

My mind wanders, as it often does, to the park across the street from my school. I wish I were there right now, watching these guys—they call themselves b-boys—dancing on large pieces of linoleum thrown atop the concrete. The b-boys dress so fresh, in matching

T-shirts, fitted Lee jeans, and fat laces. They spin on their backs and heads. They glide on their palms and uprock like Apache warriors. Watching them dance is like watching Bruce Lee fight himself in *Enter the Dragon.*

The b-boys and b-girls catch fame, too, arguably more than some of the graffiti writers on the scene. They have def names like the writers and wear them in brass and silver on their belts: Doze, Crazy Legs, Frosty Freeze, Kuriaki. There's a girl, Baby Love, I want to battle. Freeze is mad cute, and so is Kuriaki. Doze and he could be in Menudo, and that beautiful writer Mare139, too. Mare139 has the best chance to get into Menudo, with that silky hair of his. The rest of the writers look kind of like ducks. In my eyes, LEE is the only writer who's an exception to the rule. It doesn't matter what he looks like because he's the most famous writer in New York City, even bigger than Menudo.

I imagine myself doing footwork on the linoleum flooring, looking all high post and shit, when I make the same mistake on the piano.

"If you do tha' *again,* I'm going to *throw* you out the window," Papi yells.

If Papi had a tag name, it would be Trujillo215, the boogeyman Mama used to talk about.

"Eduardo, *please*," Alice says, "don't say those things."

My hands are shaking. I try to play whatever classical piece Ms. Kaufman assigned me that week—they all start to sound the same after a while—slowly, correctly.

I fuck up again.

"I'm going to throw you out the window, you *understan'*?"

"But Papi, I'm trying hard."

He springs up from my bed and punches me in the back of the neck with such force that I start seeing two of everything. I am grateful that he's using his fists this time and not the orange metal ball hopper or the antique wooden chair that matches absolutely nothing in the apartment.

My head is spinning faster than a windmill. My back is numb, my eyes are heavy, but I do not cry. Like the graffiti writers, the dancers, and all the other kids nobody wants, I resist tears.

"Eduardo, *please.*" Alice is frowning at Papi from the kitchenette but does nothing to stop him.

"You going to be like *dose* ga'bage Dominicans on welfare—like your moth'a," he screams into my right ear, sending me further off balance.

"But Papi, I'm—"

"I hope one day you cry tears of blood," he says, his eyes bulging out of the sockets. "I hate you."

I believe him.

Papi gets dressed and leaves. He disappears—he jets for an hour or two almost every night—ignoring Alice when she asks where he's going or where he's been.

I stop playing.

As Papi slams the door behind him, his dental school graduation photo falls from atop the old black china cabinet onto the floor. I jump on the photo, screaming, "I HATE YOU. I fucking HATE you, you motherfuckin' asshole!"

"Rachel, *please,*" Alice says, "don't talk like that."

I stop. I don't want her to tell on me. Thankfully, she doesn't.

"Why do you let him hit me like that, Alice?" I ask.

"Because he's your father, and he can do whatever he wants with you," she responds.

I lie down on my twin bed and close my eyes. I continue the fall down, down, down a damp well whose bottom is endless, never reaching the bottom. The throbbing up and down my neck and back awakens me.

I stare at the small clock-radio on the junky night table next to my bed. I'm alone, finally alone in my makeshift bedroom. I turn on the radio.

"Ninety-eight-point-seven *Kiiiiiiiiiiiiiiiiiiiiiiiiiiiiiissss!*" pronounces the raspy voice through the static.

I feel electricity run through my body. I don't move. The DJ—his name is Red Alert—is mixing the same music I hear blaring from boom boxes at the park by my school and the handball and basketball courts in Inwood Park. It's the kind of music that sends b-boys

flying through the air, taking control of their bodies as if they're pup-
pets suspended and controlled by magical strings. It goes BOOM-
BAP, BOOM-BOOM-BAP, BOOM-BAP, BOOM-BOOM-BAP. The
music is called rap.

"God is smiling on you but he's frowning too / Because only God
knows what you'll go through." It's Grandmaster Melle Mel. His voice
pours out of the speaker with the force of a *brujo* invading my head.

The lyrics feel like they were written for me, almost like a sound
track to the movie of my life so far. The music delivers me from the
suffocating darkness in here, from Papi's fists and Alice's indifference.

The music sounds different here than it does outside. Out there,
everybody thinks I'm stuck up because I play a "white girl's sport,"
and piano, and because I live on Seaman Avenue with a white
woman. Some of the kids at school swear I think I'm better than they
are and am intentionally drawing a line where I'm standing alone on
one side, looking down at them. It's worse when Papi makes me bring
my medals and trophies to school to show my teachers. Up here and
at tennis, I feel like no matter what, I will never be good enough or
rich enough. I don't feel like I fit in too many places. Grandmaster
Melle Mel gets it.

Xiomara is the coolest mom at St. Thaddeus: everybody loves her. And
a couple days after I spotted her laughing with Papi at a parent-teacher
conference, she started paying special attention to me. One morning,
Titi—she told me to call her that—brought me Entenmann's chocolate
chip cookies and rice and beans for lunch. I felt so special because she
began treating me like she did her own son, David, for no apparent
reason. I don't know or care what Papi said to her the other night, but
I don't want to mess this up. Maybe people will finally stop making fun
of me every time Alice comes to school looking crazy in her flammable
polyester getups.

Titi looks more Puerto Rican than Dominican. I'm not sure where
she comes from; her accent doesn't give her away. David is a *jabao*
version of Titi, with light skin and coarse hair. They live on Academy

Street, near Post Avenue. I can see the 1 train zoom by their second-floor apartment window.

I fall in love with everything about her, even her bottled strawberry-blond hair, cut short in a pristine DA. She wears a lot of makeup and tight-ass jeans that look really good on her except for the perpetual *pan de agua* she rocks between her legs. I don't dare ask Titi her age, but she must have had David really young, like they do in D.R., because she had it going on. And she cooked so well I didn't want to eat out anymore.

I feel like a duck living on Seaman Avenue, away from Titi and life east of Broadway. I love going to her apartment. From Titi's window, I can see young guys rocking DAs and tight Caesar haircuts and girls wearing long mullets. In the summer, couples dress in matching two-toned Lees and Le Tigre shirts and leather bomber jackets, sheepskin hats and coats in the winter.

I overhear women *bochinchando* in front of Titi's building. I hear there's a brothel in the old lady's apartment with the black window curtains in the basement. We all know something weird is going on in there because these creepy-looking guys, almost always *blancitos*, come and go like they're giving away free money and crack at all hours of the day and night. I never see any women enter or leave the apartment, but I hear these *sucios* in there are fucking girls of all ages.

I start noticing something else: more and more adults who look out of place, walking around with big cameras filming and taking pictures on the block. One day it happens when we're running back to Titi's apartment because I have to use the bathroom. People with big cameras and colossal attitudes won't allow us onto Titi's side of the street. They have a permit, so we have to wait until they finish filming a scene of a movie they are calling *Body Rock*. A bunch of kids from the area are recruited to walk behind the movie's star, pretending to be a part of his posse. I've seen the dude before on *The Love Boat,* but now he's dressed in a long black leather trench coat with a wickedy-wack piece on the back that reads CHILLY D in fluorescent colors.

Chilly D is wearing a girl's spike bracelet on his wrist with a pair of matching black boots and high-waisted stonewashed jeans. Take after take, Lorenzo "Chilly D" Llamas is acting like he thinks he is the coolest guy to ever step foot in the 'hood. It's so crazy funny, I forget I have to pee.

Good things happen when I win. For one, Papi does nice things for me even when he isn't trying to show off in front of Titi. Papi is hanging out more frequently with us while Alice holds down a nine-to-six. Work must be slow for Papi right now, because he always manages to make early appearances when Titi, David, and I are hanging out at the park or her place.

I'm playing so well these days that I become part of the Reebok Junior Tennis Academy, where they lace me with eight pairs of sneakers and a big tennis bag full of clothing to represent them. It's too bad that Reebok sneakers, except the high-top classics, are strictly for toys.

For my eleventh birthday, Papi takes me to see *Beat Street* at the Alpine on Dyckman. I'm wearing the gray Lees he and Alice bought me from the huge habibi Supermundo store. It's my favorite one in the 'hood because they sell BVD shirts and Lee jeans for just $11.99. I'm so nervous. I wonder if Freeze is going to be at the Alpine tonight, or any of the writers from the Manhattan Subway Kings. I hope Papi doesn't embarrass me.

It's love at first sight. This time it's with the man on the large screen, RAMO, who I think should audition for Menudo as soon as possible because he's almost too old. They should have replaced Ricky Meléndez with RAMO: His long black DA and those high cheekbones make him look like an *indio,* as if he moved from Puerto Rico to New York City just to conquer the trains. I look over at Papi, who fell asleep soon after we sat down, and I completely lose myself at the Roxy.

"What are you *doin'*?" Papi says, half awake. "Why are *you* crying?"

I don't answer him. RAMO just died, electrocuted on the third rail of the train tracks.

"What happened?" Papi asks me again.

"Be-be-cause RAMO died on the third rail and, and—" I whisper.

"*Stap* crying," he snaps, "you are *so* ri-di-culous with *your* monkey business."

Papi falls asleep until the final scene, where Grandmaster Melle Mel and the Furious Five rush the stage at the Roxy to perform the film's title track. Papi is jolted awake by the music. "What is *this*?" he asks me, pointing at Melle Mel, one of the few people who could roll up into any 'hood wearing tight leather pants and boots.

"That's—"

"What, is he—a *nice*-looking boy dressed like that?" he asks.

"He's not gay, Papi, that's—"

"What *time* is it? We have to wake up early for tennis tomorrow."

I don't respond. I won't let Papi ruin the celebration of RAMO's life.

CHAPTER FIVE

An Awakening

It's exhilarating to be alive in a time of awakening consciousness;
it can also be confusing, disorienting, and painful.

—ADRIENNE RICH

I BEG PAPI AND ALICE FOR A SHEEPSKIN IN THE WINTER OF 1984.
I'm playing the shit-brown piano really well. A few months ago, I ran
through Clementi's "Sonatina Op. 36, No. 1" like it was nothing during a recital at the Wellington Hotel. I'm also winning more tennis
matches and tournaments and learning how to pretend that I don't
hate every second on the court. And on the nights that don't end violently, I use my dance routines to make Papi and Alice laugh. I throw
myself from my bed to the floor and do the worm across the living
room. The worm, for some reason, makes Papi laugh hysterically every
single time I do it.

"Ask *her* what she *wan's* to be when she grows up, *dah'ling*," Papi
says to Alice.

"A breakdancer, I'm going to be a b-girl. And I'm going to write rap
songs for Roxanne Shanté," I respond.

"She *wan's* to be so Black," Papi says, laughing.

"Eduardo, *please*," Alice says, "you know that it's not only Black kids who are doing that dancing."

I want a sheepskin so badly I don't challenge Papi's hip-hop miseducation. He promises that we'll go to Delancey and pick one up before it gets cold, but that doesn't happen. Instead, Alice comes back from visiting her sister upstate with a shopping bag that contains the ugliest coat I've ever seen. It looks like a dead polar bear.

"Look what Anni gave me to give to you," Alice says to me, holding up the dark blue fur coat in front of my face.

"But that thing isn't a sheepskin. You *promised—*"

"Rachel, *please*, it's the same thing."

"No, it isn't," I say. Tears are beginning to rush down my cheeks. I wish Titi were my stepmother. She'd never let me look like such a *campesina* at school.

"Nobody will know the difference, Rachel," Alice says. "It's a perfectly good coat."

"*Stap* with that *monkey*-business crying," Papi says.

We've been enjoying a rather warm winter. For a while I can get away with wearing layers of clothing under my uniform and Reebok jacket instead of the blue polar bear, but I dread the inevitable. First I became the laughingstock at school when the other kids started calling me "Steel Back" because of the bulky-ass brace Papi made me wear under my uniform, when I could have just worn it to sleep, after I was diagnosed with scoliosis. Then, things went from bad to worse when I came to school with bad *graho* after forgetting to put on deodorant after tennis one morning.

The first time I'm forced to wear the polar bear to school, everyone does poke fun of me except my best friend, Claudine Jean-Baptiste. She lives in the Dyckman Houses with her mother, a nurse born in Port-au-Prince whose English I pretend to understand.

"It's not *that* bad," Claudine says. She's trying hard not to laugh while consoling me in the girls' bathroom.

"I look like a fat-ass fucking polar bear," I say, staring at myself in the mirror from every angle. "Everyone is fucking with me again."

"Well, at least it's different, Raquel. Everybody already thinks you're on some other shit anyway, right?"

Something happens that makes my polar-bear coat take a backseat. The conversation shifts to an entirely different topic, one that will consume every adult in my building and teacher at school, the tennis players in the park, Papi, and even a few kids I know for months and months.

"*Venga aquá loco,* did you hear what happened to those dudes on the steel horse?" I hear someone say as I'm leaving school a couple days before Christmas break.

"Yeah, someone shot those motherfuckers right there in front of everybody like nothing," says another dude. I only halfway pay attention, thankful that there are no rumored gang fights preventing us from leaving school again. New York City reported dozens of robberies and assaults on the train every day this year, so the drama rang like any other story at first. It becomes real when I see the kids on FOX News appearing from the station on stretchers. Adding to the mounting suspense, the shooter is incognito for days.

Suddenly, the nerdiest white man the city has ever seen in handcuffs, with thick glasses and a detached gaze, turns himself in. In the beginning, Bernhard Goetz is lionized as a working-class hero for carrying out what many straphangers who've been terrorized on the train have only fantasized about. He confesses to shooting the four Black teens in the seventh car of a number 2 subway train on Fourteenth Street because he felt like they were about to jack him. Goetz had had enough. He was mugged by Black kids before, and the police, he felt, did shit to help him. The guy is dubbed a subway vigilante, a modern-day David, an avenger with the blood of these street toughs, four Goliaths, splattered on his face and hands. Many people feel that by shooting the boys, Goetz somehow took back the streets of New York City from the public's most bloodthirsty enemies.

Throughout, the man remained as cool as Clint Eastwood in a Western flick. "You seem to be doing all right," he allegedly told one of his victims, "here's another," before pumping a second bullet from his Smith & Wesson .38-caliber revolver into a nineteen-year-old *moreno*'s back, paralyzing him.

At the *bodegas* around the way, folks start playing 14, 7, 38, 1, 9, 8, 4, and every imaginable combination of numbers associated with the incident. Goetz is on TV every night and on the cover of every daily newspaper for a long-ass time. The Guardian Angels, a group of mostly Black and Latino unarmed citizen crime patrollers in their teens, raise thousands of dollars for his defense. Even after he gets off on attempted-murder charges—Goetz was saying all kinds of crazy shit a lot of people were thinking, after all—people still show him love. Papi does too, though he's never gotten mugged and rarely takes the train. Papi drives to his job in the Bronx.

I stop complaining about the polar-bear coat. I have—*we* have—bigger issues to worry about. Bernhard Goetz has convinced me that everybody in the city, not just Papi, feels that Black and Latino kids are no better than subway tunnel rats. Around our way, the resentment we feel encourages kids who may not have otherwise fucked with each other to form alliances. Hip-hop, this thing we love that loves us back, is our lingua franca.

Papi's mother, Ercilia Rabassa, starts visiting us from Newport every summer, breaking the monotony of my life, which revolves around tennis and piano. On the surface, she's the dullest woman I've ever met, with the strangest Dominican *apellido* I've ever heard.

She doesn't speak a lick of English except for "t'sank you" every once in a while, and Alice's Dominican Spanish is wack, so they communicate by smiling. When Papi translates, he repeats everything in broken English and Spanish, filling in the many awkward moments of silence. Alice enjoys Ercilia's visits even if she doesn't understand everything that is said because Papi won't leave them alone as much to go on his nightly *diligencias*.

Ercilia sleeps on the pullout bed stored beneath mine. I make her bed nightly and store it away every morning as she sits with her back to me, praying and reading her Bible. She sleeps with her back to me too, having conversations with God until she falls asleep. Ercilia sometimes smiles in my direction but never asks me to call her "Mama." Come to think of it, I can't remember one single time when she's spoken directly to me. The only reason why I know she isn't *muda* is because I can hear her praying. Her voice is faint and supplicant, her Dominican accent thicker than a stack of pancakes at IHOP. I listen closely for her to break out into the strange language Papi says she knows, hoping she'll say something that will clue me in to who she really is. It never happens.

I stare at the back of her head, trying to imagine what lead Ercilia to her holy-rolling present. I try to picture her as a child, walking beside her parents in the Dominican Republic, though I've never seen a photo of her parents or anyone on her side of the family. When Papi talks about her, the stories always contradict each other. In some she wasn't adopted, and in others a wealthy couple took her in from San Pedro de Macorís, where she was born. I've heard Mama and Papa say that people in Santo Domingo referred to Ercilia's mother as *la prieta* Francisca because she was darker than the night sky; she supposedly stood in stark contrast to her white husband, Don Pedro Rabassa. The only consistent thread in Ercilia's story was how badly her mother and siblings treated her. I think it had something to do with the abiding sadness Papi's mother shouldered. I promise, listening to Ercilia snore the night away, that I'll never allow myself to become a dejected church lady.

The times Ercilia does feign interest in me, she speaks as if I'm in another room even when I'm sitting next to her.

"Eduardo, the girl is getting big," she almost whispers. Ercilia never refers to me by name.

Papi nods in agreement. "It's the tennis. Have you seen all her medals and trophies?"

Ercilia strains to form a smile.

End of conversation.

Ercilia looks like she may have been gorgeous once upon a time. Her face is shaped like an oval, with perfectly proportioned eyebrows and lids that slant down like mine, covering part of her large, deep-set chocolate-brown eyes. Her thick wavy locks, now cut short like her son's, must have looked luscious back in the day. Her nose, neither wide nor narrow, is in harmony with her fleshy lips. Papi's father must have loved kissing them back in the day, before they deflated and settled into a frown.

I've never given Papi's father a thought until now, when I try to imagine Ercilia locked in a passionate embrace with a man. I've never seen a photo of him. I've never been curious about whether he was as handsome as Ercilia or as tall and lanky as his son. I bet they were like any other Dominican family, with members spanning from the bluest black to the lightest beige, despite Papi trying to front like he is different from virtually everybody else on the island. The only thing that makes my family stand out is how disconnected and fucked up they were to themselves and each other. I can't imagine I would recognize myself in Papi's father if I saw him on the street. What I do see is that Papi suffers from something I learned about in school: low self-esteem, a profound sadness that switches into fits of rage faster than I can make Ms. Pac-Man swallow power pellets. The low self-esteem and sadness come from Ercilia. I'm curious from whom Papi inherited his short, violent temper.

Where Ercilia is more religious than Pope John Paul II, Papi isn't at all. He makes me to go to church with his and Mami's old friends Miguel and Clara and their spoiled-ass daughter, Carmencita, only because they pressure him to let their pastor work his magic for the salvation of my soul. Otherwise, I don't think Papi believes in or cares much for God. He falls asleep in the pews just like I do on the rare occasion when he meets us at Clara's church, snoring right through the homily and the passing of the money tray. My holy-rolling Sundays—spent playing Truth or Dare with the boys and flashing our prepubescent *tetas*, pussies, and tiny dicks in Carmencita's pink bedroom after church—are short-lived.

Like Papi, I'm not so sure God exists. He—I'm told God is a He—never visits me. I've seen spirits in my dreams ever since I was a little girl living with Mami on Seaman Avenue, but they looked more like *indias,* with long black hair, like a young Ercilia and her daughter, Perla. I used to have a recurring dream before moving in with Papi and Alice. In it, Woody Woodpecker uses his beak to poke holes in my face. When I feel like I can't survive another peck, a very tall *africana* with tight curly hair, dressed like a Spanish *dama,* sweeps me to safety by shooing the bird away with one hand and hiding me under her huge skirt with the other. When Woody flies away, she holds me tightly against her *tetas.* The *dama's* cleavage holds magic that heals the wounds on my face.

I never dream of being saved by any of the blond men portrayed on the stained-glass windows at St. Thaddeus. Those gods, I'm convinced, don't know the language of the people begging for their divine intervention.

Toward the end of Ercilia's visit, we take a walk in the park after dinner. I straggle way behind, trying my best not to be seen with them. In the distance, I can see the group of tennis players Papi embarrassed me in front of sitting on a bench by the courts. Papi walks by them without saying a word. Alice and Ercilia are holding hands and trailing behind him.

"What are you doing with dose *lou'sy* Dominicans," Papi hissed at me last week, although at least one of the players was South American.

"I just finished playing tennis," I said, at once nervous and hopeful that the men would jump Papi and beat him at least as badly as he had hit me.

"Let's go play now!" he screamed.

"Eduardo, excuse me, she played all afternoon with us, Rachel is—" Jose said, but Papi cut him off like he did everybody.

"Get up, I say," Papi demanded.

I didn't say goodbye to the guys and followed Papi to the courts in the back.

"I'm going to fix you with this when we get home," he said, pointing at his racket. *Fuck Papi,* I thought every time he threatened me. The notion of returning the favor one day became my motivation to live, to survive. Every beating, I thought, brought me a step closer to freedom.

"But I was just doing what you told me to do. You know, it was that creepy pervert Mike Cohen who told me my stomach looked soft like Madonna's and that he wanted to stroke it, not these—"

"Shut your *mou'se*! Go run around the park."

Exhausted, I walked over to Diamond One. The tennis players looked away just like our neighbors did on the mornings when they heard me screaming for Papi to stop pummeling me.

Now the same guys are staring at Ercilia as she walks by, hand in hand with Alice. I imagine they're thinking what I'm thinking. Ercilia's whiteness is a figment of Papi's imagination.

The closer I am to finishing my bid at St. Thaddeus, the more I feel like I'm living in a pressure cooker fueled by hate. I hate Papi. He hates me. I hate my teachers. They hate me. I hate Mami. She has long since forgotten I exist. I hate being called a "spic bitch" by white kids on my way back from school as much as I hate being called a "wannabe white girl" by Latino kids for playing tennis and living west of Broadway.

We all may have made the trip from the islands and live together here, but we are crazy divided. Once folks make enough loot to fill their *apartamentos* with more black-lacquer bedroom furniture and porcelain tigers than the next person, their attitudes get icy. It now takes something remarkable like a crack giveaway or the discovery of a dead body in the alley to bring people together. However, nothing does it better than the miracle of Jesus making an appearance on somebody's window. And He does drop in from time to time. The apparition of His head, always in a crown of thorns, surfaces in the form of a misty outline on some poor disciple's window facing the street. The word spreads even faster than bad news.

"*Ay, Jesús e'tá aquí,*" Jesus is here, someone screams, sounding the alarm.

"*Jesús* is here to warn us!" an old woman says.

"No, *Jesús* is here to *save* us," another church lady says.

"It doesn't matter why He came but that He's here. ¡*Qué bendición!*" says another voice in a growing crowd.

As soon as I hear Jesus is in town, I run down to Post Avenue and find a spot toward the back of the large crowd to see Him for myself. A group of revelers in the front row are on their knees with fingers twined in prayer. They are reciting the Lord's Prayer: *"Padre nuestro, que estás en el cielo. Santificado sea tu nombre. Venga tu reino . . ."* Others are on the side, pointing up at the window and crying. With a piece of John's fried chicken in hand, I try hard to focus my gaze in a way that will enable me to see what so many believers do, but I fail miserably.

I've been training one hour before class at an armory in Harlem and several hours after school at the park for a while now. By the time school starts, I'm too drained to care what's happening around me. I can hardly make out the brick lining of the building's exterior or the nondescript tile floor adding to the sad institutional feel of the joint.

My eighth-grade teacher, Sister Catherine, is a young androgynous woman with the prudish demeanor of a person three times her age. One morning she calls me over to her desk to read a note she's written to me. "Are you high, Rachel?" it starts. "Your eyes are always so red." Sister C. smiles nervously at me.

I feel as if someone has punched me in the chest. Like our school's namesake, who never answers my pleas for help, this bitch doesn't care to understand me. There are people in my class who are flying high, but I'm not one of them. I've seen a couple of girls come out of the bathroom stalls with white powder covering the tip of their noses, snorting and laughing as they wash their faces in the sink next to me.

I lean over and scribble something below her note, smiling. "I don't know a crack dealer named Peter," referencing the pusher in Boogie Down Productions' "9mm Goes Bang" and "I'm more interested in what happened that brought you to this place, Sister C. Why do you always look so sad?"

Sister C.'s face flushes with anger. I keep smiling at her as she slouches into her chair, frowning. "Go to the principal's office right now," she whispers, pointing at the classroom door with her bony index finger.

• • •

I usually fall asleep during religion class and lectures with buzz words like "Thanksgiving," "Christopher Columbus," or anything involving missionaries. I hear words like "primitive," "savage," and "extinct" used interchangeably to describe almost everyone we learn about who isn't of European descent or a sellout. The "savages" our teachers talk about usually look like most of my classmates and me.

More often than not, I'm thrown out of class if I challenge Columbus or the Catholic dogma they feed us. We aren't encouraged to think for ourselves and ask questions. We are expected to accept what they teach us as infallible truths.

"But isn't it messed up to force another group of people to believe what you do and make them slaves if they don't give in?" I ask one day.

"It isn't the same. The missionaries were moved by their love of God and the Blessed Sacrament."

"But it's wrong to go to someone's house and force them to hand it over to you, learn the language, and love your God, isn't it?"

"That's enough! Go downstairs to the principal's office, you're disrupting the class!"

I survive the remainder of my time at St. Thaddeus by fantasizing that I'm no longer there. I stop asking questions. Sometimes I spend time in the gym practicing my footwork with Martin and David. During lunch, I pretend that I'm on deadline to write battle rhymes for Roxanne Shanté, Sha-Rock, and MC Lyte. In my spiral notebook, I scribble rhymes and words that I think sound nice from other songs and English class.

I come across a discarded copy of *The Autobiography of Malcolm X: As Told to Alex Haley* at school. I decide to read it because of the fine redheaded man gracing the book's cover.

I'm forgetting everyone in Santo Domingo. It's been years since I've spoken to Mama and Papa. In New York City, I'm creating my own identity, one in which hip-hop culture, now in full effect, is at the core.

The beatings continue.

"Please, Papi, stop. *Please,*" I scream as loudly as I can.

Alice now retreats into the bedroom, closing the door, so I can see the reflection of him kicking, throwing, and punching me in the mirror fixed to the door.

I hear someone knocking on the front door. I know it's the police, I can hear static and voices coming from a cop radio. Papi shoots me a warning with a raised eyebrow as he collects himself and walks toward to the door. "You don't want to go live with that *lousy* mother of yours and become a maid and babysitter for all her children, do you?" he asks me. We recently found out that Rocío gave birth to two more daughters.

The last time I spoke to her was some months ago when Papi threatened to throw me out the window after I lost a tennis match. He dialed her phone number as Alice stood by frowning in silence, and then he began pleading into the receiver for Mami to come to New York City and pick me up before he ripped me apart.

"*Please* pick me up," I said, not expecting her to, "or he's really going to *do it* this time."

"I told you when you left me for *him* that you would go to hell, Raquel," she said, her voice almost too soothing for the situation. "You have to learn how to listen to your mom."

The next day, to my surprise, Rocío showed up with a tall *trigueño* who I assumed was her latest boyfriend or husband, dripping with gold like a *jodedor* by her side, to rescue me. I hardly recognized her aside from her thick wavy locks and curves galore. Rocío's expression looked as if she'd been living hard; her face was weathered by experience. I didn't see the glint of intellectual curiosity in her eyes anymore. This guy looked like he was half a step above the last one.

Something always happened to prevent me from leaving with her. Besides, Mami didn't put much of a fight. She stood quietly watching the drama unfold in front of her, not saying much to Papi or Alice. Papi would start to panic and change his mind. He'd beg me to stay, and I did. I always do.

Papi opens the door. "Can I help you gentlemen?" he asks the cops.

"We're getting reports again about possible domestic disturbance at this residence. We need to come in and ask you and your daughter some questions."

I'm sitting on a chair, my legs are shaking from side to side out of fear that if I tell the truth, I'll have to go babysit Rocío's kids. If I lie, I'll have to stay here with two people I've grown to fucking loathe with the same intensity I've learned to love this city. This is where I was born, and I'm not prepared to leave.

"I was behaving badly, Officer," I say.

"Are you sure?" asks one of the two cops standing over me. "You don't have to be afraid to tell us the truth."

"Yes, I'm sure. I-I-I'm just being lazy and dramatic," I say.

Papi walks over and smiles at me and then at the officers.

"Okay. Have a good day, sir," a cop says to Papi.

They leave.

When Public Enemy releases *It Takes a Nation of Millions to Hold Us Back,* it ignites me, gives me life. I feel free to express myself, using their seething vocabulary and attitude to articulate what I'm feeling. Something about the music and lyrics speaks to my anxiety. It compels me to question everything I'm being taught at the Catholic high school I'm attending in Yonkers.

Public Enemy's message makes more sense to me than the gospel of obedience and servitude I learn at school. It's like Chuck D is directly speaking to me. "The enemy could be their friend, guardian . . ."

I feel like a hypocrite for letting my enemy, Papi, hit me. I'm going to fight back one day. "You *not* putting enough spin on your forehand," he screamed at me last time during practice. "Come *on*—your back-hand is flat—use your slice. *WAIT* until we get home, you—" Papi's threats reverberated from one court to the next, intensifying with each slap of his thigh and stomp of his foot until he morphed into an overgrown toddler throwing a tantrum.

• • •

I'm hanging out with a couple of my girls, drinking nasty warm Olde English malt liquor and playing with Lupe's baby on Sherman Street after school. Caridad is a Cuban and Puerto Rican beauty with skin like a cinnamon stick and the temper of a rabid Chihuahua. She has huge brown eyes like that of a deer and these fly-ass freckles on her chiseled face that draw attention away from her fucked-up teeth. Caridad has gotten thrown out of school more times than anyone I know because she just can't let shit slide. I wished I were more like her.

"You're an African queen," I say to her, passing Lupe the forty-ounce bottle.

"Listen, you're cool, even though you're a little fuckin' weird, Rachel," she says, "but listen, if you call me a nigga one more time, I'm going to have to fuck you up."

"But Caridad, I ain't trying to call you out your name. I just think we have a lot in common with—"

"You're light-skinned. You don't understand shit but that uppity-ass shit you play in the park."

"We're all still women of color regardless of our complexions," I try to reason with her. "Sis, I wasn't trying to disrespect—"

Lupe chimes in, "Just don't say that shit, okay? Rachel, she don't like it."

"But Lupe, don't you sort of date that Black rapper with the light eyes or something like that?" I ask. "You have knowledge of self, you understand I wasn't trying to—"

"Drop. It," says Caridad, now visibly irritated. Lupe breaks the tension by stepping between us and handing me the bottle to swig from. I pass it to Caridad as a peace offering, hoping she won't use it to crack my head open.

I decide to stop fighting a losing battle uptown.

Soon I become a walking contradiction. I begin to call any Black and Latino girl I meet at my high school "sister," even if I despise them and they me.

"I can't understand why you like all that Black shit," Susana says to me one morning on the bus ride to school.

"What do you mean 'Black shit'? Hip-hop is *our* shit, too."

"Na, freestyle is *our* shit," she says.

"Shannon is Black, so is Joyce Sims. What the fuck are you talking about, sis? That half-Italian blood is making you loopy."

"You just hate anything white, don't you?"

"What, are you—Wait, I like Jared from Bailey, and isn't he like Albanian and German or something?"

"Come on, girl, you like him because he dances like he's Black and he sort of looks like RAMO from *Beat Street,*" she says.

I look out the window at the nondescript streets we're driving through in Yonkers, ignoring Susana for the rest of the ride. I resist the urge to fuck her up. I look over at Socorro, the only Dominican girl living on Sherman Avenue who wears her hair teased big like the Italian girls at school, and I try to guess what she'll say at lunch today.

Unlike me, Socorro could pass for a straight-up *morena* if she kept her mouth shut, but you couldn't tell her that. The hair relaxers she uses are so strong they make her smell like she's on fire all the time. She is the only girl I know who is as delusional as Papi, if not more so. Yesterday at lunch, I gave her dap for the fresh electric-blue eyeliner she wore to school.

"Socorro, that blue makes your eyes pop," I said.

"Yes, thanks," she said, "it brings out the blue around the edges of my eyes." She angled her face in closer for me to see what she'd done. I laughed, thinking Socorro was joking because her eyes were almost black, but she wasn't. She was serious. I didn't understand people like her or Papi. Socorro went to another Catholic grammar school in our 'hood. I wondered if she believed the shit they preached in religion class about "savages," and wanted to look more like the God-fearing missionaries who brought, with their Bibles, civilization to the New World. I leaned in a bit closer to see if I could find one speck of blue in her dark eyes, but I couldn't.

"Yeah, Socorro," I said. "I think I can see it now."

CHAPTER SIX

Jesus Christ and the Freakazoid

In all chaos there is a cosmos, in all disorder a secret order.

—CARL JUNG

ROCÍO IS ON THE PHONE.

We rarely speak to each other unless she has major news to break or Papi calls her during one of his violent fits. I try to guess what kind of news she's going to drop on me this time: the birth of child number seven; a new boyfriend or husband; someone is sick or, worse, dead. My stomach churns at the thought that something may be wrong with Mama or Papa. I feel light-headed.

"*Ello*, Raquel," she almost whispers. "This is your *motha*. How *are* you?"

"Life is beautiful," I lie. "What happened—have another kid?"

"Does something have to be *wrong* for me to call *my* own dau'hta—my *first*born?" she asks. Rocío sounds different from the last time we spoke. She's now dragging her A's and dropping her R's while still failing miserably at shedding the weight of her Dominican accent.

"Something usually is when you call. Why are—"

"Oh, Raquel." Pause. "I was wondering if you wanted to visit us fo' a while," she says. Her voice is grave, almost foreboding. "You never show *any* interest in your brothers and sisters."

"I don't know them, remember?" I respond. "I didn't even know about kids number three and four until they were three and four." Since, she's had a set of twin boys.

"Well, anyway, I spok' to *your* fa'tha, and he says you can come for a visit before school starts."

"But I don't want to go to Boston."

I'm pissed. I don't know when or how they ended up living there. It's August 1988, and I want to spend my last month before school at the park, watching the hot boys run up and down the basketball courts.

"It's settled."

"This shit is wack, yo!"

"Don't speak to me like *that*—I am *your* moth-a," she whispers.

The following week I find myself sitting on a plastic-covered couch in a household brimming with small children, including the oldest, Giselle, who's now nine. I hardly recognize her except for the remarkable likeness she bares to Papito, which turns me off. Her wide bright smile scares the shit out of me, like a circus clown or Dr. Bunsen Honeydew. I no longer feel compelled to protect or share a room with her, much less the other tiny strangers running around the house.

I watch one of the girls play with dolls in the living room, fascinated by how much she looks like a Chinese boy. The girl has hair that's thicker and straighter than any of the other kids', and her eyes are small and slanted. Some of the other children entertain each other by playing tag until one dashes out the back door—the others stop what they are doing to follow—into the small backyard of Rocío's rented house. I stay sitting, the back of my thighs are stuck to the plastic covering, and pretend to do my summer homework.

There are words on the page I'm sure I should be memorizing, but I'm frozen in another dimension, one where I'm trying hard to feel something new, a warmth toward the people I'm visiting. I feel like I'm not normal. There's a fuse that's gone out in me, something I cannot turn on for any of them. I close my eyes and try to concentrate, but no matter how far I travel and tell myself, "*This* is your family, *this* is your mother, *these* are your brothers and sisters," nothing happens.

Rocío is sitting in the kitchen with a friend, talking about the poor health of her premature twins, who are about three. Her friend comforts her over what smells like a cup of Bustelo. She calls Rocío *una santa* for sacrificing so much for the boys while their father, a good-for-nothing *comemierda*, parties with other women. I assume they're talking about the tall brawny guy dripping in gold with whom she showed up with last time Papi threatened to throw me out the window.

Sometime since I last saw her, Rocío has chopped off her long wavy locks. She is noticeably heavier, and in this saintly incarnation looks too matronly to be a woman in her early thirties. Her eyes carry enough *miseria* to satiate a pew full of dolorous church ladies.

A newspaper sticks out midway from a bin filled with Spanish- and English-language magazines in arm's reach of the sofa. I pull out the paper, folded to a black-and-white photo of Rocío and her brood. If it weren't for the children, I wouldn't have recognized her at all: morbidly obese, curly hair styled like an unkempt poodle's, and grinning from ear to ear like a scary cartoon character. I couldn't believe it. Her twins were much smaller, and the girls were dressed like Rocío, in dowdy clothes. Below the photograph, the caption read: "Mother of the year . . . with her five children . . ."

Rocío was being rewarded for the outstanding care she took of her preemies, for reasons I didn't care to read. I was more awestruck by her ability to balloon to that size in the first place, and how she managed, in a relatively short period of time, to shed a whole person in fat. I placed the paper in my textbook, counting and recounting the number of children in the photograph. I read and reread "her five children" and nothing else, tracing the border of the image with my middle finger. Five children. She bore six.

Rocío created a perfect world in that photo, one where children behaved perfectly and kept their Sunday best spotless. In this picture, good mothers were martyrs, caring for their children to the point of abandon. In this world, the child Rocío cursed and sent to hell on Arzobispo Portes simply didn't exist.

I want to go back home to New York City. I want to hear Exposé and Michael Jackson blasting from the handball courts, kids—not these kids—screaming in the playground. I want to see Angel Lizardo, especially now that the former chubster surprised everybody when he strutted onto the court taller and kind of muscular right before I had to come here. He must have worked out like a maniac when he visited his cousins in La Romana earlier in the summer.

I'd do anything to escape Boston and go to Washington Square Park for just a few hours. It's like church for baseheads, rappers, skateboarders, cult members, freaks, and super-straight folks I recognized from my 'hood, sitting in homosexual embraces on the surrounding park benches. When Papi and Alice went to work, I sometimes jumped on the A train and headed downtown when I was supposed to be practicing tennis in the park, or at home watching MTV or Video Music Box in their dingy-ass bedroom. The park downtown was way more interesting. From the benches, I could see everything. There were girls who looked like boys in ripped jeans, rubbing each other's *tetas* and dry-humping on the lawn and against the trees. Sometimes I'd see someone I wanted to meet like Russell Simmons and Run-DMC cutting across Washington Square west to east. "I'm going to work for him one day, writing rhymes for his artists," I said to myself.

Once I saw a group of white boys with funny haircuts who called themselves Hare Krishnas circling the park, draped in matching uniforms like Mahatma Gandhi, but in shades of washed-out orange and yellow with foreign letters. They appeared to be synthetically happy, almost lost. They danced around the fountain without paying any attention to rhythm while chanting "*Hare Krishna, Hare Krishna, Krishna Krishna, Hare Hare, Hare Rama, Hare Rama, Rama Rama, Hare Hare,*" until one by one they started looking like they were passing a *santo*. Sometimes, whoever was tripping off heroin on the benches got it together and joined in the dancing. Boston, in comparison, was corny beyond comprehension.

I call Papi, but the phone just rings and rings. Rocío's monotone voice is lulling me to sleep. I carefully place the newspaper back where I found it and start making my way upstairs.

"Raquel, what's wrong? Why aren't you outside playing with your brothers and sisters?"

"Maybe it's because I'm fifteen and not interested. I'm sleepy."

"But *i's too* early for bed—I was planning on taking you all in the *ca*- for a drive and ice cream."

Ice cream. Rocío thinks this is *The Brady Bunch.* "No, thank you. I'll be up when you get back."

"*Ay,* she is so disrespectful, Rocío," says her friend.

"Oh, it's okay," she says. "Raquel is just angry because I was right about what would happen if she went to live with her father. God will open her eyes one day and deliver her back to me."

Rocío got it all twisted. Hell is right here in Boston in her suffocating and delusional universe. Everything about her is fake, especially that wack Boston gringo accent she struggles to speak in. I sit on one of the twin beds in the room and try focusing on my textbook, but after a few minutes, the humid air in the room drags me to sleep.

I wake up back in New York City but can't figure out how I got here. I'm sitting on a swing in the 207th Street playground. Nobody is here. The sun above me is so radiant, I cannot see the seesaw I know is only feet in front of me. The tennis and handball courts have disappeared. The streets, the buildings to the east of me, everything has been absorbed by the light.

As I hold on tightly to the twisted steel ropes suspending the swing and rock back and forth, I start to feel a presence. I can see the outline of a short round figure with long wavy hair making her way toward me.

I immediately recognize Ercilia when she appears before the park gate.

"Why—What are you doing here?" I ask, suspecting I must be dreaming.

"I came to say goodbye and ask you something," she says in Spanish.

"Why say goodbye to *me*? Where are you going?"

"I'm sorry for being so cold to you—"

"Where are we?"

"I am leaving. I want to go," she says. We are in the hospital corridor. "I'm dying, and I want to walk into the sun, but I can't go peacefully until you forgive me."

"Fine. I forgive you, but only if you promise never to come back to me for a visit. Are you afraid of dying?" I ask her. "Does it hurt?"

"Not as much as I'm afraid of living. I was cursed at birth and tossed away like garbage."

"Are you Jewish? What's that strange language Papi says you know how to speak? Why is he so damn mean?"

Ercilia smiles. "Maybe one day you will want me to visit you again," she says, walking out the gate and into the light.

I'm awakened by the giggling twins playing at the foot of my bed. They are scrawling in my textbook with the black pen I used as a bookmark. I am furious. I snatch the book from one of them and the pen from the other and stomp into the living room.

"I had the craziest dream," I tell Rocío. "Ercilia visited me in it."

"Oh, *that's* something," she says. "Do you want to go with me and your brothers to the hospital for their treatment?"

"I think she wants to die," I say.

"You should get dressed while I put them in the *ca'*," she says, only halfway listening to me. "You can't imagine how stressful it has been for me to take care of my babies all alone." I don't want to go. I'm even more disinterested in Rocío's litter of kids than I am in her.

"Not really. I need to call Papi."

"Well, you *ah'* coming," she says. I don't know what's worse: Alice's "Eduardo, *please*" or Rocío's irritating monotone.

Two weeks later, I'm back on Seaman Avenue for real. I rush up the stairs to drop off my stuff so I can race back down to Post Avenue and buy a number 1 fried chicken combo at John's. Maybe I'll eat it upstairs at Priscilla's. I swear she thinks I had something to do with her grandmother dying, like I put a *fukú* on her or something. I dreamed that Priscilla was at a funeral several weeks before it happened and warned her, but now I wish I'd never said a word. She called me a *bruja* at school and has been acting like a bitch ever since.

Thinking about the crispy skin and the aroma of fried and roasted chicken at John's makes my mouth water. I'll go upstairs and say hi to Priscilla's mom, Milagros, afterward.

I unlock the door and find Papi slumping in a chair and Alice standing over him.

"Hi," I say. There's something in the apartment that feels more ominous than usual. "What's wrong?"

Alice says nothing, but her painted-on eyebrows furrow as if she has something heavy on her mind. Papi doesn't look up at me. His eyes are red. I start to wonder if I did something wrong. I'm either getting a welcome-back beat-down, or he got caught cheating again and Alice has retaliated by speaking only in Finnish to him so he can't understand her, driving Papi mad.

"Ercilia died," Alice says. I feel my organs drop down to the bottom half of my body; the weight is making my knees buckle.

"What? How? When?" I ask.

"Why are you asking me?" Papi says. "You don't care."

"She died last week when you were in Boston," Alice says, "during open-heart surgery."

The light. My head is spinning. The hospital corridor. Was this my fault? Would she have pulled through surgery had I *not* forgiven her and released her spirit? First it was Priscilla's *abuela* and now Ercilia. What's wrong with me?

"I'm going to go eat at John's," I say. I can't bring myself to offer any sympathy. I can't tell Papi about my dream now that Ercilia's dead. There's something about the way he's sitting, in agony, that I find gratifying.

The day is beautiful. I walk up 215th Street to Park Terrace West and make a right, thinking about Ercilia's visit, still not understanding why she chose me. I continue walking on the hill overlooking Seaman Avenue, taking the scenic route to fried chicken heaven.

Why me? Why am I seeing the dead like some freakazoid? The only thing I know about Papi's father is that he read cards when it moved him. He considered it a privilege to throw cards for people, to be able to see what so many others could not. It's hard to believe any of it, because the only people I met on Papi's side of the family were so hot for Jesus.

I continue strolling down the hill, people-watching along the way. I spot a group of girls, including two I went to St. Thaddeus with, walking on Isham toward the park. Another girl who looks familiar is carrying a stickball bat. "Yo, Zenaida!" I scream. She doesn't hear me.

I arrive at John's. I rush in and order an extra piece of chicken, sit down, and eat. I missed New York. I'm never going to Boston again, no matter what. From the window, I can see Priscilla crossing the street with her little sister. She's gotten even fatter in the short time I've been away. It's too bad; her face is so pretty in the summer, when freckles dot her topaz-colored face. Her legs look like tree stumps, and I can see the sides of her stomach moving in a sluggish side-to-side rhythm from the back.

I decide to go upstairs and say hi to Milagros before going back to Papi and Alice's prison.

"What are you doing here?" Milagros asks me. "Come in, hurry up."

"What's wrong?"

"Did you see Zenaida and those girls outside?"

"Yeah, I tried to say hello, but she didn't hear me—why?"

"They were looking for you. I heard them downstairs in front of the building."

"But why? I was in Boston this whole time."

"I know, *mi hija*. They made a big deal about Pumpkin's boyfriend looking at you in the elevator and you smiling back."

"Who's Pumpkin?"

"*Una idiota.* They said you think you're better than them because you have money, living up there," she says.

My heart starts racing. "I'm going to have to kill somebody for them to leave me alone. Everybody wants the next person to be as miserable as them," I say. Rage is running like an electrical current through my body. "My father's mother died last week, when I was away—I dreamed it all the way up in Boston on the day it happened."

"I'm sorry, *mi hija,*" Milagros says, coming out of the kitchen with a glass of water from the faucet. "Go to my room and take a nap. Cry if you have to."

I wake up to Priscilla unlocking the front door; her chubby sister waddles in behind her. They look like pregnant penguins.

"Did you hear about Zenaida and that other girl?" I ask Priscilla.

"Yes. They also said something about you saying that Cielo's apartment burned down, and you know that's Zenaida's *prima hermana.*" She smiles.

"But I wasn't here."

"Fucking sucks for you, then, right?"

I put my sneakers on and leave.

I stand in front of the building on Post Avenue, waiting for the girls to come back. I look up and see Cielo looking out her mother's window.

"Yo, I hope your fucking apartment burns down," I scream up at her.

"Fuck you, bitch, that's why you're going to get your ass kicked."

"We'll see about that."

I put on my Sony Walkman headphones, cue LL Cool J's "I Need Love," and press Play.

Weeks go by and nothing happens.

Somehow I receive a scholarship to a swanky tennis academy on Long Island. I hate the place. The kids I meet only talk about money and being something called a JAP. The first time I hear the acronym is on one of the indoor courts in the back.

"I'd never be seen in public with any girl other than a JAP," this kid says within earshot while we're picking up balls after a drill.

"Yeah, I hear you. My mother would kill me if she even thought I was interested in anyone else," replies another kid, glancing over at me. "Those are the only girls I like, anyway." One of the girls on the court tells me that a JAP isn't short for Japanese but an acronym for Jewish-American prince or princess.

I am not a JAP, but that doesn't stop me from developing a crush on Simon Goldstein. He's arrogant and temperamental on the court, like McEnroe, tall and wiry, with wild long hair. He's not a cookie-cutter rich kid like the other boys. I think he may like me, too. He doesn't ignore me. In his world, I exist.

Simon's mother is skinnier than a thirteen-year-old girl. She looks like she works out a lot, and her skeletal face is always done in shades of frosted makeup. Everyone notices Mrs. Goldstein from the moment she walks through the glass doors because she is more overstated than any of the other parents, even the rich ones. It looks as if Fendi, Louis Vuitton, and Gucci have thrown up on her all at once. A little girl, my future sister-in-law, usually runs in behind her.

"Can you watch my sister when she goes to the bathroom in the women's locker room?" Simon asks me.

"Yes, of course," I respond.

He smiles warmly. "You know, you look like a younger version of my baby sister's nanny," he continues. "Are you from Central America or someplace like that?"

"No," I respond, deflated.

"Anyway, you're sort of hot in an exotic way. Maybe one day you'll work for me and we can fool around." He laughs.

"You mean maybe you'll work for *me*."

"Come on, let's be realistic. You could be my cleaning lady."

"Fuck you. I'd rather be a cleaning lady than walk around with that stupid ugly-ass hook nose."

"You better watch it before I tell someone you're anti-Semitic."

"What the fuck does that even mean?"

"You don't want to know, *mami*."

Simon and I never speak again. His mom and little sister don't even glance my way when they walk past me anymore. They also begin to ignore Papi.

"What happened with that nice boy?" Papi asks one afternoon on the car ride back to the city.

"Nothing. I don't know," I respond.

"You must have said something stupid. You always embarrass me."

I say nothing. One of the girls told me what it meant to be "anti-Semitic," and I've realized nobody will ever take my word over a JAP's in this place, not even Papi.

I start running into Marie Christophe at Carrot Top on Broadway that spring, after the yellow and gray snow melted away. She graduated from St. Thaddeus a year after I did. Like Claudine, whom I lost contact with after she moved to Hollis, Marie was born in New York City to Haitian parents.

Visiting the Christophe family feels like entering a parallel universe. When I come over, which is almost daily, there's almost always somber country music playing in the background. "Hello, Mr. and Mrs. Christophe," I say. "I hope all is well this evening." Marie's dad is sitting in a chair talking to her mom, who is cooking dinner in the kitchen. " '*Allo*, Raquel, *you* ar' so well mannered," he says to me in an accent I understand somewhat better than I did Claudine's mom's. "Marie should be mo'r like *you*." Marie's eyes roll to the back of her head.

"*Yo*. I just saw my dad with that Cuban lady from across the street and her fat-ass daughter," I say, entering Marie's room.

"You're crazy, girl," she greets me in, oddly enough, a heavy Dominican accent. "What chu' got for me, *mami*?"

I throw myself on Marie's bed, covered with freshly laundered clothes, and open a bag to trade with her for the week. We pool together our wardrobe in order to look fresh to death when sneaking out to Greenwich Village. Sometimes we go to the park or walk by Unique Clothing Warehouse on West Broadway to check out the guys airbrushing T-shirts in the front window. On other days we just roam around, pretending to be drunk off of flavored Bartles & Jaymes wine coolers, and watch clans of white homeless teenagers with dreadlocks and tracks on their arms beg for money on the street.

Our mutual homegirl Sheeba is the tallest girl both Marie and I know. She lives on the other side of Carrot Top with a mom I've never seen smile, in an apartment as dark as Papi and Alice's. She has her own room and more gear than Marie and I put together. Her dad, whom I never met, is from some country in West Africa. That may be why Sheeba, despite those pimples that make her nose look way bigger than it is, looks as if she's chiseled from an otherwise perfect slab of Champlain black marble.

Marie and her friend Sabrina and Sheeba and I are people-watching on one of the concrete benches surrounding the water fountain at Washington Square Park. I glance over at Marie, noticing her red lipstick perfectly framing a set of full pouty lips. I wondered if we would have been friends had we been living in D.R. or Haiti. I imagined thousands of friendships disintegrating into the arid Caribbean air—POOF—before they could even begin. Teenagers, separated by an imaginary line, who will never laugh together or share fresh clothes. I can't imagine it.

All the bullshit Dominicans talk about Haitians rushes into the foreground of my mind. I am embarrassed by it. Marie finds it confusing that the *plátanos* over here spewing the worst venom about the *prietos* back on the island often look just like them. It's part of the baggage our parents and grandparents lug over from the *madre patria*.

"Oh my fucking God, that's Plug One and Plug Two from De La Soul walking toward us," I whisper loudly to the girls.

No one responds or looks in their direction. I forgot for a moment that part of our thing was to look jaded. But I couldn't play along. *3 Feet High and Rising* recently dropped.

"Yo, that 'Buddy' remix is the craziest song ever," I tell Marie. She shrugs. "It's cool, I guess," she says.

"They ain't no Redhead Kingpin," Sheeba says.

"Are you crazy? He's corny," I say. "Fine like Malcolm X. But sounds like hip-hop fusion for elevators."

Sabrina offers nothing. As usual, she's borderline lethargic.

"Did you hear that girl with the English accent—Monie Love's flow in it?" I say. "She's so dope. I want to write lyrics for her one day."

"You're smoking crack," Sheeba says. "You'll never write for any of them."

"Yeah, and when I do, you'll be the first to catch the vapors," I shoot back.

Russell Simmons is trailing a few feet behind them, talking to someone who looks like Plug One, aka Posdnuos.

They walk over to us and lean on the other side of the concrete bench. Sheeba's long flawless legs and model-thin body must have Posdnuos open because he can't stop staring at her and cheesing. "Hi, I'm Pos," he says to us.

Plug Two, aka Trugoy, hair styled into his signature high-top fade with a crown of dreads, smiles and nods hello, exposing a rotten tooth. He stands next to Pos until Russell Simmons makes his way over to our group, fixing himself between the two, totally ignoring our side of the concrete slab.

"Hi, I'm Lucky," says the guy who looks just like Posdnuos. They're brothers.

Soon Russell Simmons trails off toward Broadway. We are all left standing. "Where are you guys from?" I ask, pretending not to know they're from Long Island.

"My parents are Haitian," says Trugoy.

"That's dope. Sabrina and I are Dominican," I say, "and Marie's parents are from Haiti, too." Marie and Trugoy say something to each other in Kreyòl. I try to follow, but only a few words are familiar.

"You don't look Dominican," Lucky says. "I thought you were Puerto Rican and something, or, like, Black and white."

"Really?" I respond. "What about me isn't Dominican?"

"You're hanging out with Haitians, for one," says some tag along from the peanut gallery outside our cipher. "And the way you dress—you don't dress like no hick."

Angel looks even hotter now than he did last summer on the basketball court. He lost more inches around his waist and shot up to almost six feet in height. I floss on the tennis court, putting extra spin on my forehand and my one-handed backhand to get his attention. I can see him watching from my periphery. A well-dressed older woman who looks related to Rocío, with shoulder-length brown hair, is watching us. When I'm done playing for the afternoon, I rush off the tennis courts trying not to make eye contact with Angel. The older woman stops me. "*Hola, ju sink* he's look cute?" she says, pointing at Angel. "He' my son."

"*No, señora,* I was just saying hello."

"You look like a nice gu'l. I see you play tennis here a lot."

"Oh, yes, I do."

"Angel, come here." She formally introduces us.

"Yo, can you talk love if I call you tonight?" Angel asks me.

"I can talk love, I can talk *anything,*" I respond, immediately regretting how silly I sound.

"Your father isn't going to freak out, is he? He's really fucking *loco,*" Angel says.

"We're only talking, so it's no big deal." I'm lying.

CHAPTER SEVEN

Ave Maria, Morena

> Simultáneamente me miraba la cara desde distintos ángulos
> Y mi cara, como la realidad, tenía un caracter multíplice.
>
> Simultaneously, I saw my face from different angles
> And my face, like reality, had multiple characters.
>
> —GLORIA ANZALDÚA, *BORDERLANDS*

A FEW WEEKS LATER, OVER A SINGLE SCOOP OF CHOCOLATE ICE cream, Angel says he wants to ask me a question. We walk into the small empty lobby at Apple Bank across the street.

"I want you to be my girl," he says. "I promise to be good to you."

"What do you mean by *that*?" I ask.

"I'm falling in love with you—yes, it's happening mad fast, but I can't help it." He leans in and whispers, "I'm not like these other Dominican assholes."

"I think I'm falling in love with you, too," I say. Angel leans in closer until we are locked in a heated, lip-sucking first kiss.

"What the hell are you doing?" Papi is screaming from the door, waving his oversize graphite tennis racket with his right hand like a madman. "What are you doing with this *lousy* Dominican?"

"Papi, we were just talking."

Angel is frozen. He can't move.

"I saw the whole thing from *there*," he says, pointing at Golden Rule, where Alice is sitting, frowning with her entire face, by the window. "You're supposed to be practicing, but I find you here, acting like a *cuero*. You're just like your *lousy* moth'a."

"But—"

Papi raises his tennis racket up to Angel's face. "Stay away, you and your *lousy* moth'a." Still paralyzed with fear, Angel is unable to move or defend Maria's honor. A crowd is beginning to gather by the door.

"STOP! STOP IT!" I yell. "Leave him alone, or you'll be asking for problems!"

Papi grabs me by the forearm and drags me across the street. I look back at Angel. He hasn't moved from the spot where Papi threatened to beat him down with his tennis racket.

"She's going to be on welfare with a bunch of kids, like her *lousy* moth'a," Papi says to Alice.

"Eduardo, *please*," she says. If she frowns any further, Alice may morph into a Shar-Pei.

"Go sit over there," Papi screams at me, pointing to a single booth on the other side of the empty restaurant. "I can't look at your face."

"I really hate you," I yell back.

"I'm going to fix you when we get home."

"If I don't manage to fuck you up first," I mumble to myself. I hate it when he compares me to Rocío almost as much as I hate it when Alice introduces me as her daughter to the people she works with.

When Papi and Alice aren't around, Angel and I become inseparable. I see less of Marie and everyone else.

Suddenly, freestyle music doesn't taste like bubble gum anymore. I finally know what it's like to yearn for someone. When Exposé sings "I'll sacrifice tomorrow / Just to have you here today," it takes on a whole new meaning. I can't remember life before Angel. I can't imagine a future without him.

More than being Angel's secret girlfriend, I become his mother Maria's de facto daughter. And her man, Casimiro, becomes, by default or kismet, a father figure.

There must have been hundreds of thousands of women from the Dominican Republic bearing her name, as many as there are stars strewn across the tropical night sky. Many Marias have found themselves in New York City, working in factories assembling hats and sewing buttons on shirts, as maids and home-care attendants, doing whatever to provide for their families here and back home with the bit of money they scrape together every other week.

This Maria was no different from the others—that is, until I came into her life. Maria rescued me, *una recogida*, from Papi. To me, this made her extraordinary. She was hardly the wealthy person Papi pretended to be, but she took me in nonetheless, setting a place for me at the table whether I dropped in for dinner or not.

Not since living with my grandparents in Santo Domingo had I felt wanted. Once trapped in a golden cage with Rocío and now living with Papi's fury and Alice's baffling indifference to it, I was little more than a street kid myself. Back in Santo Domingo, I used to see them running up and down El Malecón, barely surviving by cleaning windows, selling *maní*, newspapers, and their asses to European and American tourists if need be.

Every day since moving in with Papi and Alice, I had prayed for a mother. And finally, Maria fell into my life. She came in a handsome package with a gift card from the universe that read: "You are meant to be, despite how you got here; you'll see someday. In the meantime, handle this lady with care."

Maria looks young for her age. She never divulges exactly how old she is, but I guess by looking at her eldest son when he comes to visit, Maria must be somewhere in her early fifties. Her flowing skirts and dresses make her thin frame look elegant, and her lips are always stained in earth tones to match her thick and wavy reddish-brown mane. Maria stands out from the rest of the women living at 512 Isham in that she never wears the spandex shorts and super-tight jeans that give the other women severe cases of *pan de agua.* Their crotches—especially Charo's on the fourth floor—look as if they are always crazy horny.

Maria is as bitter a person as she is an attractive one. She was duped into having three sons with three different men. Her first love, she tells me, promised to marry her soon after she gave birth to his son in *la capital.* Months later, without warning, the older man married another girl around the corner from where Maria lived with her family. The son she bore from that man, Roberto, is studying to become a gynecologist. Pussy, he says, is the only thing he feels passionate enough to dedicate his life to. Maria brags about him to everyone in the building. *"Mi querido hijo,"* she says, "is going to help me retire while I'm young enough to enjoy life." The fact that he keeps failing the board certification never comes up.

Maria doesn't talk about Chino's father at all, and she barely talks to him, even when he's sitting in front of her. He tries desperately to bond with Maria, sometimes leaving his girlfriend, Blanca—I forget her real name, but everybody in the building calls her Blanca as a joke, because she's mad dark-skinned—behind in her small one-bedroom apartment on 137th Street, pissed off and alone. Chino is a sensitive slender man in his twenties with soft curly hair and skin that looks like toasted cacao beans. Usually, I find him sitting in the kitchen drinking espresso and recounting his day to an apathetic mother who always changes the subject to one of her other two kids.

"*Hola,* Chino, where's your lady?" I greet him, expecting the usual wicked response at Blanca's expense.

"*Tú lo sabé,* I love women others find too ugly to be seen wi's in *público,* because they never treat me bad," he says, laughing.

Angel's father, Emilio, looks exactly like Angel before he lost his baby fat in Santo Domingo. I usually find him, Casimiro, and Maria sitting around the kitchen table, eating Casimiro's *bacalao* with *mangú* and onions. The whole building knows when Casimiro is home because you can smell the onions, first soaked in vinegar, sautéing with the *bacalao* from the front door of apartment 1B.

I let myself into the apartment—it's rarely locked—and walk by an elaborate gold-framed painting of San Miguel slaying a dragon on the right side of the wall behind the door; it hangs there for protection. On the floor directly below the painting are a coconut, candy, a cigar, and a stone head with eyes and a tiny mouth made of cowrie shells resting on a small plate. Next to the stone head Casimiro calls Ellegua is a cigar and a tiny bottle of half-drunk Bacardi rum he sprinkles on the stone head every Monday.

I steal a piece of caramel candy from Ellegua's plate and proceed down the endless dimly lit hallway. The aroma of *bacalao* and onions guide me to the first opening on the right, the kitchen and center of Maria's universe. Angel's dad is sitting with his back to me, laughing like a jolly Buddha about something with his ex-wife and her current love. Casimiro is mashing the boiled green plantains with mounds of butter and hot water from the pot.

"You remember Angel's dad, Emilio?" Maria asks me.

"Yes. Hello, sir," I say. Emilio nods, making absolutely no eye contact with me. I don't think he's ever addressed me directly. I sit on the other side of the round wooden table.

"Angel's dad used to be a vegetarian when we were together, but now he eats fish," Maria says. I can't imagine someone with Emilio's rotund stomach, protruding over his jeans, without a piece of *pernil* on his plate.

"A Dominican vegetarian, are you joking?" I ask her.

"Yes, we *jused* to be Hare Krishna," she says. "Angel even have that little *cola* growing from the back of his clean-shaven head."

"But why?" I think back to Washington Square Park, trying to remember if I heard any salsa or merengue versions of their incantations. "They are so phony."

"Why not? You have to open your mind," Casimiro says. I feel one of his D.R. history lessons coming on. "There were Muslims and Africans who brought *los misterios* with them during slavery, Taíno animists in the mountains, and Jews who worshipped in secrecy. The Catholic conquistadors—there are all kinds of people with different religions who are *dominicanos, chica.*"

"I guess I didn't get that far in school."

"They are not going to teach you that, Raquel, but the information is yours if you want it," he says.

"*Ay*, Casimiro, don't involve her in your *brujería*," Maria snaps. "Do you know one of his *putas* left something at my door, *una cabeza de chivo*, a fucking goat's head in a box, and I lost a belly. She would have come after Angel, like you. That beech *cabróna*—"

"STOP IT, Maria," Casimiro yells. "*Now* is not the time." Maria doesn't respond. Emilio doesn't look up from his plate during her rant. He's in another world, a state of culinary bliss.

"*Bendición*, Papi." Angel appears in the doorway, his T-shirt soaked from an afternoon of playing basketball. Sweat is dripping down his rust-colored arms and his newly developed muscles. I really don't want to fuck this relationship up. I gave Angel my virginity several months after we started seeing each other, on my sixteenth birthday, to prove it. The only thing I remember about it was my favorite song, Soul II Soul's "Keep on Movin'" was playing in the background. Unspectacular as it was, and as much as I almost immediately regretted doing the nasty with Angel, I didn't want to risk losing Maria, Casimiro, and 512 Isham. Besides, I feel that Maria may need me as much as I do her.

After school and tennis, I spend most afternoons at Maria's apartment, cleaning the kitchen, doing the dishes, and picking up after Angel. Sometimes I accompany Maria to the welfare office, where she volunteers me to translate for other women in the building, which I really fucking hate doing. During the warmer months, I'm also the one who accompanies her to one wake after the other at the Riverdale Funeral Home on Broadway, right next to Golden Rule. We rarely know the deceased, but that doesn't matter to Maria. She finds peace among the dead and the mourning.

On the days when Casimiro is home from work as a custodian and handyman at the Four Seasons, he spends almost the whole day in bed reading science fiction books he buys at the Strand Central Park kiosk during his lunch breaks. On the days when Maria wakes Casimiro up by screaming at him about a foreign scent she's picked up on an undershirt or a telephone number without a name she found while looking through his uniform or wallet, he leaves the apartment like a Jedi knight, without fighting back. The rumor on the block is that he, like Papi, prefers to fish in the local pond for company. They are both too damn lazy to cheat outside their 'hood.

One day I walk in on Casimiro, reading one of his science fiction books in bed.

"*Hola*, Casimiro. Can I watch TV in here?"

"*Ay, coño*, I got goose bumps," he responds. "When you walked in through the door, I saw one of your guides, *un indio*, walk in behind you."

"What are you talking about?" I say, looking over on the left side of the bed to see if his bottle of mamajuana and shot glass are on the floor next to his stack of books.

"Raquel, I saw my *madrina de santo* today and she gave me a reading *con los caracoles*. You came up. She says you will be the one."

"The *one*? Like *Moíses*?" I ask.

"The one to carry on our tradition, who will communicate with others who we really are to the world," he says. "Your guides are strong enough to carry you even if you don't recognize them now."

"Let me read *you*, Casimiro," I say, halfway joking. "I can tell you now that you guys are all *mierda*. Why do you make Maria suffer so much? Why are you playing her dirty with that short fat bitch around the corner? I'm pretending not to know shit, but I hear you have a kid with her."

"That's my burden to carry here in this life. Women destroy me. I allow them to."

"But you are one of the smartest people I have ever met. How can you invite so much drama into your life?" Papi, who embarrassed me when refusing to shake Casimiro's hand the other day on Seaman, didn't possess the understanding or curiosity that his nemesis, this uneducated raven-complected *campesino*, from Dajabón did. "You are so much more worldly than Papi. I hate him. I am sorry he wouldn't shake your hand. He thinks he's better than everyone."

"Leave that man alone. He's lost. He's ashamed of who he is," Casimiro says. "You have been born blessed, chosen to do something here, Raquel. Listen to what I'm saying."

"*Cabrón,* I hear you have a son." Maria walks in screaming. "I saw him. He looks just like you but with fucking light green eyes."

"Maria, please don't fight with me. I—"

"I curse him and you, *maricónaso.* I've accepted all of your fucking little bastards, and this is how you repay me?" she screams, clawing at Casimiro with her nails. Droplets of blood surface through the welts on his face and bare chest. Maria's eyes are wild, her ponytail wet. "Raquel, get dressed. There's a wake on Broadway, and I think I know the poor kid's mother." I don't want to go, but I know better than to say that right now.

The boy's mother, sitting in front of the open casket, looks familiar to Maria, but she can't place her or the teenager, lying in eternal slumber in a simple wooden casket, with certainty. She sits in the back, tears streaming down her face as she looks straight ahead at the dead kid. He looks to be around the same age as Angel. I have a feeling she isn't crying for the deceased, his family, or the street violence doing more to wipe us out than any *tyrano* back in the old country could. Maria is crying for herself. She's crying for the circumstances that led her to this cold and unwelcoming city, into the arms of a cheating prick. She's crying because Roberto is probably not going to be her golden ticket to early retirement. She's crying because she may have missed destiny's revelation to her. Surely, Maria wasn't meant to take care of crazy old senile men like Leonicio and, by default, his *tecato* son, Jesús, for the rest of her life—or was she?

I try to understand where Maria is coming from. Leonicio lives on the Upper West Side with his crackhead son who stripped their tiny apartment bare and who, Maria told me, sucked dick in their hallway when there was nothing left to sell. Their apartment was almost totally devoid of life. Leonicio slept atop a mattress on the floor at night and sat on an old plastic-covered chair for hours during the day. Maria, whom Leonicio confused for his long-dead wife, Mima, used some of the money from her paltry paycheck to buy him a small used TV set, one of those shitty ones that Jesús couldn't exchange for crack on the street.

I recently went to pick her up at the old man's apartment. There he sat in thick diapers under his shorts. "Mima, I have to go to the bathroom," Leonicio yelled at her. "Now, *hija de puta!*"

"Control yourself for *un minuto*," she said, "and I'm Maria, not Mima."

She struggled to peel the old man from the plastic-covered chair. I stood, frozen, by the door. When she did finally get him up, shit started running down his leg and onto the floor, making a trail to the bathroom. "*¡Puta madre!*" Leonicio screamed. From where I stood, I could see Maria wiping his ass and flushing the toilet before helping the old fleshy man into the narrow shower stall. She bathed him like a baby, helping him to the bed before cleaning the foul-smelling shit from the linoleum floor.

Leonicio cackled from his mattress as Maria cleaned up after him. "That's all you good for, Mima, you piece of *chit*." Maria held her tongue. Her shift was almost over. The old man's gaze shifted toward me, and the room became silent, only the sound of the tiny fan whizzing an insignificant stream of air in his direction filled the air. Leonicio stared through me and started sweating as profusely as Ms. Mabel used to.

"*¡Mira viejo sucio*, stop doing that right now!" Maria screamed at him.

Leonicio was jerking off under the covers. I was his unknowing muse.

"Thank God Jesús wasn't here, or he may have join in *también*," she joked anxiously. "*Less* go out of here."

None of Maria's sons understand how fucked up and degrading her job really is, not even Casimiro. Here, at the funeral home, she is free to cry without guilt or judgment. It doesn't matter to her that I'm sitting here. Maria lets it all out. I think she is jealous of the kid in the coffin. If she were fated to clean Leonicio's shit for the rest of her life, Maria preferred to die.

"*Oye, nena*, you look like one of them mixed Black chicks from the seventies with your big curly hair and that dashiki top," yells Blackie out the fourth-floor window as I walk up the stairs to 512 Isham. Blackie and his thunder-crotch wife, Charo, must be the last *boricuas* on the block, certainly in the building.

"What's a dashiki?" I yell back, not understanding that the colorful shirt I'd bought at Antique Boutique had a name. "It's that Native Tongue shit, 'black medallions, no gold.' know what I mean?"

"Sure, whatever," he yells back over the salsa blaring out of his apartment. When Charo isn't home, he turns the music up, way up. "You look like you could be from anywhere, Rachel. Yesterday you looked Egyptian or something, your face looks like this photo I seen in my *National Geographic.*"

"Really?"

"Oh, and I read this story about this African tribe in Senegal, and one of the women looked just like Natalie—dark and round, with fine features, wearing a long-ass weave."

"Word? I guess Natalie *could* pass for an *africana,*" I yell up at him.

"I swear. I'll bring *el deso* down if I find it," Blackie says. "Is Maria home?"

Nobody in the building gets Charo and Blackie's relationship: They are opposites in every way. He's skinny and looks like a cross between Bobby Valentín and Oscar D'León, mustache and all. Charo is tall and fat, with hair the color of *avena* and light-colored eyes and could easily be mistaken for a white girl if not for her hair.

Blackie may be the happiest doorman in the city. He works at one of the fanciest buildings on the Upper West Side, where he opens doors, signs for important packages, and stores dry cleaning—even the occasional bag of weed and coke—for a juicy list of famous people. In return for his discretion, Blackie is so well laced with money, liquor, and drugs during the holidays, it's the only time of year he can afford to buy peace from his mean-ass wife without sacrificing any of his vices.

Charo is a social worker for the city, but since she got her master's degree and a promotion to manager she's started to force-feed her husband's balls to him every night. He makes more money than she does, but Charo's job, she thinks, takes more brains and therefore yields more power. She's so devoted to her work that she brings it home with her, talking to her husband like the social workers do their clients at the welfare office: as if they're worthless.

Blackie is even-tempered and a jokester. Charo is brutal and clumsy in her own skin, the bearer of bad news and *bochinche*. I swear it was Charo who told Maria about Casimiro's son around the corner. She wants everybody to be as miserable as she is.

"I've got the munchies," Blackie yells down. "You think Maria has a little something extra for me?"

"Of course. You know she cooks extra food in case anyone drops by," I yell back up. "Come down."

"What?"

"Come. Down."

Blackie runs down four flights of stairs so fast we arrive at Maria's door at the same time.

"Peace, my sista," he says, laughing and pumping his right first in the air. Blackie's breath reeks of alcohol.

Maria is cooking white rice and *pollo guisado* for dinner in the kitchen. Natalie, Maria's next-door neighbor, is sitting next to Raquel, the prettiest woman ever to live at 512. A tiny light-brown Chihuahua is resting on Raquel's expensive high-heeled leather boots. She looks exactly like Dorothy Dandridge, an actress who starred as Carmen Jones in one of those old movies Alice forced me to watch with her when I was younger. I love that we share the same name.

Because of the patronage of the white man who lives in her apartment sometimes, everything Raquel wears is really dope. She is so well paid that when she heard me talking about Antique Boutique and Basic Basic with Marie the other day on Maria's phone, she paid me in clothes to take her down to the Village. On the train, Raquel showed me thousands of dollars her boyfriend had given her crumpled up like garbage at the bottom of her Gucci bag. "It's dirty money," she said, laughing. "That's why I treat it so poorly." In a few hours Raquel spent almost every hundred-dollar bill she had in the bag. We headed back uptown with just enough money for a couple of tokens.

Raquel is a kept woman, though I imagine she could have made stupid loot as a supermodel. Instead, she plays different men into buying her clothes and shoes, paying for her hair appointments, rent, and food in exchange for her company.

Raquel likes her job. She enjoys being in the company of men, even the ones who don't speak Spanish, because she can't stand being alone. Natalie, who introduced us to her, told us that Raquel's mother abandoned her as a child for six years in a *campo* in Moca with her father. Apparently, Raquel took too long to load into the car with her other siblings.

"That's *cold*," I said. "Natalie, how did she end up in New York, in 512?"

"Raquel met an American tourist in Santo Domingo who promised to take her to New York City and enroll her in English classes," Natalie said, "but his real plan was to take advantage of her."

"How it happen?" Maria asked.

"Well, don't tell her I told you," she said, "*pero* the motherfucker took her directly from JFK to this dirty apartment and locked her ass in there—bolted the windows shut, left her with the clothes she came in, no food, *nada*—and he was married!"

"*Ay, Dios mío que estás en el cielo,*" Maria screamed, holding on to her chest as if she were about to throw up her heart. "Oh my God, I have to make some *cafécito.*"

"He tortured her, raped her, starved her until one day she decided to play along and fuck him real good," Natalie said, pausing to finish the plate of *moro con pollo* Maria had made that night, "and when he fell asleep, she took his keys, locked him in, and ran out of the apartment in the snow with nothing but his shirt on."

"I don't believe it, Natalie, that's wack as hell, but—" I said.

"I swear. Her sister confirmed the story," she said. "So finally, she found a cousin here who took her in and set Raquel up in a factory job only to steal her money. Her family is real fucked up."

"How did she end up here?" I asked.

"She met the old man who owns this Dominican restaurant she ate at one day, and he fell so hard for her that he set her up here."

I almost felt bad that we were making so much fun of how fucking strange Raquel acted sometimes, but we couldn't help that she gave us fodder for our jokes, usually at the expense of Chino and his physically challenged assortment of girlfriends.

"*Mira*, Raquel is giving us this little baby Chihuahua," Maria says to me. "She's *rabiosa* like you, and even has your face, but we need to give her a different name so we don't confuse her or anyone else in the house." Everyone, except me, explodes in laughter.

"Oh my God, she does have your face," Blackie says. He's become a fixture at dinner over the last several months because Charo is working late to complete some special project.

"And look, she has *your* wife's face, Blackie, but on the other end of her *culo*," I snap back.

"Don't listen to them, they're just bothering you," Raquel says. I don't know how she communicates with her white boyfriends, not knowing a lick of English. The conversation abruptly shifts to Chino, as it often does when Raquel is over.

"You just missed Chino, did you see him downstairs?" she asks.

"No. I didn't."

"He was with that other *prieta*, Lesbia, the one who is taller than he is by half a foot and looks just like a man."

We brace ourselves for what Raquel may say next. "You know he likes ugly girls," Blackie says. "He must be fighting with Blanca again."

"Oh, I would give anything to watch them make love on the roof," Raquel says. "I would have to wear panties so I don't wet my jeans."

We are stunned, dumbstruck by the mental picture Raquel has drawn for us, especially in front of Maria. Natalie doesn't look up from her plate.

"I wonder if she has a penis," Raquel says, laughing. "I bet you she has something interesting down there or she would be too boring and ugly to fuck."

"Raquel, where do you come up with these things?" I ask.

"It's just my imagination. Have you seen her in jeans? Not even *your* wife looks *that* bad," she says to Blackie, who's snooping around the cabinet looking for Casimiro's stash of mamajuana.

"My wife is beautiful, maybe not as much as you or the Chihuahua's twin, but she is a bad—"

"Come on, Blackie, just because she has *Children of the Corn* hair and the complexion of a Glo Worm doesn't make her pretty," I say.

"That's the only thing that saves her," Raquel says. "I wish I was a natural blonde."

Angel walks in and says, *"Bendición, mami,"* giving Blackie a pound. *"Que Dios te bendiga,* my son," Maria says, frying her second stack of *maduros* over the hot stove. Something is different. He doesn't make eye contact with me as he washes his hands in the sink. He smells kind of funky, like Night Queen oil and sweat.

"You know, I don't ever wonder what you and Raquel look like when you two make love because you're both too pretty, so boring," Raquel says to Angel. I'm red with embarrassment, hoping she leaves soon. Angel looks at her and smiles. He doesn't respond.

"My baby son doesn't do that," Maria says. "Come on, Raquel, stop." Blackie doesn't look up from his second plate. Raquel giggles while standing up and reaching for her Gucci bag on the floor next to the dog. *"Gracias* for the food, Maria, I don't want my baby to shit all over your new kitchen floor," she says. "I'm taking the bitch for a walk downstairs before I drop her off for good with you."

"Raquel is so weird," I say after she leaves.

"But she sure does have a fine ass," Blackie says. "She's almost as hot as my wife."

Charo walks through the front door, knowing Maria's apartment is locked only on weekend mornings to keep the Jehovah's Witnesses from inviting themselves in. A bit ruffled, she appears in the doorway of the kitchen.

"I knew I'd fucking find you here, *lambón*—did it occur to you that I'd be hungry by the time I got home from doing real work?" she says to Blackie. "Hi, Maria, kids." We nod. Blackie's head hangs low, weighted down by humiliation.

"Here, Charo, I saved you *un plato*," Maria says. "Raquel, set a place for her over here."

"Thank God for Maria, or I'd starve to death."

"Please, Charo. Relax," Blackie says, almost whispering.

"Maria, I think I saw Casimiro down the block going into the building on the corner."

"Shut up, Charo," Blackie says. "Mind your fucking business."

Maria doesn't say another word for the rest of the night, retreating to her bedroom to read through the latest edition of *Sucesos* before Charo and Blackie leave. Maria's hung up on *Sucesos*, a weekly tabloid for those obsessed with all things macabre, detailing all the crazy shit that goes on in rural D.R. with headlines like "Woman Sets Husband's Mistress and Their Children on Fire" and "Man Machetes His Girlfriend and Lover to Death in a Jealous Rage," with accompanying color photos. She stockpiles them underneath her side of the bed.

"Dominican men will only lead you down a path of self-destruction and death," Maria says, showing me an article she's reading, which, like the rest, ends badly.

"Haitians, too," I say. "The whole island is full of cursed men."

"No, it's us that are cursed," she says. "We are stupid enough to fall for their *mierda*."

Now that it's springtime, we're no longer forced to wait for the bus in the cramped lobby of Apple Bank with other high school kids. I spend most mornings, afternoons, and evenings thinking about Angel and little else now that he's been accepted to Temple University, all the way in Philadelphia. I try to imagine life without him here and whether or not Maria or Casimiro will lose interest in me once Angel leaves the city.

I'm so distracted that I can't listen to Frankie Ruiz's *Más Grande Que Nunca* without getting emotional. Casimiro and Maria tried to teach us how to dance salsa to that record, but we couldn't get it together. I can't listen to Bobby Brown records, either. If I even think of how sweet Angel sounded, his voice cracking, singing: "She'll make the toughest homeboy / Fall deep in love," I get misty-eyed and have to rush to the girls' bathroom before totally breaking down.

This school year has been really tense so far. It happened right before school started at the end of last summer, but the Yusef Hawkins murder in Bensonhurst at the hands of a crew of Italian-American wild cowboys is still a fresh, open wound on my mind. I try to keep it together as long as I can. I don't say a word when some white boy jokes about how Mayor Dinkins should stay away from his 'hood or risk catching a bad one like "that other monkey" in Bensonhurst. It doesn't take long, however, for something in me to snap.

It's on my way to Maria's that I hear someone yell, "You better keep walking, you fucking bitch." I turn around and see Danielle, a redhead from St. Catherine's who I thought was my friend, standing with a large group of white boys. Some of them are carrying stickball bats.

"What did you say?" I ask her, smiling.

"I said you better keep walking, you fucking dirty spic," she says.

I want to stop and fight, but something tells me the smart thing to do is ignore her if I want to arrive at Maria's in one piece. One of the guys in her crew yells, "Why don't you fuck that nigga spic up, we got your back, Dani." They laugh as I pick up the pace and almost jog down Isham Street with tears streaming down my face.

The next weekend, I see Danielle in the park during tennis practice. Angel is playing basketball when she enters the court and starts flirting with him. "I'm a nigga spic, Danielle, right?" I ask, walking toward her with my tennis racket in hand. I don't give her a chance to answer before hitting her knees with my racket and wrapping my hands around her neck. She falls forward, and her face has started to turn blue when Angel yells, "That's enough!" One of the regular ballplayers grabs my legs, another my waist, and yet another starts punching my wrists until I let go of Danielle's neck. One of the tennis players tells me to go home before the cops come.

A few hours later, Papi bolts through the door, panting. "I hear that you were fighting like one of those street *ga'bage*," he yells. "Why are you starting with people?" He doesn't let me answer before smacking me across the face. I don't cry. "You're going to be a nobody, like your lousy *madre*." He leaves me sitting on my bed, stroking my cheek.

The taunting of this new Black Muslim girl named Amina at school is especially irritating because the ringleader is a guidette named Anastasia Perillo. She looks like a blowfish, with hair that's teased to the ceiling and brown eyes that are too small for her huge face, set on either side of a pointy noise. Anastasia never went anywhere without a bottle of Aqua Net and a tube of vaginal itch cream sticking out of her leather purse.

One morning I hear Anastasia referring to Amina as a monkey before class. "Did you see how hairy that bitch's legs and arms are?" she jokes within earshot of the girl. "Don't those people believe in Nair?" I'm not sure if Amina hears, but I don't care. I calmly walk over to Anastasia's desk, pick her up from her chair with my left hand, and slap her several times with my right before a teacher pulls me off her and sends me to Dean Kelly's office. I don't understand what a Muslim girl is doing attending a Catholic high school, but it doesn't give anyone the right to make fun of her for not shaving her legs or hiking up her skirt to thigh-level. Dean Kelly isn't hearing it, and I receive my first warning.

The only other thing that matters to me right now is A Tribe Called Quest's *People's Instinctive Travels and the Paths of Rhythm*. Nothing is as creative as what comes out of the Native Tongues. I press play and rewind dozens of times to listen to "Bonita Applebum" on my Sony Walkman every morning on the bus to school, full blast until my ears start ringing, followed by "Can I Kick It?," which I like because I just met Mayor Dinkins at the tennis courts in Inwood Park. I memorize all the lyrics on the album and write verses for Queen Latifah, Monie Love, and MC Lyte in my notebooks instead of doing any work at school. Writing keeps my soaring temper in check and my fists from pounding some girl harder than Papi does me.

Soon after slapping Anastasia, I see Dean Kelly again. An angry and obese chick named Yesenia, whose parents fled Cuba, begins popping shit because she thinks I'm crazy for calling her "my sister." She let me know it every chance she got. I let it go for the first two years of school, but all of a sudden I begin to see Papi in Yesenia's fat brown face.

"You're so fucking stupid with that 'my sister' shit," she says one morning in the girls' bathroom.

"Why does it have to be like that?" I ask the fatty.

"Because I fucking hate you, you fake Dominican bitch," she says, laughing as the crowd starts amassing around us.

"You're acting like one of those savages we learn about for no fucking reason," I say. "And you were born here, just like I was, and you call yourself Cuban."

"Oh shit, Yesenia, you're going to let that bitch talk to you like *that*?" yells a voice in the crowd.

"You better get out of here with that *Different World* shit before I smack that played-out 'We Are the World' taste out yo' mouth."

"Please, don't force me," I say, making my way out of the bathroom and back to typing class. I think of Papi slamming the orange metal ball hopper into my back and sides. I think of Alice standing there, watching. I think of my strong hands around Danielle's long neck, her face turning shades of blue. I think of the Dominican hick Fredericka from Aquinas, who lives by the 1 on Dyckman and of beating her up so badly I was sorry for it. She accused me of making moves on her nerdy boyfriend when I never even noticed him before.

I am light-headed in class, overcome with a sinking feeling that something awful is about to happen. Casimiro told me that these heavy feelings are our Indigenous and African spiritual guides intervening, warning us of danger. "Intuition is everything," he always says. "Listen to her." I start rapping "Bonita Applebum" to myself. The bell rings.

We pour out of class quietly because the chapel across the hall may be in use, and the dean's office is only feet away. There, Yesenia rushes me with Yoanka, a friend from St. Thaddeus, and a third girl I've seen around school.

"You wanna act tough *now*, bitch, right?" Yesenia yells. She tries to rip my skirt off, revealing a sliver of the red shorts I'm wearing underneath.

"Wow, you, too, Yoanka?" I ask, punching her with my right fist, snapping her head back. I turn around and grab Yesenia by the back of the head, landing a right in her face. The other girl starts crying and rethinks jumping in. "Yo, Rachel got pretty legs," I hear my friend Freddy yell in the background.

I start dragging Yesenia toward the chapel door, where I intend to slam the door on her neck. I figure she's brainwashed, anyway.

The assistant dean runs over as I'm about to open the chapel door, alerted by the cries of a few girls yelling for me to stop and guys encouraging me to finish what I started. Blood covers sections of the floor and our clothing like sweat during a basketball game.

"I've had enough, Ms. Cepeda," the assistant dean yells, pulling us apart. I don't explain who started it or that I was just defending myself. "I'm calling both your parents to deal with this."

The next morning Yesenia and her mother and Papi and I are sitting in Dean Kelly's office, waiting for her to finish making the morning's announcements.

"We are going to put you in a pot with Yemaya," Yesenia's mother whispers to us. "You're going to see."

"I think you're crazy, lady," Papi says loudly. "You don't want to make empty threats."

Dean Kelly walks in and hears Papi responding to Yesenia's mother. "What's going on in here?" she asks.

"*Ay*, I don't know why he is being so rude," Yesenia's mother says.

Papi and I decide not to explain the situation. Yesenia is off, dismissed back to class. Dean Kelly asks us to stay behind.

"I think it's best if you don't return next year," Dean Kelly says to me. "I heard about the girl from St. Catherine's and an incident with someone from Aquinas, then the poor Perillo girl, and now this." She doesn't allow me to respond. "And did you know that Rachel wrote a pro-choice paper in English class at *this* school?" she asks Papi. He doesn't understand what Dean Kelly is talking about. I shrug. "You start too much trouble. Why are you so angry?"

CHAPTER EIGHT

God Bodies and *Indios*

> *All* that we see or seem
> Is but a dream within a dream.
>
> —EDGAR ALLAN POE, "A DREAM WITHIN A DREAM"

ANGEL MOVED TO PHILLY AT THE END OF THAT SUMMER.

Maria submerged into an abysmal depression months later when Casimiro ran off with Charo. Nobody, not even the ancestors and spiritual guides, could have known to tap me on the shoulder beforehand and whisper in my ear that this tidal wave of betrayal would come to strike Maria down.

I walk into 1B and find Maria having another *ataque de nervios* at the dinner table. Natalie is sitting next to her, and Blackie is making coffee.

"Maria, he was good for nothing, don't cry over that guy," Natalie says, reaching over the table to hold her hand.

"I was so good to him," Maria sobs.

"Too good," she says. "He didn't contribute a penny to the house, never gave you anything."

"But I loved him, was so loyal," Maria says, crying hysterically.

"He is an ordinary man who isn't worth it, and that woman was never your friend," Natalie says.

"*Ay,* Maria," Blackie says, "we're better off not wasting time with people who don't give a shit about us."

Only Blackie looks happier than I've ever seen him. He comes by almost every night after work to comfort Maria over dinner with stories about the articles he read in *National Geographic.* Maria is usually unresponsive.

I start senior year at the same impossibly large high school in the Bronx that Angel went to. I feel like I'm entering a prison every morning. Thousands of other kids in the yard are cluster-fucked into cliques by ethnicity or sport.

It's easy to tell which Dominicans are *campesinos*—the newest arrivals. The guys yell instead of speaking to each other, and sport Jheri curls. Many of them speak in dialects I barely understand and say words I can't begin to try and spell. They sport shoes and sneakers with no socks, even in winter. And the girls usually wear their hair fried so severely straight they smell as if they're on fire, even more so than Socorro did, when you pass them in the hallway or yard. With several notable exceptions, Asian kids stick together, as do white and Black-American kids.

Then there are the Latinos born in New York City, who don't give a fuck about the *plátanos* as much as they don't care about us. To many of the tens of thousands flooding the city, we're gringos, fake-ass Dominicans, though they are just a few years away from becoming as American as they perceive us being. In the time in between, the rift between "us" and "them" has become more volatile than standing on a fault line during an earthquake. Many of us born in New York City who feel like we have nothing in common with the *campesinos,* and assume they've come straight out of the farms and shantytowns of rural D.R., began choosing sides.

Some of my classmates from the Caribbean, West Indies, and

Central and South America are tipsy off of the American Dream Tang that their parents served them daily. Teachers like mine, who force-feed us more misinformation about our history than we can process, further ingrain the idea that white friends and hardcore mainstream assimilation will bring us a step closer to realizing our parents' *sueños*.

I don't quite see it that way. Yusef Hawkins, Bernhard Goetz, that poor old crazy lady Eleanor Bumpurs, Simon Mandel, Papi—realizing the American Dream for some means a living nightmare for others. In my world, the bogeymen usually get away with murder.

A couple of weeks before I start working at a clothing store downtown after school, I try to hang out with the Dominican *campesinos*.

"Yo, you look so stupid, hanging out those hicks," points out one of my friends whose mom is Puerto Rican and dad is Black-American. "It's so obvious that they don't even like you. Plus, you're blacker than me, *beeyatch*, and they don't like that shit."

"But I'm trying to connect with them," I say. "Maybe I can talk to them about knowledge of self. You know, like 'a supreme mind will take you out of your paralysis'?"

"Wow, you're really weirder than people think," she says, "if you think quoting Lord Jamar is going to get you anywhere with those hicks. They scream over each other too loudly to even hear what you're saying."

"Those people are ours, too, you know," I say.

"No, they're not. They may be yours, but they ain't mine."

Soon I give up. Maybe homegirl is right. Besides, the *campesinos* don't even notice when I stop hanging out with them.

Angel was born again in Philadelphia. He changed his name to Infinite Reality, and with his new name came a totally new identity, one I only vaguely recognized as that of my first love.

"Yo, why are you working for those devils?" he asks me. He's sitting next to me in the kitchen, eating *concón* with red beans and rice. Maria sets down a fresh plate of fried *maduros* in the middle of the table. This is the first time Infinite doesn't reach over to lick the sweeter slices, burnt on the edges and oozing grease, only to put them back on the plate before anyone else can take a few.

"They don't have knowledge of self. They don't understand that we are the Nation of Gods and Earths, so they treat us like slaves," he says.

"*De que tú 'ta hablando,* Angelito?" Maria asks. "You no God."

"No, Ma, God is right here in all of us."

"Well, I work because I need the money, and your mother buys things for you using my store discount," I say. "Maria needs all the extra money she can spare right now, especially with her 'cancer'—"

"But you and I and everyone else knows there's nothing wrong with her," he says. We all knew Maria's a hypochondriac, but it's gotten worse since Casimiro split and Angel left for college. "Ma, what's wrong with you now?"

"I used to had *un* cancer in my right *seno,*" she says, "and then my *doctor* say it go away, and now it might be in my left. *Ay, Dios libre me.*"

"You know, the other day when Natalie was here for dinner, your mother heard us talking about *SIDA,* and she told us she had it in her left middle finger but it went away," I tell Angel.

"So she's the first woman to have AIDS in one finger, and then just like that, it went away?" he says. "You know, Ma, you have to stop listening to what the white devil doctor fills your head up with."

"I *s'ink* he was like a Indian," she says, cupping her left breast with her right hand. "I couldn't understand him too good and his *boca* smell like curry."

"Are you in the same religion or club or whatever as Brand Nubian?" I ask Angel.

"True indeed. The Nation of Gods and Earths."

Angel traveled all the way to Philadelphia to become a part of the Nation of Gods and Earths, though they've been in our backyard all along, founded just fifteen minutes downtown on the A train by a former student of Malcolm X in 1964. Clarence 13X clashed with the Nation of Islam on the true identity of God. He believed that God was a direct reflection of the Original People, those of African descent. Clarence 13X also believed that 15 percent of the world's population possessed the truth about the nature of God and that only 5 percent were destined to shed light on those still in the dark.

Clarence 13X delivered an ideal of self-determination and improvement that found an audience with a younger crowd of disenfranchised Black-Americans who found his so-called Supreme Mathematics and 120 Lessons palatable.

At the dusk of the 1980s, and now, the onset of the '90s, social awareness is at the forefront of rap vérité. Hip-hop storytelling, illustrated most vividly by N.W.A. on the West Coast and Public Enemy on the East, is starting to eclipse its other expressions by assaulting all those who'll listen with the fucked-up truths about society's mores and politics. A spirit of resistance is being captured in the zeitgeist. The aftershocks of the crack era shredded our families and, in turn, sent us into our communities looking for role models in all the wrong places. Police brutality, while hardly a new phenomenon, was finally caught on video in the savage beating of Rodney King in Los Angeles. Shit is tense, and there's been no time in hip-hop like the present for a revival of Clarence 13X's Five Percent ideology.

"You know, I heard Brand Nubian over a year ago in New Rochelle before they dropped *One for All*," I say, trying to make conversation with this stranger before me. "My tennis friend dates one of Lord Jamar's best friends, the god Mellicon."

Nikki is one of the few tennis players whom I've befriended off the courts. She loves hip-hop as much as I do. She looks like one of those *Essence* cover models, tall and thin, with her mother's Chinese-Jamaican eyes and her father's bronze skin.

"Yeah, they're dope, but listen to the message over the music," he says, quoting Grand Puba on "Wake Up": "'The maker, the owner, the cream of the planet earth.'"

"You think they didn't have to work with a few devils before they were able to release an album on a record label?" I ask. "We all have to work the system or, like in Maria's case, a discount to get what we need."

"Sometimes," he replies with the utmost gravity, "we have to dance with the devil if it enables us to get a greater message out there." He pauses, glancing down at my legs. "Why are your clothes so tight? Don't you have self-respect as an Earth, a mother of civilization? Are you cheating on me when I'm in Philly?" His voice is rising. "Since you like Brand Nubian so much, listen to what the gods say and "Slow Down."

"Why are you wilding out?" I ask. I always ditch the Girbauds for tight jeans when the man I once knew as Angel comes to town.

"*Ay*, Angel, leave her alone," Maria says.

"Listen, the white man is our collective oppressor," Angel says, "all over the world. Look, even in the D.R., the Taíno and Carib Indians and the Original Asiatic Black man had to contend with those white devil Spaniards. And now look at how we embrace the Spaniard and call ourselves Spanish and white, even when most of us obviously are not."

"You're the first Dominican I've ever met down with the Five Percent Nation, but I can see the link," I say. "My only thing is that I've also met Black and Latino devils, and how about those Black cops who took part in Rodney King's beat-down?"

"They're just brainwashed—they're part of the eighty-five percent who live in the dark about their own and our collective identities."

"Casimiro made the connection explicit—maybe you should have spoken to him more. He could have told you how they couldn't kill our culture completely, even though Columbus wiped out all the Native Indians and—"

"Don't say that *maldito* man's name in this house!" Maria screams. She slams one of the dinner plates we bought at the 99 Cent store into the sink, cracking it in two pieces. "You see what you make me do?" She storms into her room and doesn't come out for the rest of the night.

Angel goes back to Temple, back to the gods in Philadelphia. I find out some time later that he's moved on with a new so-called Earth who doesn't mind that he has a girlfriend at home. I am devastated.

"Maria, Angel is living with some chick in his dorm," I tell Maria and Natalie, sobbing. "Something told me to cut class and go call him."

"*¿Y que paso?*" Natalie asks. "What happened when he picked up the phone?"

"He didn't. This girl did and said her 'king' wasn't there."

"He's just going through a *morena* girl phase," Maria says. "Be patient, *mi hija,* and he'll come back."

"I should have stabbed him that time I chased him around the block after catching him with that ugly-ass girl from the Caroline."

"Why would Raquel want to wait around?" Natalie asks.

"Yeah, fuck that asshole, I don't want to waste my life with someone like that."

"My son is not a fuck-ass, don't talk about him like that," Maria screams at me.

"How can you defend that behavior, especially after all you've been through, Maria?" Natalie asks. None of us have touched the chicken *guisado* or rice on our plates.

"That whole situation was Charo's fault," she yells. "That *puta* stole him from me!"

"I thought you cared about me, but I can tell you see me through Angel's eyes, like a piece of shit," I say, crying.

"Well, he is my baby, my son, and you are nothing to me but *una recogida* into that *brujería mierda* Casimiro fed you," Maria screams. "You know, maybe you liked him, too!"

"*Maria*—" Natalie yells.

"I can see why Casimiro left you," I snap.

"Get out."

I storm out, down the long dark hallway, past the image of San Miguel slaying a dragon and an old dry coconut on the floor. Casimiro must have left it there in haste.

I can't hide my hatred of tennis anymore and become bolder with Papi when he screams or threatens me.

"You're terrible, *never* will you get in college playing *lousy* like that," he says one day after practice.

"Well, then kill me," I scream back, "or kill your own self."

"Nobody can deal with you, not even that woman you pretend is your mother."

Alice doesn't say anything, not even "Eduardo, *please.*" She has remained nothing more than a spectator ever since I told her Papi was cheating on her again with the *cubana* across the street who looks like Rocío.

"Get out!" Papi screams at me.

He locks me out of the apartment for hours. The last time it was overnight. I walk around the park and sit on the benches, looking at the river for hours, wondering why I haven't been raped or killed.

Ever since I discovered *The Village Voice* downtown last summer, I've wanted to become a music writer, replacing my dream of writing lyrics for female emcees. I never cut English class, hoping Ms. O'Connell will one day notice my writing and take an interest in me. In the meantime, I bring copies of the alternative newspaper to class and spend the period reading them cover to cover, even the classifieds, while the other kids crack jokes and fuck with Ms. O'Connell until she explodes.

The bell rings. Nothing happens. "Can we start class?" I ask Ms. O'Connell.

She looks in my direction, uncertain who in the overcrowded class made the request. "I can't wait to stop having to teach you bitches," she says. The kids break out in laughter as Ms. O'Connell stares out the window for the rest of the class. I break out and never return.

Maria has left an urgent message for me. Surprisingly, I see it on the crowded table in Papi and Alice's suffocating apartment. It reads, "Come to house, *urgentemente.*"

I walk over to Maria's apartment that evening during dinnertime, when I know other people will be there. The door, as usual, is open. Natalie is sitting in the kitchen.

"*Ay*, Raquel, I have to tell you something, *sientate*," Maria says, serving me a plate of food. She's wearing the same thing I last saw her in: an oversize pastel T-shirt with a robe on top. Her deep auburn hair looks freshly dyed.

"How have you been?" I ask.

"My left breast—I think I have the cancer again," she says. I guess this is Maria's way of apologizing. I look at Natalie and make small talk.

"I hear you've been walking around the street late at night because of your *idiota* father."

"He's all I have."

"Why didn't you come here?" Maria asks. Natalie glances up at me. On the wall to my right is Sheeba's telephone number scribbled in Angel's handwriting. She sees me looking at it and says, "Angel is doing so well in college."

I don't respond to that. Sheeba, my "sister," always wore Night Queen oil. That bitch. "I read a note that you had something urgent to tell me," I say.

"I had a terrible dream with you a few nights ago," she says. "You have to leave New York City *por un rato*."

"Why?"

"I dreamed that you were in the elevator of the Caroline with two cops. They were being bad to you, and you screamed at one of them. The guy shot you dead. I only saw your back, never your face, but I'm sure it was you. You have to go."

"You sure it wasn't Papi who killed me?" I ask, chuckling to break the tension.

"Listen to her, Raquel," Natalie says. "Maria's dreams are real."

I do. That week I walk into the empty guidance counselor's office. There, I find a catalog of colleges and universities around the country and lug it to a round table. I set the book in front of me and close my eyes. I don't know why, but I start praying. To whom or what, I don't know.

I wish I had spoken to Maria before I took the SATs. I took them last Saturday, after another tennis-related fight with Papi. I was so exhausted and angry that I filled in my name and put my head down for the rest of the period. I didn't realize how important that test was until now.

I open the book to a random page with my eyes still closed. My right index finger falls on the right side of the fold, to a university in a city called Pittsburgh, somewhere in Pennsylvania.

I don't know how it happened, how I got here.

I mean, I know how I got here, but it doesn't seem real. The eight-and-a-half-hour bus ride with Papi was crazy tense, even though we barely spoke and sat in different rows. Sometimes Papi would walk by when he wanted to stretch out, staring at me as if he wished he could lay me out right there in front of everyone for almost breaking his arm several weeks ago.

"You wasted all of my money and my time," he screamed at me from his dimly lit bedroom, now stuffed with dental equipment and framed photographs of people I assumed were Alice's family members. He was upset that I didn't have the drive to become the next Gabriela Sabatini, or at least get a full ride to the university, after all his hard work.

"I'll be out of your place soon, and you won't have to worry about me at all after that," I yelled back from the bathroom. I didn't care about having to take remedial courses. Anything was better than this.

Alice said nothing. She sat drinking a cup of Sanka. The noise she made gnawing on a Stella D'oro breakfast treat was crazy loud.

"I'm tired of your shit," I said to Papi, now standing by the doorway.

"What did *you* say?" he screamed as he reached for my hair and dragged me to his bed. Papi punched me so hard, I blacked out long enough to see black, then red, then a series of thunderbolts flashing before me. This was it. I felt something pass through me.

"This is the last time," I said when I came to. I lunged at him. I punched and kicked and scratched and grabbed Papi's wrist with the intention of breaking his arm. He yelled for Alice, who was already in the room.

"Rachel. *Please*," she yelled. "He's your *father*."

"I'm not going to sit here anymore and take your shit," I said to him. "Next time the neighbors will be calling the police on *me*. I don't give a shit who you are."

Papi ran to the bathroom, holding on to his right arm and yelling, "*Dah'ling,* I think *she* broke *my* arm! I think she broke it!"

We barely spoke to each after that. I spent almost every night at Maria's until Papi and I boarded the first local bus out of Penn Station headed to Pittsburgh. I didn't say good-bye to anyone except Maria, Blackie, Natalie, and some of the other neighbors who came by to eat dinner with us the night before.

Before leaving the city, I've traveled around the country only by plane, to compete in tennis tournaments, barely taking in my surroundings before winning or losing the game and then heading back home. This was the first time I'd seen other parts of America from this angle. My heart sank when we rolled out of New York City and into the downcast city of Newark and then Philadelphia.

I imagined Infinite and his Earth living in one of the houses or apartment buildings we drove by. I looked for them, dressed in matching red, black, and green kente cloth outfits. I was sure her locks were hidden under a head wrap high enough to pierce one of the clouds looming above us. I looked for Infinite in every face standing out in front of the corner stores we drove past. Surely he was somewhere, devouring a pressed Cuban ham, cheese, and garlic sandwich, away from the disapproving gaze of the other college boys who discovered God in themselves and white coeds. I tried to look into every brown face on the way out of the city but never found his among them.

I fell asleep en route to King of Prussia and woke up sometime after departing Harrisburg to miles and miles of unchanging landscape. I couldn't believe how depressing the scene looked from my window. I started regretting listening to Maria's warning. I could have flown to and from Santo Domingo in the same amount of time it took me to get here.

While I first find it unsettling, Pittsburgh also means a break from the violence. Here, I'll be able to finally sleep through the night in my own space. I'll be far away from Papi and Alice and the cops who brutalized me in Maria's dreams.

Almost as fast as we hail a cab to Forbes Avenue, Papi's ghost. "Good luck," he says, shaking my hand. He reaches into his pocket and gives me a wad of singles—under twenty dollars—and some loose change. I don't get a chance to thank him. The man disappears into a group of students and families rushing the Towers entrance, leaving me and all my possessions, stuffed into two suitcases, at the top of the steps.

Freshmen are whizzing by me in the Towers lobby like Flash Gordon, most with their proud fathers and frantic mothers in tow. I'm alone and lost, standing by the revolving doors, watching strange faces smile nervously, running in every direction to what I think are their assigned dorm rooms. I'm disoriented and hungry.

"Hey, excuse me, you look like you need help," says a voice in the mob. Jane Mintz is a sophomore from some town outside Philadelphia I've never heard of. Her face is bright red, and her hair is long and wavy. Jane has pretty big hips for a white girl. "I first noticed you from across the lobby because I thought you look like a girl that me and Egypt would have."

"Who?"

"He's Black, from Cleveland. What are you?"

"I'm Dominican, from New York City."

"Is that like biracial?" she asks. "Or like a Puerto Rican?"

At home, Papi said I wanted to be Black because I love hip-hop, and a low-class Dominican because I like graffiti and b-boys. The kids at St. Thaddeus said I wanted to be white because I played tennis and lived with Alice. Casimiro said I needed to recognize and embrace my native *indios* and *africanos* in order to strengthen my spiritual guides, whom he likened to my intuition. Caridad told me I had a vibe of a Black and white gringa. And Blackie said I could be from anywhere. But I like being Dominican, sort of, especially one born in Harlem who likes to wear socks in the winter.

I don't know how to answer Jane.

"I know you ain't completely white or Black but somewhere in between, and you are so pretty," Jane says. "Egypt is going to think you're so pretty, too, and the AKAs are going to want you to be down."

"What the fuck *is* that?"

"Oh, I can tell you're from New York City with that mouth," Jane says, laughing. "Let's go to the pool hall later, when you settle in."

I can barely get a word in on the short walk to my barrack-style dorm room, but I do learn plenty about Jane. First, that she wants to be an FBI agent. And ever since learning American history in a Black Studies class here, she's been ashamed of being white, so much so that "I'd never pledge anything other than a Black sorority" and "I'd never marry a white boy, regardless of what my parents say."

Jane leaves me at the ground floor of my new residence. I walk up a couple of flights and open the door to my tiny room. There's only enough space for a set of bunk beds, one dresser, two desks, and one tiny closet. I stare at the beds. I hadn't realized I'd be living in this box with a total stranger. I almost feel like I'm back on Seaman Avenue, back in prison.

Before my roommate arrives, I drop my bags atop the bottom bunk and leave to take my first walk down Fifth Avenue in search of a school cafeteria that might be serving food. When I finally return to my room, I find my roommate, Tanaisha from Philly, looking through my clothes.

All the beatings, tournaments, traveling back and forth to tennis practice, early-morning private lessons—none of it pays off. Alas, I can't fake my drive or enthusiasm for the sport and receive only an itsy-bitsy partial scholarship. In the first few weeks of school, I report to tennis practice. I can almost see Papi on the sidelines, standing next to the coach, shaking his head every time I miss a volley or ram a backhand into the net. I can hear him screaming: "Add more spin to your forehand! Attack the net! Serve and volley! More power on the serve! Come on! Come *OOOONNNN!*"

Watching Number One play like Chris Evert in a Steffi Graf world, I'm floored to see how little it takes to get a full ride to a division one school. What's even more confusing is that Number One and I aren't allowed to play practice matches against each other like the boys are. One afternoon when I think our coach won't show his face, I challenge her to a match.

After winning fairly easily, I'm beckoned to the sideline and chastised by the coach, who showed up after all. "You have a bad attitude, Cepeda."

"But we were just playing," I say. "This isn't a tournament."

"I need you to sit out for a few," he says. His blue eyes are cold and angry. "What did I tell you about playing her?"

The coach doesn't scold his star tennis player, especially not in front of his homeboy, her dad, who drops by often and unannounced.

When we hit the road, I learn a whole new lesson about team camaraderie and humor. On an off day, one of the girls relaxing by the pool calls a few of us over to share a joke her mom just told her on the phone.

"My mom is so funny," she says to us. "Okay, check this out—"

"Yeah, okay, I'm game," I say.

"So we just bought a new dishwasher." She pauses. "His name is Juan."

She starts laughing. The other girls chuckle, except Number One and me.

"You don't think that's funny?" she asks, still laughing.

"Um, what exactly did that joke mean?"

"Dude, she's Hispanic," says Number One. "That was kind of a stupid joke."

"How was I supposed to know what she was?" says the jester. "And I was talking about Mexicans—she doesn't look like one of them."

"Your mom taught you that?" I ask. "Does she keep Juan shackled all day to your dishwasher and then to a tree at night?" I laugh. "What's wrong, massa?"

The jester bolts up and retreats to our room without a word. A couple of the other girls follow.

"Fuck them," Number One says. "Let's go for a drink. I'll use my fake ID. They never ask us white girls to prove anything, so it was easy-breezy to get the DMV to issue me one." We laugh all the way to the bar down the block.

Back at the room, I notice that all of the jester's jewelry has been cleared from the dresser. An alpha female, she encourages some of the other girls to do the same. Most of them avoid eye contact with me for the rest of the trip, including the only other person of color on our team, one of the few Black-American guys on campus to pledge a white fraternity.

When we arrive back on campus, Number One confides that some of the girls have been complaining about not feeling safe around me.

I start skipping tennis practice on a regular basis, spending more time with my college soulmate, a country boy named Chris, from a small town outside of Pittsburgh I've never heard of called Washington.

Chris and I met at the pool hall, where I stood checking him out so hard, he couldn't help but notice despite the sophomore, junior, and senior women standing around him, cracking stupid jokes and vying for his attention. I found his tight curls irresistible and his freckles unusual. I began counting the flecks one by one until I made him uncomfortable enough to walk over to the pillar I was leaning against with Jane.

"Where are you from?" he asked.

"New York City."

"*Ahhh*, a city slicker," he said with an accent that wasn't quite urban or country. "Are you Native-American?"

"Negative. The Spanish cowboys killed our Indians, bro," I said.

"Are you Puerto Rican? I met one on campus once. Or are you mixed?"

"I'm dominiyorkian."

He's never heard of the place. "Is that in the Bronx? I'm part Black-foot Indian, part soul-broth'a," he said.

"That's a mighty fine mix," I flirted back. We sat in front of the steps outside the hall talking until the sun came up the following morning.

From that morning on, we spent almost every night together, mostly talking about where we came from: two different planets in the same orbit. At some point, I'm not sure exactly when, we fell in love.

Chris lives almost at the top of a steep hill in a two-story frat house on Chesterfield Road, minutes away from campus and closer to my new dorm at Lothrop Hall.

I moved in right next to Jane on the thirteenth floor. Finally, I had my own space, my own piece of real estate to do as I pleased. My slice of heaven—a decent-sized sixteen-by-eight room with my very own sink—used to be a nurse's residence, but the building feels more like a converted hospital with spirits roaming the halls. I sense that someone died in my room. There is one spot, right above the wooden head-board, that is always freezing even on days when the heat is pumping steam into my room. I'm not scared of it as much as I'm intrigued by what makes this thing linger.

At night when I can't sleep I reach for the cold with my right arm, piercing through it with my fingers and then my hand. "Why are you here?" I whisper. "Do you know Casimiro?" I ask. "Are you one of those guides he told me about? And if you are, what the fuck am I doing here?"

I close my eyes and try to clear my mind. I focus on listening for anything close to a response from the invisible cloud hovering above me. I hear nothing, I never do, but somehow the thing makes me feel protected. Outside these walls, I don't feel so safe.

I can always tell when Egypt crosses the border from his backwoods in Ohio into ours. I'm transported back to Rocío's golden cage every time he does. Tonight, through the flimsy wall separating our dorm rooms, I hear the familiar sounds of him fucking, then beating, then fucking, then beating Jane.

I can hear her begging him to stop. "Please, Egypt, please stop." SMACK! Then she screams.

I run out of my room in an oversize T-shirt and sweatpants. I don't care whom I wake up when I bang on her door, yelling, "Jane, are you okay, girl? You want to sleep in my room?"

Jane cracks the door open. Her face is flushed and streaked with tears trickling over streaks of dry salt underneath. "Everything is fine," she says. "We're just playing."

"It sounds like he's fucking you up," I say.

"You don't understand," she says, almost whispering. "He loves me."

"You don't find it weird that he comes only after dark?" I ask. "Or that most of his songs are either about how the white man is the devil or his African queens?"

"That's just for show," Jane says. "He doesn't believe in that stuff."

She closes the door in my face. I feel helpless, not understanding what she sees in a broke-ass unemployed wannabe rapper who creeps to her room after dark when everyone else is asleep. I can't help her anymore. I begin to spend less time in my room and more on Chesterfield Road with Chris.

Chris has neighbors down the road who seem to hate people of color, especially those who look racially ambiguous or mixed. They stare ominously at anyone who makes them think and challenge their notions of what race here in Wonder Bread country should look like.

Weather permitting, they sit on their porch and glare at me from the moment I appear at the base of the hill, walk as fast as I can past them, and continue on to Chris's house. As I race up his front steps I turn around and can still see them wrestling to figure me out. They don't care that Chris is gawking back at them.

"Fuck 'em," he says to me, "they're just looking for a fight."

"They look crazy sinister," I say.

"You think that's bad?" he says. "You should see how these crackers act back home in Washington."

"The baddest white boys in my hood—even the Albanians over on Kingsbridge—have nothing on these guys," I say. "Their hate is on a whole other level."

Some months later, I'm on my way to Chris's for a party. The same guys and their friends are drinking beer on the front porch. I can't tell them apart because they all have shaved heads. One of them is smiling at me. They stop talking when I'm within earshot, and for the first time, one of the guys, the one smiling, says something directly to me.

"Hey you, brown sugar, I wonder what your pussy tastes like," he says.

"Fuck you," I yell back.

"Yes, please," he says. "I'd love to fuck your brains out." He pauses. "Literally fuck your brains out. Get it, bitch?"

By the time I reach Chris's house, I'm out of breath and shaking. Nobody notices. People are hanging out on the front porch. A number of guys from the basketball and football teams are grinding with sorority chicks to Luke's "I Wanna Rock." Chris's frat brothers are screaming "Face down / Ass up" so loudly that he can't hear what I'm trying to tell him. My distress makes it apparent that I have something serious on my mind that cannot wait.

"Are you pregnant?" He chuckles. "Why are you looking at me like that, city slicker?"

"No, asshole," I say, recounting what just happened down the road.

Chris doesn't respond. The music stops abruptly. He picks up a loose brick on the kitchen floor and runs out of the house. Almost everyone follows.

"You got something to say?" he yells down the road.

"Yeah, boy we sure do," someone yells back.

"Then why don't you come up here and say it, cracker?"

Minutes later, the guys run up and into Chris and his frat brothers like a pack of hungry wolves. "Fuck that nigger up," I hear one of the white boys yell to another.

Chris starts pounding some guy with the brick while another jumps on his back.

I run into the house and come out charging with a broomstick, swinging it in every direction until one of Chris's frat brothers drags me back into the house.

Eventually, cops arrive on the scene. They admonish the guys for starting trouble. It's a miracle that Chris wasn't badly hurt. He can barely stand, his legs are trembling with anger, and his heart is pounding out of his chest. After the boys in blue drive away, Chris picks up the brick and stands in the middle of the street, staring down the road.

Nothing changes on Chesterfield Road except that the bald guys do not speak to me so much as throw daggers with their eyes, piercing my breasts and ass every time I walk by their house. I don't tell Chris.

Not long after the fight on Chesterfield Road, Chris and I start growing apart.

It doesn't take long before I fall into a serious depression in the Pitts. It's as if I'm wearing a wet bathrobe over my clothes—the extra weight is making me miserable. I miss New York City. I miss eating dinner for breakfast at Maria's place and the classic salsa blaring out of Blackie's window.

I move off campus and survive off of school loans while interning at an urban music radio station. I hate school. My English professor spends more class time looking at my *tetas* than anything else. I don't know exactly when, but I unofficially drop out of school, spending hours repeating my ABCs as clearly as I can because I'm promised an on-air gig if I manage to lose my "New York Puerto Rican or something" accent.

I lie down, and looking out my window ask the universe for a sign that it's time for me to go back home. I don't want to lose my accent. I don't want to become someone else.

I doze off and wake up in a dream. I'm riding in the passenger seat of Chris's navy blue Volkswagen Rabbit. We are in front of his swanky new apartment building in an upper-middle-class section of the Pitts. Chris pulls up to the building and double-parks. He has a surprise for me.

"I gotta go upstairs, city slicker, to pick up these tickets for a comedy show I'm going to take you to," he says. "I'll be right back." He pecks me on the lips and disappears upstairs.

"Hurry up, please," I say. "I still love you."

Chris doesn't hear my muffled voice.

A black SUV drives by slowly until it stops in front of Chris's Rabbit. The passenger window goes down. Eventually, all of the windows are down and two machine guns start spraying bullets in my direction. Bullets fly through the windows, my face, my hands. My brain oozes out of my head like water out of a fountain.

I am stunned awake by the buzzer. It's Chris's frat brother Martin, the one who recently graduated from weed to crack. He's looking for Chris.

"It's five o'clock in the morning," I yell into the intercom.

"I need to speak to Chris," he yells back. "NOW."

"He isn't here."

"Then I'll wait until he shows up."

Not long after I page him, Chris finds Martin pacing back and forth like a basehead in front of my building. My dream compels me to act. I start packing what I can fit into the suitcases I brought here and leave everything else behind. Something will happen to me if I stay here. I'm sure of it. I catch the next Greyhound to New York City, back to 512 Isham.

CHAPTER NINE

There's No Other Place . . .

I am not at a crossroads;

to choose

is to go wrong.

—OCTAVIO PAZ

"*¿QUE TÚ HACE AQUÍ, MI HIJA?*" DOÑA AMPARO ASKS ME. "DOES Maria know you're back?" No, she doesn't. I've been sitting here for about an hour, inhaling the floral smell of detergent and fabric softener floating out of the new Laundromat on the corner. Doña Amparo places her groceries on the ground and sits next to me on the steps, taking out two Coronas. We sit in silence, sipping the cold beer and watching people walk by.

Doña Amparo lives with her son, Moncho, and his wife, a morbidly obese reputed cokehead whose name is also Maria, on the third floor. Fat Maria and Moncho, a rail-thin man of average height, look like the number 10 when standing next to each other. It's hilarious.

Maria and I feel sorry for Doña Amparo, who moved to 512 from

Santiago not long ago, kicking and screaming, after her husband died. The poor lady suffered from *ataque de nervios* brought on by the stressful move to the city and made worse by not being able to visit her old man's grave at leisure. We hear that the elderly woman was prescribed a cocktail of uppers and downers for what was diagnosed by one of those gringo head doctors from the neighborhood clinic as manic depression. Soon enough, Doña Amparo became addicted to Xanax, meprobamate, and ethclorvynol. Her purse was like a portable pharmacy filled with pill bottles that her son and daughter-in-law dipped into every now and then. She should have stayed in the Dominican Republic. Here, Doña Amparo was reduced to a guinea pig with a muted personality and a swollen face.

"I thought you were living in Pennsylvania," Doña Amparo says, breaking the silence in the Spanish patois I missed hearing in Pittsburgh.

"Yes, I was," I say, "but it wasn't for me."

Doña Amparo offers me another beer. "Angel is doing so well out there, I hear," she says. "It's too bad you two didn't get back together." Angel recently traded in a life in the Five Percent Nation for a career in the military and law enforcement. We rarely run into each other anymore.

Like a hot knife through butter, Maria's shrill voice cuts through the cacophony of taxicabs blasting bachata and screaming children playing tag. "Raquel, is that you?"

"*Sí*, Maria, it's me," I yell back.

"How long *has* you been downstairs?"

"Just a couple hours, catching up and drinking a Corona with Doña Amparo."

"*Ay, que bueno*, you have great timing," she screams, "*el doctor* may have found something in my *seno*. Come upstairs."

There is something morose about Maria's demeanor. She's more melancholy now than when Casimiro left a couple years ago, spending more time in bed flipping through old issues of tabloid magazines and watching telenovelas instead of taking Tiffany for walks around the block and talking to her *vecinos* downstairs.

Natalie later tells me that something happened to Maria when I left that may explain why she's been so detached. Fat Maria waited for all of us to be out of the building before wilding out on Maria. One day when she stepped out to buy Tiffany a fried chicken breast from John's, Fat Maria defied all logic and almost flew down the stairs of 512 in her *bata* and *chancletas*. The corpulent woman chased Maria, an older woman less than half her size, down to the front of the building.

"You're after my man!" Fat Maria yelled.

"*¿De que tú hablas, estúpida?*" Maria replied. "You're crazier than you look if you think I'm after your *borracho* cokehead husband!"

Fat Maria grabbed her elder's thick auburn bob and began pouncing on her. She kicked, scratched, and bit whatever exposed flesh she could sink her teeth into. Maria wailed and screamed for someone, anyone, in the growing crowd to help her. Surely someone she fed over the years or made me translate for at the welfare office would step in to rescue her. Doña Amparo yelled at her daughter-in-law to stop, but the pleas fell on cocaine-fueled ears.

Fat Maria tore the front of Maria's button-down linen shirt almost completely off, dragging her across the pavement and kicking her frail body under a parked car.

Only after Doña Amparo returned with Moncho, who was at the bodega around the corner playing the numbers, did the beating cease. Moncho broke through the crowd, screaming for his wild-eyed wife to stop. "*¡Carajo gorda,* what are you doing!" he screamed, jumping on her back. "Why didn't anybody stop this?"

Maria never told me about the incident. I don't think she told anyone. I felt like I failed her for allowing a *tecata* like Fat Maria to treat her worse than a piece of garbage tossed into a landfill.

What Fat Maria did to Maria was horrible. It reminded me of what happened to the nice old white lady living on Tenth Avenue and 207th Street when I was still at St. Thaddeus.

I'd see her on my way back from school, watching the 1 train run down the avenue, and sometimes I'd see her sitting in front of her building on a foldout chair. Her daughter was a total bitch. She hated us "Spanish people," I heard her say once on my way home from school.

It was a gorgeous late-spring day. My bare legs didn't feel numb from the cold anymore, even with my uniform rolled up to midthigh. After school, I ran into people gathering around several police cars and an ambulance.

There she was. Strands of bluish-white hair drifting in the air like dandelion seeds. Her face had been rubbed off on impact, and pieces of limbs—a foot here, an arm there—were strewn about the street and sidewalk with empty beer bottles, candy wrappers, and dog shit.

The only recognizable part of the old woman were her creased pastel polyester pants, still connected to her small torso, spilling out what looked like spaghetti pomodoro sauce onto the shoes of the man who picked her up and tossed her body into a black plastic bag. On her way to Pathmark, the old lady had been run over by an eighteen-wheeler.

I imagine the neighbors looked at the two Marias like they did the old lady's mangled body: in awe. Plus, many of Maria's neighbors were jealous of her. Maybe they thought she was rich because she always had enough food to feed anyone who walked into her kitchen.

Maria now turns off the lights in the hallway and living room before we sit down to eat dinner. The front door remains locked all day, and I'm instructed not to open it when someone knocks to visit or share a juicy morsel of *bochinche*.

Doña Amparo, too old and fragile to deal with not knowing if I'd snap at any moment, stopped visiting Maria shortly after I came back. Fat Maria, who once watched me chase Angel around the block with a kitchen knife after catching him with another girl, was ghost.

One night after dinner, I convince Maria to go for a walk to get ice cream.

"Do you remember when we thought you had been found dead off the Henry Hudson Parkway?" Maria says, breaking her silence.

"How could I forget that?" I say.

Raquel was discovered slumped over the steering wheel of a car right off of the Dyckman exit by Fort Tryon Park. Nobody knew what happened or why.

I was still in Pittsburgh, and Maria was in Santo Domingo visiting family, when she received the call. She was inconsolable, crying and yelling my name when not sedated with Valium. Only my voice on the other end of the receiver calmed her *nervios*.

"Ma, what's wrong?" I asked. "What's up with the *ataque cardíaco*?"

"*¡Dios mío!*" she wailed into the phone. "Thank God it wasn't you. Thank God. Must have been the other Raquel."

I was stunned and at once saddened for the other Raquel. Nobody seemed to really give a shit about her, not even in death.

"But what happened to Raquel?" I asked.

"I have to call Angel to tell him it's not you," she cried. "You see, I was right about my dream?" Nueva York was no place for you at—*ay*, I need another *pastilla.*"

Maria was right about her dream. I needed to leave New York City.

"I felt so bad for Raquel, don't you, Maria?" I ask her as we walked back to 512.

"Yeah, I do. And anyways, you no even my daughter," she says, nonchalantly. "I just feel sorry for you like a *recogida.*"

Maria's words smack me in the face. I feel an overwhelming sense of empathy for my paternal grandmother, Ercilia. I had forgotten about that other *recogida* in the family I was born into but never really belonged in. With that sentence, Maria manages to cut the proverbial umbilical cord between us that had, over time, become infected with a wicked strain of codependency.

As sick as it sounds, I keep that conversation in the foreground of my mind whenever Maria slips into one of her dark moods.

I never find the right time to tell her that it was she and not Casi-miro who ultimately taught me to believe in the power of dreams and spiritual guides. I want to tell her about the realization of the dream that brought me back to New York City. Soon after I came back from Pittsburgh, Chris called to tell me that the windows of his Peugeot (not the Volkswagen in my dream) were shot up by thugs driving a maroon SUV (rather than the black SUV of my dream) in a fit of road rage. Thankfully, he wasn't in the car when it happened, he was upstairs picking up tickets to a comedy show.

Had Maria not pushed me out of her nest, I might have never found myself. I get a job at a quasi-Afrocentric novelty store in Greenwich Village, selling watered-down fragrance oils and Ron G mix tapes, and I start spending more time downtown. I hang out at Washington Square Park and the surrounding areas, rediscovering the neighbor-hood, collecting flyers, and meeting people down with spoken word and hip-hop, the lines of which are practically seamless in the early 1990s.

I've been writing poetry for as long as I can remember, but I never think about reading any of it out loud until I start to frequent open mike nights at the Nuyorican Poets Cafe on the Lower East Side. After watching how viscerally the poets onstage connect to the audience with their words, I start writing feverishly again. A friend from Pitts-burgh puts me onto a poetry night he hosts at the Fez Under Time Cafe on Lafayette Street, where poets and hip-hop artists perform in a room filled with rappers, hip-hop journalists, and executives, in-cluding Russell Simmons. There, I catch Freestyle Fellowship's Mykah Nyne and Aceyalone perform "Inner City Boundaries." In unison, they rhyme: "Once we have the knowledge of self as a people then we could be free . . ." That performance inspires me to dive headlong into the deep end of the hip-hop-inspired poetry scene.

Soon thereafter, I become the poetry editor at *New Word*, an urban lifestyle magazine ("urban" being the code word for all things Black and Latino). I begin publishing poets and spending more time in Clinton Hill, Brooklyn, where the magazine is based, not far from the home of the Notorious B.I.G., whom I meet through a mutual friend. Brooklyn is becoming the center of my universe.

Under the *New Word* banner, I start producing poetry readings around the city. Sometimes, with the masterful beat boxer Rahzel, I cohost poetry gatherings featuring Jada Pinkett, muMs, Mos Def, Lauryn Hill, and many other actors, rappers, and artists down with spoken word. Almost every night brings with it a new experience, a hip-hop or poetry event, and an impromptu slam in Washington Square Park or on the corner of a Harlem or Brooklyn block. Had I not been so hungry, working mostly for free at the magazine after quitting my gig at the novelty shop, I may have never ventured back uptown to Maria's kitchen. And when she was out of town in Santo Domingo or visiting Angel, who now lives in Virginia, I had no choice but to crash at Dad and Alice's place.

Alice and Dad—I now call him "Dad" because it's more generic and less affectionate than "Papi"—didn't know I was back in the city for weeks. I barely spoke to them when I was in Pittsburgh and saw Dad only once from across the street since I've been back. He was walking down Broadway embracing a woman who wasn't Alice.

When I do show up, Dad and Alice barely say a word to me. The apartment is almost as I left it over two years earlier. The space where my piano and my bed used to be is filled with piles of junk. I sleep on a cot Dad found discarded in the basement. I find the yarmulke he kept hidden at the bottom of his dresser in the same spot I'd seen it years earlier, when snooping around for evidence that I was adopted. It was as if, except for the decaying walls and cracked bathroom tiles marking the passage of time, life came to a standstill here.

At night I use my pager for light when reading and writing poetry. The only time Dad and I speak is when he barks at me to get off the phone. Alice, too happily distracted from working at the hospital to think about what and who Dad may be doing these days, remains as emotionally detached as she was the morning I left for college.

I don't know how Rocío finds me here. I've been staying in Clinton Hill for the last several months with Jamal, a man I recently met when walking past his brownstone on Gates Avenue after leaving a nearby café. He was looking out his window when I smiled and complimented him on his beautiful huge eyes and long eyelashes. When I was almost at the end of the block, I heard him yell, "Hey, you," from his stoop. His tall stature and basketball-player build struck me. "Do you have time for a coffee?" he asked, and that was it.

After going on a few dates, I decided he was nice enough to spend a weekend with, then a week, and eventually a couple months. I try to ignore the things that irritate me about him, which is almost everything. Jamal and I can't be more different from each other but not in a harmonious yin-yang way. I'm a free spirit, a poet and aspiring journalist. He's an engineer who's almost twelve years my senior, with real bills to pay and responsibilities to assume. Jamal dresses like a suit, even on the weekends, when he visits his elderly parents in nearby Bed-Stuy. In our world, opposites don't attract but, rather, keep each other company.

"Raquel, some woman is on the phone for you," Jamal says one afternoon.

I can't think of who it could be other than Maria, and she never calls. At first I don't recognize the voice on the other end of the receiver.

"*Ello*," says a woman in a soft singsong tone, "may I speak to Raquel?"

"Sure," I say, hoping the voice is that of a magazine editor with a paid assignment, "this is she."

"It's your mom, Raquel."

How in the hell did she get my number, I thought. Maybe it was Mama who sold me out and gave it to her. She's the only person besides

Maria who always has a contact number for me no matter where I am in the world. Mama promised she wouldn't share it with anyone.

"Rocío, how did you get my number?" I ask.

"I am your mother," she says in a rhythm I haven't heard her speak in before. "Am I not allowed to have your number?"

"Let me guess," I say. "Are you with a Mexican dude now?"

"What does that have to do with anything?" she responds, laughing.

"Well, you're singing your Spanish like they do, so I'm assuming—"

"Well, *si*, I am. *Así es la vida.*"

Rocío continues calling for me the next several weeks, almost daily. The conversations are one-sided and mostly about her boyfriend and church. She never brings her other children up other than to say she would like to have more.

During one of our last conversations, the subject turns to sex.

"Do you think it's normal that he doesn't like to"—pause—"you know, *pleasure* me?"

"I have no idea."

"He likes to spend a lot of time with this guy, a friend from Ireland," she sings, "more time than he does with me now."

"I don't know what to tell you. You know," I say, "you haven't asked me once how I've been or what's up with my life. That's crazy."

"We have time for that, Raquel," she says. "Right now I need you to understand"—pause—"I have so many problems with my boyfriend, I am barely managing my situation here. I just need you to listen."

This time around, I play the role of an old friend. I am someone whom Rocío can maintain a comfortable distance with, just enough to vent her dramas to without fear of being judged. I'm relieved when she stops calling.

I see less of Maria these days.

"*Mi hija*, when you're coming to visit me?" she says over the phone. "Your twin sister, Tiffany, no stop barking because she miss you."

"Yes, I miss her, too," I say, "I promise I'll try to come by soon."

"Forget that writing stuff," she says. "You don't even speak good English."

"I'm going to become a famous poet and writer," I tell her. "Do you want me to read you something?"

"Yes, but make at least some of the words Spanish," she says.

I explain to Maria that some of the racial dramas I experienced in Pittsburgh are playing themselves out again in Brooklyn. The idea of fitting into a Black or white mold was something I never did well. Life is so much more colorful than that, at least in my community.

"This poem," I tell Maria, "is about a poetry reading I went to in Harlem where some folks didn't get it."

She doesn't understand. "Get what?" she asks. I begin to read a part of the poem to her:

Entered the room full of my brothers and sisters
Beautiful faces
Different shades of Black and Brown races
But those faces hint traces
                    of hate when I enter the place
Guess my hair is too straight

But I'm Black,   as Black as my master permitted
From Spain, the man was acquitted
Of the crimes he committed against my ancestors
Against my *tatarabuela*
But people give *muela*
When I enter the place   like I was a disgrace to my race
And welcome me with shade to make me seem darker
Más oscura, que locura
                    nunca puede ser . . .

Maria laughs. "You always a dreamer, always trying to get *pee'po* to see things when they no ready," she says. "Anyway, *por favor*, come and write here, *mi hija*. We miss you."

I don't come for a long time.

Months turn into a couple of years at Jamal's brownstone. Living with him is like running through a revolving door; I often find myself on the outside looking in. Sometimes friends come to my rescue and make room for me on their couches, and when I wear out my welcome I stay with Maria back uptown. It becomes a routine. After a few weeks, Jamal tracks me down at Maria's, where I always find him sitting in the kitchen with Tiffany resting atop his expensive shoes, waiting for me. He wins me back each and every time by taking me on shopping sprees at Saks Fifth Avenue and to dinners at Mr. Chow or whatever restaurant is hot at the moment. It only takes a few days, though, to feel suffocated once more by Jamal's constipated outlook on the world and his controlling nature. I'm even more weighed down by my own guilt for essentially using the guy for a place to live and work out of.

Somewhere along the way, I make the transition from spoken word to hip-hop journalism, making a slight detour into a paying job as a music publicist. Jamal, sick and tired of my writing for free and bleeding him financially, called a music industry friend who got me the job.

I start saving money with the intention of freeing myself from Jamal's conservative grip. I want to come and go as I please and continue to flow in hip-hop's current without being questioned by someone who doesn't get it. I want to write like Robert Christgau and Joan Morgan and Greg Tate and Lisa Jones, all journalists whose contributions to the *Village Voice* replaced the played-out textbooks I barely cracked open as a high school senior at the onset of the '90s.

I develop my voice and begin to write for papers and magazines about hip-hop and R&B music, and cultural criticism, but something happens along the way that throws my plan a bit awry. I step out on Jamal out of boredom and have a fling. In the spring of 1996, I find out I'm pregnant.

CHAPTER TEN

Whitewash

> There must be something beyond slaughter and barbarism to
> support the existence of mankind and we must all help search for it.
>
> —CARLOS FUENTES, LAST TWEET

NOT LONG AFTER MY DAUGHTER, DJALI, IS BORN, MARIA STARTS
spending more time in Florida, where her eldest son relocated. She's
terrified of living by herself because of the World Trade Center attacks.
A couple of months later, when American Airlines Flight 587, bound
for Santo Domingo, falls above Queens, killing everyone on board,
she takes it as a sign that it's time for her to go, and starts planning
her move down south. New York City has become a miserable living
thing to Maria. She was convinced it would swallow her whole if she
stayed put. I try to dissuade her but I'm no match for her paranoia and
Casimiro's ghost haunting her empty bed at night.

Maybe it was a good time for Maria to leave. After all, the neighborhood has lost its *adobo*. It now has the flavor of a piece of dry toast,
with people hiding under a saccharine veil of political correctness. It's
most evident during the rush hours. In the morning, people anxiously
ride the train downtown, afraid that it may blow up at any moment.

Then, after a long and stressful day at work, the menacing glare of racial profiling goes into overdrive on the way back uptown. The tension between people is palpable, and the ideal of what it means to be and look American becomes a preoccupation to folks around the country, including me.

As is the case with many first- and second-generation children of immigrants, we are stuck in between the old-school social and cultural standards of our parents, their respective homelands, and this American one, the latter growing increasingly hostile to our presence. People across the nation are freaking the fuck out.

As a group, many American-born Latinos exist in a kind of liminal state. For one, although different Spanish-speaking groups have been migrating here since at least the 1800s—the exception being Mexicans who were here well before the first Europeans arrived—we are still being treated like personae non gratae in our own home. The thing is, mainstream society isn't sure who they're discriminating against—are we all the way white, Black, or Native-American? Are we Arabic and, therefore, presumed terrorists?

One evening on the A, my *comadre* Gigi and I are headed uptown and notice that we're being given dirty looks by a white woman sitting across from us. At first I figure that something unrelated must have happened earlier in the day to make her sour, but soon I realize that we are the sources of her unease. "They must think we're Arabic," I whisper to Gigi, "especially since you're rocking that caftan-style dress."

The white woman sucks her teeth as we step out of the train. I walk up the steps behind her. "Excuse me, but we are both Latina, darling."

Embarrassed, she smiles back nervously and says, "Oh, I wasn't sucking my teeth at you—I, I just—"

"No worries. Every time I see someone who looks like Timothy McVeigh, I freak out and assume she or he's a terrorist too," I say. "Besides, I don't think my friend or I mind being mistaken for Arabic women."

This woman made me long for the tough-as-nails Irish-American chicks I grew up with. At least they were brutally honest with their feelings, regardless of what side of the divide they stood on.

Many Latino-Americans from all over the city must have been feeling the same way Gigi and I did. One morning on my way to the 1 train, I see a white T-shirt with bold black letters that read, "I'M NOT A TERRORIST, I'M DOMINICAN—on the window of a mom-and-pop clothing store. I start to eavesdrop on conversations and overhear other Latinos recounting stories of being harassed because of how they look, especially when venturing downtown.

I secretly wished one of those accounts had come from Dad. We'd been, for the most part, civil since Djali was born, but now Dad began to jump on the anti-Arabic bandwagon though he could easily have been mistaken for a Middle Easterner. I was torn. If it wasn't for Dad and Maria's intervention, I might have lost my head to an almost crippling battle with postpartum depression, made worse by the fling-cum-forced-relationship I felt stuck in with Monk. Dad stepped in and helped me escape a miserable environment when Djali was still a newborn, despite Alice's protests to let me fend for myself.

"You're never going to lose the weight you gained carrying Djali," Monk would say. "You're never going to succeed as a writer." I was quickly sinking into emotional quicksand. I believed everything Monk said, despite the fact that we didn't know each other well enough to engage in any kind of psychological war of attrition. I began to think it was true that I was incapable of being a good mother because I never really had one. I believed that I should think about getting a "real job" because I'd surely fail as a writer. I bought all kinds of shit from Monk, a very well-spoken and frustrated rap music producer I suspected had a split personality disorder. Being with him made my insides feel like they were stuffed into a pressure cooker that was my body. *Fuck,* I thought, *I'm becoming Rocío.* Just as I began totally imploding, Dad called me. "I will do what I can to help you and the girl," he said. He couldn't pronounce Djali's name correctly until she was almost two. "Please stop your worrying." So

Monk led me, by way of our daughter, back into Dad's life. Everyone, I suppose, has a purpose.

And yet, despite his intervention, a greater part of me wants Dad to feel what it's like to be persecuted for being something he is not. I want him to feel the pain and confusion I did all these years for simply reminding him of what he was, *un dominicano.*

Maria gave up her apartment and sold everything in it before moving to Florida. Everywhere she looked, Maria was reminded of what she wanted to forget. She never did recover from Casimiro's betrayal, even after she exacted revenge. The curse Maria delivered with her sharp tongue against Casimiro's illegitimate child had come to pass. The boy with the most beautiful algae-green eyes I'd ever seen had been spotted talking to himself, *como un loco de remate,* on the block.

Blackie followed Maria down to Florida, and eventually, most of the neighbors who used to frequent her apartment for dinner and *bochinche* also moved away. Many relocated to the South, back home to Santo Domingo, or because they were being priced out of the neighborhood, to the outer boroughs of the city.

On a particularly humid summer day in 2003, my cell phone rings. I notice Maria's area code on my caller ID and pick it up. "*Hola,* Maria," I say, sitting down on the ledge in front of McDonald's. "*Mira,* it's hot as hell and smells as bad as sweaty balls out here. What's up, Ma?"

Maria doesn't laugh like she usually does when I paint gross mental pictures for her. I can hear her breathing on the other end.

"Raquel, *por favor,* come see me," she says. "I'm dying from the cancer *otra vez.*"

I don't believe her. I just saw Maria a couple months earlier, when she came to visit us for the week. She looked as radiant as she did whenever she came back from vacationing in Santo Domingo. "You don't look like you've been sick or undergone chemo, Ma," I said to her. Her locks were thick as ever; Djali was kneeling behind her on my bed, using her small fingers as a comb and pretending to braid it. Maria responded, "Well, my cancer went away again because of the treatments, but I'm sure they'll find something else very soon." I've lost count of how many times she claimed to have cancer, AIDS in certain body parts, and all other sorts of ailments she miraculously bounced back from.

"I have *some'sin* you like I going to give you," Maria struggles to say, "the dark yellow and red scarf I got when Angelito's father *y yo estábamos jodiendo con los* Hare Krishna downtown."

"Okay, Maria, hold it for me," I respond. "When I come, you have to tell me the details of how you got entangled with them."

Maria laughs, then coughs and sighs. I've heard this despondency in her voice before.

"*Yo tengo* your magazines on my night table," she says. "I knew you could do it."

"It's extremely busy up there right now," I say to her. I started my post as editor in chief of *Russell Simmons' Oneworld* magazine at the end of August 2001, and each page we produce is like birthing a litter of children every couple of months. I rarely take time off.

"I know you're busy. Do you go to all those countries where that *basura* is popular?" she asks. "You should put Eddie Santiago or Sergio Vargas in your magazine."

"I love them, but this is about hip-hop and its *poder a través el mundo entero.*"

"Yes, I hear rapping down here in that reggae the Puerto Ricans sing."

"Are you hanging out in the club, Ma?" I joke.

She struggled to speak. "I may be old, but I'm not dead. Yet."

In a few weeks' time, I thought, she'd be back to her normal mercurial self.

Maria died weeks later.

Today I recognize 512 only as a relic of its former self. It has lost its soul now that Maria isn't there to feed her neighbors. And it really doesn't matter, because the people here have long since started to bolt their doors at night and look down when walking by their *vecinos*.

PART II

~

PART II

CHAPTER ELEVEN

Truth, Reconciliation, and Time Machines

> Our heirs, whatever or whoever they may be, will explore space and time to degrees we cannot currently fathom. They will create new melodies in the music of time. There are infinite harmonies to be explored.
>
> —CLIFFORD PICKOVER, *TIME: A TRAVELER'S GUIDE*

"SO, DAD, BACK TO THE MORLOCKS AND ELOI," I SAY OVER RICE and beans at the Dominican joint in our neighborhood. "This whole ancestral DNA thing is exactly like time traveling."

"What?" Dad asks, holding a piece of grilled chicken in his right hand and a glass of Pepsi in the other. "What you're *talking* about?" He looks over at Djali, now a freshman in high school, doing math homework when she's not picking at her plate of rice and beans. Although Djali and I are so close that we can sometimes communicate telepathically, she has no clue what I'm talking about, either. "Tell your *mo'tha* I already said I would think about it," Dad says. Djali shrugs. "Just do it, Papa, please," she says, "unless you want her to keep going."

145

• • •

There's no more time to think about it. Just a few months ago, Dad was reclining in a hospital bed, looking as terrified as I did when I was living like a scared animal under his roof. Djali, the conduit responsible for thawing our frostbitten relationship, lay down next to Dad, eating the chips we bought him at the deli. Alice sat on the edge of the bed, talking about everything and nothing, as usual. "I should go get shrimp for the turtle, *oh,* and my sister called; her husband is better. I spoke to the girls at my old job, and Karena got into an argument on the train, and if I order rice and beans from Mi Pequeña, I can walk to get the shrimp for the turtle down the block and . . ." My husband, Sacha, sat quietly in the large moss-green chair, talking to Dad about the latest television pilot he was producing.

I looked over at Sacha from the doorway where I was leaning and wondered how many people had sat in that very chair and watched their own fathers expire like cartons of milk languishing in the back of the fridge. The hospital room was as cold as dead skin, the hallway crowded with lost souls and reeking of illness.

Dad wouldn't allow anyone to help him out of the hospital bed. He forced himself up on his elbows, then rolled on his side before lunging up while holding a pillow close to his heart. From his grimace, I could tell he was in excruciating pain. I think Dad wanted to feel the pain, to feel his body cry, an urgent reminder that he was still alive. I pretended not to notice.

"So, I wan' to *say* bye, jus' in *case.* Just. In. *Case,*" he labored, walking over toward the doorway. His hospital gown had slipped off his spindly shoulder; it fit him like a Snuggie. His already thin legs looked like stilts poorly supporting their unfortunate wearer. The heat emanating from his body was weirdly assuring. I allowed Dad to lean against me for support. I couldn't let go and watch him fall to the floor, even though I had often fantasized of revenge, of one day degrading him like he did me.

"Let me give you a hug. Come on, my daughter," he continued. "My daughter." I could count on both hands the times he'd addressed me as his daughter. I couldn't remember him ever offering to hug me, and the thought sent chills through my body, making the hair on my arms stand on end. Dad had gone under the knife before because of his heart, but this time something felt different. I tried to figure out what I found scarier to grapple with, the potential loss of my dad—despite being unable to stand him for most of my life—or that I found myself giving a shit.

The afternoon before checking him into the hospital, we were sitting across from each other at our usual table at the Dominican restaurant, having another heated argument.

"I belief in mass *depor'dation*," he blurted out in response to a *Telemundo* news report blaring from the restaurant's TV, about yet another Latino getting jumped for no other reason than because he *looked* Latino, whatever the hell that meant. "Dey *shou'* take them *all* out o' here."

"Do you even understand that dozens of American territories were Mexican not that long ago, or that the border is just an imaginary wall imposed on people who have lived in those territories for centuries, Dad?" I asked.

"That don't matter," he replied, as he usually did right before deciding to tune out of the conversation.

"Dad," I tried to reason, "don't you think it's hypocritical that Americans, both Black and white, call Mexicans 'illegal,' although they were here first?" Don't you feel any outrage at all for how 'they,' who will spill over into the collective 'us,' are treated?" I waited for an answer. Dad remained silent for a few seconds and then changed the subject.

Even though Dad and I argued more often than not, I couldn't help but feeling moved for him at the hospital. He extended his arms over my shoulders, panting for air as he leaned in to me. In midwheeze, he fixed his lips to kiss me on the cheek. "I love you"—pause—"in case of," he managed. "Love." I didn't recall him ever using that word when it came to me. It sounded almost inappropriate, even foolish, all these years later. Alice, still sitting on the bed, looked down at the floor, and Djali let out an uneasy chuckle because, after all, the display of affection coming from her papa toward me was sort of absurd.

"Come on," I whispered, wiping the wetness from my cheek, "that's gross." That's all I could say. As I was leaving, it hit me. In one of those "duh" moments, I realized that in addition to our shared deadpan, sardonic humor, my dad and I possess an awkward sort of love for each other. Maybe we do have a little something in common. We have both dealt with our pasts by not talking about it and, perhaps consequently, have grown equally detached from most of our relatives.

I've been too busy running away from the violence and abandonment that marked a big chunk of my childhood to revisit it. However, as resolved as I was to forget the past, I found myself determined to excavate it. And if Dad didn't pull through his surgery, then a part of me would die with him. I needed Dad to help me uncover an important part of our family's history. By using the science of ancestral DNA testing, I'd be able to start piecing together the puzzle of our history that had eluded me all these years: our ancestral origins. All it took was one scrape of his cheek. Where the results would lead me was anybody's guess.

Dad was released into our care after his heart surgery. Watching him sleep during the day, I thought of how to broach the subject of ancestry without getting into a fight with him. Every time he awoke from a nap, I tried to bring it up, but since his operation he'd been showing interest in only one topic—time—or, more specifically, time *machines.* I hadn't heard this talk in a while, not since he first sprang it on me a couple of years ago. He said the idea had come to him in a dream: building something that "will change and correct the past and save a lot of people." Time machines had become an outright obsession.

"Can *you* jus' imagine if we could go *back* in *time,*" he said one afternoon as he was resting upright against a stack of pillows on our bed. Every time he brought it up, I acted as if it were the first time he'd broached the subject, perking up in my seat.

"I don't imagine going back in time at all. I don't think I can do that again," I said.

"I have a dream again las' night about my machine," he said. "Imagine if we could go back through history to find and put Hitler in a prison. Everything would be different. All of history."

"That would be something, Dad," I said, hoping he wouldn't work himself up.

"The government can use my machine to catch all the criminals in the world and, and—"

"Dad, the government may not be the right set of people to trust with a machine like that."

"I don't *care*." He struggled, his voice escalating.

Djali, consumed with everything but time machines, zoomed past my bedroom, trying not to get swallowed up in Dad's madness.

"Eduardo," Alice said, standing at the door, "*please* stop with that talk already."

"*Dah'ling*, shut up!" he snapped. "I can say what I want to in my daughter's house."

"Well, if I could go back, I would burn that hideous polar bear coat you and Alice forced me to wear in eighth grade, when you promised me a sheepskin."

My father wasn't amused, and Alice, as usual, frowned with her entire face. "*Everytheen* to you is a joke. I am going to have the *last* laugh when I *make* my time machine."

I thought about it. I may have found a way in. I'd invite Dad to take a trip back in time without actually having to go anywhere.

"Dad, speaking of your time machine, there's a way we can do that—travel back—without having to build anything or spend too much time looking for the parts to build it."

My father's interest was piqued. I decided to pitch time travel, but my version of it. Like H. G. Wells's narrator in *The Time Machine*, we'd be traveling through time and space. However, rather than jumping into the unknown world of the Morlocks and Eloi, we'd be making a direct link to our own history with our own saints and sinners. "And," I tell Dad, "all it'll take is a swab and a couple scrapes of the insides of our cheeks to get going."

"Let me think about it," he said. I let it go.

"Listen, Dad, there is no more time to think about it," I say, drinking a second cup of *café con leche.* "How many lunches do I have to buy you to get an answer already?" Dad doesn't have a clue that I already ordered and received the kits.

"We'll see. There are *no* needles, right?" he asks yet again. I already answered the question several times over the course of a month. Dad grins like he does when he's either withholding something or satisfied with himself.

"No, Dad," I say calmly, "no freaking needles."

The science of ancestral DNA is something I'm learning about myself. DNA, an acronym for deoxyribonucleic acid, is the material within us that carries our unique genetic information. Spencer Wells, an Explorer-in-Residence at the *National Geographic Society,* director of its Genographic Project, and a rock star in the field of population genetics, traced the patterns of human migration out of Africa by analyzing the Y chromosome in his documentary *Journey of Man: A Genetic Odyssey,* named after the book the film was based on. In it, Wells describes DNA in the most accessible way for a neophyte like me to understand: "Our DNA carries, hidden in its string of four simple letters, a historical document stretching back to the origin of life and the first self-replicating molecules . . ." We human beings "are the end result of over a billion years of evolutionary tinkering, and our genes carry the seams and spot-welds that reveal the story."

Based on genetic evidence, every human being on the planet today descends from a single man who lived in Africa about sixty thousand years ago. About ten thousand years later, human beings started migrating in waves out of the continent.

The first people who left followed a coastal migration route on the south coast of Asia and ended up in Australia. Another band followed a different route that ended up in Central Asia. Once there, Wells and his team learned that about thirty-five to forty thousand years ago, this band of people branched off. Wells found a man living in Kazakhstan today whose direct ancestor lived in Southern Central Asia and begat all Europeans, many Indians, and ultimately, Indigenous-Americans.

About fifteen thousand years ago, an ancestral group of eastern Russian Chukchi people made a leap across the Bering Strait during the ice age and walked into Alaska. About thirteen thousand years ago, between ten and twenty of these folks found their way into what is now the United States. In only eight hundred years, they peopled both North and South America.

Lucky for me, Bennett Greenspan, the founder and CEO of Family Tree DNA, has the kind of patience I can only dream of possessing. Perhaps more important, he doesn't tire of talking about genetics in a way that is comprehensible for people like me who don't subscribe to *Popular Science*. My ethnic background is intriguing to Bennett because, while his company stores the largest repository of DNA samples in the world, the Latino-American population makes up a relatively small portion.

"You just can't be sure what you'll find when looking at Latino DNA," Bennett said to me. "I mean, really, it's just a genetic crapshoot."

For a myriad of reasons, many Latino-Americans can't trace their roots beyond their parents and grandparents. For one, we'd have to travel back to our parents' respective countries of origin, and once there it's likely that we'll hit major roadblocks because the definitions of race throughout Latin America are often radically different from those here in the United States.

Here, the notion of race is static and forced; in Latin America, it's fluid. Our parents could live for decades as one race in their countries of origin and become Black or Other once they immigrate to the United States, with or without their consent. When we, the second generationers, come into some kind of consciousness, we are expected to choose sides or risk being labeled sellouts or seen as being out of touch with the cultural community. You're either all one thing or *nada* here.

To borrow a phrase carried over from the last century, "one drop," Americans are categorized as Black if they have any African ancestry. On the island of the Dominican Republic, for instance, one can make a sick joke that it's quite the opposite. If you are born with a drop of European blood, you're white. If that isn't confusing enough for someone raised in America, a person in D.R. can fit into several different categories throughout a lifetime. Money can also play a role in how one chooses to identify and how one is perceived. Throughout Latin America, racial and economic hierarchies are entangled: The higher you climb up the economic and social ladder, the whiter you become.

What we learn at school can't possibly foster a sense of pride in our heritage and the parts of our selves that aren't visibly European. If Latino-Americans accept what we're taught about our history as truth, then the indigenous peoples of the Americas were godless primitives given salvation by the grace of missionaries and their other European benefactors. And if we believe what we're taught about African history in elementary and high school every February, then we have to buy a version of the story that omits the complex and rich narrative of the transatlantic slavery experience. The truth is usually left for us to hunt and gather independently, if we are so inclined.

"Why do you need *me* for this?" Dad asks, cutting me off. "I know where I come from, and *you're* American, so why do you even care?" Djali and I say nothing but smile knowingly at each other. Dad left himself open for a barrage of disses we would have hurled at him had I not needed VIP access to the historical book he carries within his genes. Given that he has the upper hand, I'm going to try my best to answer his questions in a way that won't result in yet another screaming match. Trying to hip Dad to the overarching "why" is like trying to explain civil rights to Clayton Bigsby, Dave Chappelle's blind, Black white-supremacist character: It's stupid complicated.

Being right or winning an argument with me is never Dad's main objective. Pissing me off and embarrassing me in public is what makes him happier than a dog with a bone. Dad is sitting across from me, smiling, knowing that he has something I want so badly he can get away with saying almost anything today, and I'll just sit here and take the punches while my heart races out of my chest.

Something else is even more bewildering about Dad than the crazy shit he says: his actions. One of his favorite people in the 'hood is a West African woman, and his tennis buddies are mostly Dominicans similar to those he used to antagonize a couple of decades earlier. He lives for my daughter, Djali, who is half Black-American, despite threatening to cut me off back in the day if I even thought of dating a Black man. And Dad likes my husband, Sacha, whose mother is Haitian and father was Black-American, more than he likes me.

I know it's borderline nauseating to write that my husband is my best friend, but I don't know how else to put it. We started dating in 2003, nearly a decade after meeting each other at a Spike Lee party in Brooklyn. Sacha, a tall and painfully shy Queens native, was already writing and editing his own newspaper back then, and I was performing poetry while transitioning into journalism. He offered me my first big break—interviewing MC Lyte for his magazine, *Beat Down*—which I totally botched. Throughout, Sacha and I remained great acquaintances, reconnecting several years later when he became my editor at another magazine. We started dating soon after I invited him to submit an article about a graffiti writer that was first published by the National Arts Journalism Program at Columbia University for an anthology about hip-hop journalism I was editing. It didn't take long for us to fall in love. During the few times we split, Dad always encouraged me to give it another chance. "Believe me, I know I wasn't too *good* a husband," he told me one afternoon during lunch, "but that guy, *dat* guy is good to you and better to Djali than her own *fatha*." On one of those rare occasions, I listened to Dad. I'm glad I did.

I drink another whole cup of *café con leche*, contemplating how best to win Dad over. How can I begin to explain how empowering it is for us as a collective to explore and define our own selves to him? Dad's identity, or lack thereof, hasn't tortured him as much as it has me all these years. Alice walks in and joins us at the table. While Dad doesn't get it, curiously enough, she does.

"Wouldn't it be interesting for Dad to take an ancestral DNA test?" I ask her.

"I wonder if Finns have Mongolian blood because of our eyes and high cheekbones," Alice says. "Even those 'white' boxes on the census don't seem right to me." Alice doesn't consider herself white but, rather, Finnish and European, interchangeably.

Hip-hop—my participation in the culture as a magazine editor, critic, and documentary filmmaker—has been the proverbial key that's opened the door for me to roam this breathtaking planet. And traveling, when my racial origins almost always come up, has reinforced my desire to know where my ancestors came from, beyond my parents' homeland. When I was a kid and didn't fit into Dad's warped bubble, and his screwed-up worldview ended up being a springboard for my own curiosity. Traveling further ingrained my desire to connect to a place other than an island that is slightly older, in a New World way, than the United States, especially after I found characteristics of my face in the faces of the people in my global community.

Admittedly, I'm not the best traveler. I drink the tap water that I'm cautioned will give me Ebola or impregnate me with an eight-pound baby worm. I love buying travel books but rarely crack them open until I'm on my way back home. I don't take malaria medicine for more than two days, if that, because it makes me crazy-cranky. I go into areas I'm warned are dangerous; lucky for me, they often turn out not to be. I give away my first-aid supplies at the beginning rather than the end of my stays. And I've gotten into arguments—none provoked, I swear—with third-world policemen who make our own look like peacemongers.

Thank Buddha, Jesus, and Olofi that I possess three gifts that oftentimes cancel out my vices. I pick up languages with relative ease. I can blend in to the point of passing for a local or, if I'm dressed like a Westerner, a returning expatriate. Following my intuition has, above all else, saved my ass more than once.

The first time I visited Sierra Leone was on a preproduction trip for my documentary *Bling: A Planet Rock,* about American hip-hop's obsession with diamonds and its intersection with the country's decade-long conflict. My mission in Sierra Leone, the small West African country partially settled by repatriated freed North American slaves, was to connect with the hip-hop community there. I also wanted to hear firsthand accounts of the conflict from anyone who'd talk to me, from all sides of the divide. Just as important, I wanted to go out and experience my surroundings and see where my spirit would take me if I went with the flow.

An acquaintance who visited the country regularly warned me beforehand that I might be called "white woman." Hearing that was a shock to my system, especially because white privilege was something I'd never experienced in the United States, where I've been classified racially as an Other. He told me to brace myself, because allusions to whiteness had been made about his own light complexion despite him being an internationally renowned Black-American actor. I waited patiently for the subject of my race to come up. Somehow, *it* always does.

Our guide sort of brought *it* up in the truck after I mushed his face away from mine. He explained that he couldn't help trying to kiss me because I looked so much like his Brazilian ex-girlfriend.

Several days later, when I was venturing downtown to a beyond chaotic street in Freetown, *it* came up again.

"*Ey, how de body?*" said a local on lunch break from laying pavement under the intense African sun.

"*De body fine-fine,*" I responded to the man's greeting in Krio.

"Where you from?"

"New York City."

"I mean where you *from*?" he said.

"Oh, yes. My parents are from the Dominican Republic, an island in the Caribbean. Why you ask?" I wondered why he singled me out. I wasn't the only foreigner in the group.

"I had a feeling you were mixed, maybe Italian and Salone," he said, "or maybe Lebanese, but then you would not be here." The man handed the clerk a card from the wall behind him so I could buy what

I was there for, more cell phone credit. "There is a shade in *you* face that is familiar."

The man was right. If I were Lebanese, I probably wouldn't have been here. Freetown isn't exactly a melting pot. The Lebanese and Chinese communities lived in almost independent homogeneous states within the city, equipped with their own restaurants, neighborhoods, and nightclubs. The Italians had also left their mark here, as missionaries and doctors came over to volunteer during and after the conflict.

There was a subtext in the words "shade" and "familiar" that were spiritual to me. Perhaps he felt something spectral, like we do back home in New York City, throughout the Caribbean, and in South America. Maybe what he saw was the shadow of the *africana* I often dreamt about as a child, or one of my spiritual guides walking with me.

Being "read" by fortune tellers, self-professed seers, and spiritual people is another event that occurs frequently when I travel, be it at home or abroad.

"I have had a feeling since I arrived," I told the man, "this place is so familiar—the food, the rhythm of life and music, the culture."

"Everything started here in Africa, you know," he said.

"It doesn't feel so far away in my memory," I said.

Maria taught me to believe in the power dreams, and Casimiro in spiritual guides and destiny, when I was still a teenager. And today, my spiritual self still identifies with the *mythos*, the transcendent qualities found in Jewish Kabbalah, Sufi Islam, Indigenous and West African mysticism and religion. My rational self is drawn by the potential of ancestral DNA testing—the *logos*—to work in tandem with the incorporeal to help us make sense of our whole selves.

I ask Bennett if he can dig where I'm coming from.

"Well, as a guy who believes in evolution and metaphysics, I don't ascribe to that belief," he says, "but I have spoken to about a hundred people who have had experiences similar to those you speak of."

"What do you attribute that to?" I ask.

"I cannot explain why some people have that pull, but," he says, "you should look into the concept of *gilgul neshamot*—that may provide you with some answers."

Part of my journey will be to explore whether not the *mythos* and *logos* can jive holistically on this genetic mission.

I know I'll lose Dad if I delve too deep into the whole *mythos* versus *logos* thing, so I digress.

"Well. I'm interested in finding out more about where our people came from," I say, "*before* they went to the Dominican Republic."

"Are you sure you're not trying to see if I have any more kids out there?" Dad asks. He isn't buying my sudden interest in his family. "Or are you just trying to find if I'm from Matanga, like on *dose* shows that the president's friend hosts?" Inexplicably, Dad uses the word "Matanga" when referring to Africa.

"That's a good point," I say. "Yes, President Obama's friend has created a show where he traces the ancestral origins and genealogy of important Black-Americans, many times identifying their tribal affiliations."

Harvard professor Dr. Henry Louis Gates Jr. has successfully bridged popular culture with science since 2006, with his PBS miniseries *African American Lives,* followed by its sequel, *African American Lives 2,* in 2008, and on other shows. In *African American Lives,* he traced the ancestral lineages of prominent Black Americans by conducting ancestral DNA tests and isolating his subject's direct maternal and paternal lineages.

"I feel like, in a way, we have something in common with Don Cheadle, that actor who was in *Ocean's 11,*" I tell Dad. Cheadle discovered that he had a paternal linkage to the Chickasaw Indians through slavery. Although the Chickasaw freed their slaves in 1866, they were not offered citizenship in the Chickasaw nation. And because the Indigenous-American communities governed themselves, Cheadle's paternal ancestors weren't recognized as American citizens, either. The Chickasaw Freedmen remained stateless, in limbo—*en el aire*—for decades.

"Tha's *so* terrible," Dad says. "This country has been unfair to *many* different people."

He's finally starting to get it. I explain that many of us are finding ourselves in similar situations. American-born Latinos from dozens of countries such as Mexico, Ecuador, Chile, Cuba, Dominican Republic, Honduras, and many others, are marginalized and made to feel like they cannot claim this country as their own. What's worse is that many of us are rejected as inauthentic and called gringos when visiting our parents' countries of origin.

"Last time I was in Santo Domingo, this guy said I was *almost* a Dominican—I don't even know what that means," I tell Dad.

"I see," he says. "All right, let's do the test, already."

"The ancestral DNA kits are on my kitchen counter," I say. "Let's go there *ahora*." He rolls his eyes.

I don't want to waste any more time now that Dad is on the road to being sort of healthy and finally believes that I won't draw blood or reveal his results on some smutty talk show like *Maury*.

Once we're home, I tear open the ancestral DNA kits Bennett sent us. The contents are quite underwhelming, especially to Dad. There are no syringes or surgical gloves. Each kit consists of two individually wrapped cheek scrapers that look like long Q-tips without cotton swabs. There are two tiny solution-filled vials to place the samples in. There's some paperwork and instructions on how to use the kits, and a small padded self-addressed envelope to Family Tree DNA's world headquarters in Houston, Texas.

I go first. I scrape the insides of both cheeks as Dad watches, wearing a deadpan expression. Our kits are identical, but the information we will receive is slightly different. Because I'm a woman, Bennett tells me beforehand, I will be taking an mtDNA Plus test.

The processing of my mitochondrial DNA kit will underscore the mutations, or differences, resulting in the designation of my haplogroup, or genetic population group. When the results are in, I'll be notified by email to visit my profile page on Family Tree DNA's website. There, I'll be able to read information about my direct maternal ancestry and consult Bennett for further analysis.

The only genetic information I'll be able to receive is my direct maternal ancestry. Because Dad is a man and mothers pass their mitochondria to their daughters *and* their sons, we'll be able to discover his direct maternal ancestry and more. We ordered the mtDNA Plus Y-DNA Plus test for Dad because men inherit something else women do not—the Y chromosome, unchanged—from their fathers. This will allow me to obtain genetic information about Dad's direct paternal lineage.

My father will also be able to confirm whether he has Jewish ancestry, which is passed down through mothers. Bennett has offered to provide further analysis, he says, to confirm any suspicions we may have about Dad's background.

After Dad takes the test, I notice a look on his face I've rarely seen: melancholy. He looks as if he's wandering miles and miles within his own mind, even more than he did at the hospital before his surgery.

"What's wrong, Dad?"

"Nothing," he says. "I just need to take a nap."

I get the feeling that this, our cosmic trip, is about to go into warp drive, and there's only looking back. I'm thinking Dad may already have regretted his decision to join me.

I've been told that people don't change after forty, but I don't think that's true. Dad is in his late sixties and, admittedly, has already come a long way in the last ten-plus years. And yet, there's so much I don't know about him. I wonder if and how the results, whatever they turn out to be, will reveal how Dad arrived at his notions about race and identity.

I never quite understood it.

CHAPTER TWELVE

Things Come Together

One never knows anything about one's father. A father . . .
is a passageway immersed in the deepest darkness,
where we stumble blindly seeking a way out.

—ROBERT BOLAÑO, *2666*

THE RESULTS ARE TRICKLING IN.

Dad, Bennett says, is of Semitic descent on his father's dad's side:
haplogroup J2.

"Doesn't that mean my father descends from Sephardic Jews on his
direct paternal line?"

"There was a chance, because many Arabs and Jews fall into the J2
haplogroup, but ultimately, no," says Bennett. "That was the very first
thing I checked for. We reviewed his entire Y-37 DNA sequence and
compared his results with the massive Jewish database we sit on, and
there were no matches."

"It's interesting how so many Arabs and Jews share ancestral origins, and yet there's so much beef between them," I respond.

I pace back and forth in my kitchen, speculating which of many
ways this branch of my family may have washed ashore in the Domini-

can Republic. I can only surmise how this man arrived in Hispaniola. He may have entered the country as a crypto-Muslim or a Moor, after Spain's *reconquista* of the Iberian Peninsula in 1492. There's really no way to quantify exactly how many crypto-Muslims immigrated to Hispaniola or the rest of the Indies because they weren't supposed to be there in the first place.

The more Bennett breaks it down, the more questions and scenarios whirl through my mind.

"There's absolutely no doubt it's North African. Perhaps at some point his ancestors had Jewish cousins," Bennett says. "It's likely that your dad's direct paternal line descends from either North Africans or maybe Neolithic farmers who migrated west to Northern Africa from Iraq until they reached Spain. It's looking like he may most likely be of Berber or, rather, Amazigh, descent. Either way, it's very rare, because nobody in my entire database matches him."

I had no clue what to expect on either side of Dad's family, especially his father's side of the tracks. I still don't know what my paternal grandfather looks like. Every time I tried to talk Dad into taking the ancestral DNA test, I'd also ask to see photographs. I was curious what his father looked like, but whenever I asked for a photo, he'd respond, "We'll see," and change the subject.

I've rarely heard Dad talk about his father. What I do know is that he moved his family from the Dominican Republic to Aruba for some time when Dad was a child. Dad also told me they learned how to speak Papiamento, a local language that has more ingredients than a pot of *sancocho*: different African dialects, Spanish and Portuguese, with indigenous, English, and Dutch words. I know that Dad's father was a successful importer/exporter for a while until he inexplicably lost everything and moved to New York City sometime in the mid-1950s. And that's about it.

I'm hoping that once I reveal his direct paternal ancestry to him, Dad will become inspired to start sharing something other than CliffsNotes about his life with me.

• • •

"Can you come over after you finish eating lunch with Djali?" I ask Dad.

"Yeah, sure, but why? Are you going to make *coffee*?"

"Yes, I have some information for you."

"Oh, did you buy me a one-way ticket to Matanga?"

"I would like nothing better than to buy you a one-way ticket anywhere you want."

"Oh, you are *sooo* sweet"—pause—"like, like, a lemon."

About ten minutes later, Dad rings my buzzer.

He's wearing his trusty gray sweatpants, a bright red sweatshirt he bought in Seville with a white polo shirt underneath, and one of his gaudy fake gold watches that's too big for his delicate wrist. I don't think any of his watches tell time accurately. And then there's his hair. Sometimes it's silver, and other times it's kind of a light brown courtesy Just For Men. Today, it's freshly cut and somewhere in between.

Alice is sitting opposite Dad on the antique couch in the living room. She hands me an envelope with an old report card from St. Thaddeus, a few black-and-white photos of me as a child in the Dominican Republic, and two photos of a man I've never seen.

In the first photo, a handsome *trigueña* with eyes like mine is staring through me. She's wearing a sheer black veil over her head and a conservative dark dress with what looks like tiny light-colored polka dots. Her expression is familiar, somewhere between dignified and wretched. The woman reminds me of an Andalusian flamenco singer I once watched belt out song after song about losing it all—love, life, men, children, her mind—while exorcising the pain by stomping her feet and clapping her hands until I was almost moved to tears by the agony of it all. I recognize the woman in the antique photograph. She is a young and distant version of Dad's crestfallen mother, Ercilia.

Ercilia is holding on to a small boy's wrist with her large right hand and almost caressing part of his left cheek and ear with the other. The small boy, dressed in high-waisted slacks and a short-sleeve button-down shirt, with light hair and slanted eyes, looks somewhat like Ercilia and nothing like the well-dressed man posing with them in the photo.

"Who is *this*?" I ask Alice, pointing to the man in the photo. The

brown-skinned stocky man is standing only several inches over Ercilia's petite frame. Dressed in a dapper suit with slicked-back hair kept
in check with grease, he looks like someone James Van Der Zee would
have photographed during the Harlem Renaissance. His nose is wide,
his lips are full, and his eyes are more Asiatic than Ercilia's. She and the
man have epicanthic folds in common.

"That man is Eduardo's father," says Alice. "He's Ismael, your
grandfather."

"That's weird," I say. "Dad is lighter than both of his parents. It's like
he wasn't in the oven long enough."

"You know you can't tell what you're going to get with a Dominican
family," says Alice. "None of your father's siblings really look alike."

The second photograph is smaller, somewhat damaged by a fold
running across the young man's mouth and by mold from the rust of
an old staple. It looks like a passport photograph. This one is also of
Ismael, Alice tells me, but he is much younger in it. I can make out
the color of the well-dressed man's feline eyes, a light green, with folds
almost covering his eyelashes.

"He was very good-looking," Alice says.

"Yeah, where did you get your face, Dad—the mailman?" I ask.

Dad doesn't bite the bait. I am somewhat disappointed by his silence. He is sinking into the couch, looking straight at Alice.

I'm not really too surprised to find that Dad has Arabic or Amazigh
ancestry; I've always seen it in his face. "There's a greater chance you're
actually part Amazigh, the right word for the folks we know as Berber."

"Oh, okay," he says.

"Well, I don't have those origins, I think," says Alice.

"Oh my God, Alice, this *isn't* about you right now," I say.

"Yeah, Grandma, you sound like you did in the hospital when you
said, 'I never had heart problems,' when Dad was laid up in bed," Djali
says, rolling her eyes.

We're all laughing except Alice. Her face is bright red. "I don't know
if you know this," I say, "but you and Dad aren't related."

"You don't seem the least bit interested in your father's side, but you should be very happy," I tell Dad, looking for some hint of emotion in his eyes.

"Oh *yeah,* why is that?"

"Because for some crazy reason, Arabs are classified as being white on the census, even though many people in that community are challenging the classification. I find it odd, but then again, look at how Latinos are classified."

He looks over at Alice and shrugs.

"What do you know about Ismael's side of the family?" I ask him.

"I don't know too much about my family—my mother's side, I don't know. And I don't know my father's side, too."

"Didn't you grow up with them?"

He shakes his head. "No, I *did* not." He sinks farther into the couch and lets out a sigh. Djali looks over at Alice. What do they know that I don't?

"Let me see," he says. "Who *did* I grow up with?" Dad smiles, as he always does when uncomfortable or lying. "When I grew up, I used to live with my grandmother, my father's mother. And when I was about twelve, I came to this country. But then I had problems here with my father and the new wife, and they put me in the street after two, three months. It was summer. And then—"

"She's not talking about *that* time," Alice interrupts, "she's talking—"

I whisper, "Shut *up,* Alice, God," in her direction. "How do you know what I'm talking about?"

Dad rolls his eyes at her. "*Dah'ling,* don't get involved in my conversations, *dah'ling.* You get involved in every conversation, in everything I do."

Dad avoids making eye contact with me, preferring to stare straight ahead at nothing in particular. This man who used to scare the shit out of me when I was a child now looks like one of those abused animals featured in ASPCA commercials. I imagine Sarah McLachlan appearing like magic in our living room and, without a word, sitting down at our piano to serenade Dad with one of her crazy sad songs. The reasons why he was such a bastard of a father to me are starting to make sense. Dad sits quietly for a few more long minutes. I can tell by the distant mien on his face that he's thinking about things he hasn't in a really long time.

"My father was very, *very* well off in Aruba. He was a businessman who could not make money in his own country because of Rafael Trujillo and his brothers," Dad says, "but more important, he had natural *gifts* for reading people."

"How did he 'read' people?" I ask.

"He's no a *bad* guy, like that Walter Mercado character, because he never use his *gift* to make money," Dad says. "My father read the tarot—he knew it naturally. Whenever his spirit told him to do it for someone, he did it good and for no money."

I feel like I'm meeting someone new. Dad became obsessed with tarot cards a couple years ago, during one of his dormant time machine phases. He tells me something else I didn't know. "Some of us— we were born with these kinds of *natural* gifts in my father's family." He explains what he means by "natural." "I was born lucky. In Santo Domingo, we believe that children born with *una corona* are gifted and have a special purpose in life."

Dad was born with a caul, a thin layer of filmy membrane covering his head and face. Many caul bearers, spanning centuries and cultures the world over, are believed to be born clairvoyant and to possess other preternatural abilities. Dad believes his caul may be the reason why he was born with "too much vision," resulting in the capacity to see clearly at night. His night vision triggered terrible migraines that only an operation corrected years later.

"I was *never* afraid of the other world," he says, "or any spirits, anything that other people *say* is crazy out of their own fear."

I'm shocked but try to act as natural as possible. I try not to show any emotion or break his train of thought with my own stories about dreams and spirit guides, though it's hard not to. I wonder how much more I will learn about his and my ancestors once his mother's direct maternal lineage is traced. He pauses, so as not to leave anything out, and rests his chin on his hand to think. "I have experienced a few *things* I will now tell you."

The first *thing* occurs on Avenida Félix María Ruiz in Santo Domingo when Dad is just a kid. He has a dream that alarms him. In it, he sees his neighbors and their daughter killed in a gruesome car accident on a road en route to Santiago. Dad runs over to their home and recounts the nightmare to his friend.

"*Por favor,* stay here this weekend," Dad tells his friend. "I think you will not make it to Santiago." He spends the rest of the afternoon begging her to talk her family out of their planned excursion. The little girl is spooked enough to take heed and urges her parents to stay with her in Santo Domingo that weekend.

"But why are you so frightened, my daughter?" the girl's father asks. The girl recounts Dad's dream, much to her parents' amusement. As most adults do, they brush Dad off as a harmless little boy with a vivid imagination and decide to go anyway. The girl stays behind. En route to Santiago, her parents are killed in a car accident.

The second *thing* happens on La Ravelo in the *capital.* Dad is walking from his paternal grandmother's house on an errand when he is stopped in his tracks by the smell of his favorite drink, *café.* He notices there's a *velorio* for a teenage girl happening in the house where the aroma is coming from. Her mother can be heard yelling, cursing God for not taking her instead of her baby.

Dad, deadpan from the womb, asks the first woman he sees, "Can I have *una taza de café negro* with two sugars, please?"

"Don't you want to pay your respects to the poor child first?" responds the woman, whose face Dad doesn't remember.

He looks up at the plain wooden box holding the girl's body and suddenly feels a pull he cannot explain. He walks toward the coffin, where someone has placed a wooden box underneath so Dad can view the girl. Dad hops up on the box, places two fingers on her neck, and leans in a little closer. He listens for a few seconds and jumps off.

Dad asks to speak to the deceased's grief-stricken mother. "*Señora,*
if you allow that box to go into the ground, you will be burying that
girl alive." The mother faints. Dad jets, running down the street until
he is out of sight, somewhat annoyed that he didn't get a taste of the
sweet *café* he loved so.

The news of the girl spreads like wildfire around the *barrio*. Dad
hears she was taken out of her coffin and laid on her mother's bed
after a visit from a strange little boy. After several hours, the girl
woke up.

My father leaves the city weeks later to visit his paternal grandfather at his farm in La Torre where a third *thing* happens. Within
hours of his arrival, Dad walks around the farm until he reaches
its perimeter, marked by a row of bushes separating his grandfather's plot from the neighbor's. Dad looks over the bushes and sees
a pair of gigantic black dogs with immaculate fur making their
way toward him. They are walking on either side of a middle-aged
peasant. Dad is spellbound by the enormity of the dogs. He cannot
move.

The man and his dogs almost glide through the thick mass of bush.
"These dogs belong to San Lázaro," says the man, who doesn't exactly
look like the image of San Lázaro. Known as the Miracle Worker, San
Lázaro is a Catholic saint syncretized with the Yoruba demigod Babalú,
and is usually depicted as an old man on crutches, sometimes covered
in boils, dressed in purple or burlap rags, and accompanied by two
small dogs. Still, the energy is undeniably not of this world. The man
and his dogs walk so close to Dad they nearly brush against him. They
don't stop, almost floating past him, and then disappear before his eyes
like an apparition.

"After that," Dad says, "I never told anyone else about my experiences, because people don't believe you. But I know better. And I know
that some of us are born with these gifts."

I say nothing, listening to Dad's accounts as if he's telling me what
he had for breakfast or lunch. I don't tell him that I understand where
he's coming from more than he knows. This is the longest conversation
we've had without arguing or dissing each other.

While still in Aruba, Dad's parents separated and Ercilia went back to D.R. Ismael became involved with another woman, and his children and new piece didn't get along.

The handsome, dapper man in the photo sent Dad and his two sisters to the Dominican Republic to be raised by their paternal grandmother, Casilda, another person whose name I haven't heard until now. When Dad was about twelve, she felt it was time for Ismael to assume responsibility of his son and shipped him off to New York City. Ismael had relocated to an upper-Manhattan building with his new wife and their children after somehow losing his good fortune in Aruba.

Two things struck me about what Dad just said. First, that he could leave Santo Domingo during the reign of the tarantula in chief, Rafael Trujillo, on relatively short notice. Surely Trujillo's *monos* would have sweated the family hard before allowing them to leave the country. Second, I was surprised to hear that Dad had lived with his paternal grandmother and not Ercilia. Somehow I couldn't picture Dad in the loving embrace of a caring older woman.

Dad says he wasn't surprised by what happened once he arrived in Nueva York. In a dream, Casilda saw a period of very harsh times for him in the new city. "Be prepared, *mi hijo,*" she'd tell him often on the days leading up to his departure from Santo Domingo.

Djali embraces Dad. I'm incapable. Instead, I ask him a really stupid question with an obvious answer. "Did your father and stepmother ever get in trouble or arrested for what they did?"

"Well, no, they never got arrested. I remember they had problems. I think they had some discussion, and my stepmother said, 'Take your son out of here.' And he let me go with *no* money. *Nothing.*"

I've been stung by the stories I've heard and the images I've seen at home and abroad of discarded children because, frankly, I've seen my reflection in each of their faces. I wasn't expecting, however, to find myself in Dad, of all people. At the time he was thrown out like two-day-old leftovers, Dad was younger than my daughter is now. He was a boy who'd never seen snowfall or felt the drastic changes of the seasons on his skin. He was a child who didn't know the language or understand how easily adults could morph into scary beastly things right before your eyes.

For nearly two years, Dad lived on the streets of New York City. He slept in the subway, the park, and the hallway and entrances of apartment buildings. Every now and then strangers would take pity and let him use their bathroom and take a shower. Nobody ever asked him how he became homeless. Dad became a scavenger, picking up clothing from the streets and trash cans, and whatever food supermarkets threw out at closing time. Not one person offered to help Dad locate his parents when he walked around the city like a child lost in a department store.

One day Dad found himself back on Broadway, standing almost in front of the building where his father, stepmother, and best friend Bernardo lived. Before that day, he'd passed by the block but never ran into his friend. He'd sometimes spot Ismael from across the street, walking in and out of the building, to the bodega on the corner, and McDonald's a couple blocks down. Life hadn't stopped for his father. Dad wasn't surprised.

On this particular day, he felt something was different. For the first time since becoming homeless, Dad ran right into Bernardo, who was shocked to see his friend so tattered. Bernardo, a Dominican-American kid whose mother and stepfather shared Dad's last name but were of no known relation, said, "I haven't seen you in such a long time, I thought maybe you moved back to Santo Domingo."

"No. I don't have *no* house—living in the park and in the train and, you know, *wherever* the night finds me."

"Oh, okay" said Bernardo, "come with me."

Bernardo's parents took Dad in. I'd known that the elderly couple were related to me but wasn't exactly sure how. Over the years, I've heard whispers that they unofficially adopted Dad. Like his mother and later me, Dad became a child someone picked up off the street out of compassion, a *recogido*.

● ● ●

As I sit close to Dad on the couch, a flood of memories I've tried to suppress rush to the forefront of my mind. One took place at a computer center in a relatively swanky Freetown, Sierra Leone, hotel. One night I walked into the center and found a friend working the night shift. Already a serious woman, she looked particularly down. "What's wrong?" I asked her. "You look so *so* sad."

The young woman had taken her usual route to work that evening, walking by a street sweeper whom she recognized from a time when things were much worse in the country. The man, she said, was part of a gang of former soldiers—some of whom were children—who killed her neighbor. The noise of the woman screaming from having gone into labor earlier in the day annoyed the street sweeper and his crew. Then, she told me, the screams turned into terrible sounds she had no way of describing. The cries of the woman, who was prevented from giving birth, lasted for hours and hours. They kept the baby in the womb by ramming dozens of penises, bottles, and whatever else they could find up her vagina. Her neighbor eventually stopped screaming. The street sweeper, who likely put what he did out of his mind minutes later, smiled and nodded at my homegirl when he crossed the street.

In a New Jersey bedroom, I stood before an ancestral shrine erected by my friend in honor of her late cousin's daughter, Elisa Izquierdo. The altar, consisting of a framed picture of the little girl, a few of her personal effects, a bunch of white daisies, and a glass of water atop a wooden table, occupied a tiny corner of her otherwise messy bedroom. The shrine was next to the side of the bed I would be sleeping on that night.

In November 1995, the six-year-old became the beautiful face of the miserable failure that was and still is our city's child welfare system. Elisa, whose father had died of cancer, was isolated from her other siblings by her crackhead mother, Awilda Lopez, and her mom's boyfriend. For some reason Awilda didn't like her daughter, believing the little girl was possessed by an evil spirit. My *comadre* waged a battle against the city to adopt her late cousin's daughter. She lost. Lopez and her boyfriend starved and tortured Elisa to death.

Izquierdo's murder begat Elisa's Law, signed into legislation a year after her death by then-governor George Pataki. The press dubbed her a modern-day Cinderella, and I could see why. The girl was infectious, impressing everyone she met, including Prince Michael of Greece, who offered to sponsor Elisa's education. Unlike Cinderella, however, this child was real, and her story didn't end well. To listen to my friend relive the day she went to identify the little girl's body, to hear details I hadn't read about how Elisa's mother and her mother's boyfriend had destroyed the child, to relive the horror with her, made my insides ache.

I asked my friend if she wanted to see Elisa's mother dead.

"*No, negra,*" she said, to my surprise. "Just sober, so that she will be tormented by the snapshots of what she did to that little girl for the rest of her life."

I look over at Dad, still adrift, and try to imagine that cute little boy in the picture, suffering. I don't think that child could have imagined he'd grow up to become the same kind of animal he detested.

"I stayed with Bernardo's family in apartment number twenty-six for a long time," Dad continues. "I went to school and, you know, they helped me until I finally got into show business."

Dad lived in the same building and on the same floor as Ismael. The father and son sometimes shared elevator rides in deafening silence. On occasion, Dad used to hear Ismael crying in the hallway from his new family's crib, but he never spoke to his father again. Ismael's wife left him for a younger man and moved somewhere on Long Island. Depressed, Ismael eventually committed slow suicide by drinking himself to death either in New York or the Dominican Republic. I'm not sure.

"My father was not a bad person," Dad says.

"Are you kidding me?" I ask.

"My father was *not,*" Dad says defensively. He shoots me a look reminiscent of the days when he'd follow it up with a slap or a punch or a kick. "Even if he put me out on the street, the *problem* is the woman, because she had too much control on him."

Silence is filling the room. Dad is looking at nothing. Alice is frowning again, and Djali is looking down at the wooden floor, undoubtedly saddened by what she's hearing. Why Dad never shared this piece of his life with me is baffling. I don't understand why he speaks about it so nonchalantly, like it was all good.

As I look at Dad and think about my own childhood, my mind wanders back to that conversation with my *comadre* in Jersey, who has since died of cancer. I'd like to see Awilda Lopez confined to a cell for all eternity with her daughter's crime photos plastered on the wall, but that's not going to happen. Instead, she's alive, while her daughter decomposes in a New York City cemetery. I confess that I've never given the process of truth and reconciliation a second thought, even after witnessing it firsthand in Sierra Leone. I didn't think I was hardwired or evolved enough to grasp the idea—especially not the reconciliation part. Knowing that the street sweeper is probably still out there cleaning the streets or maybe even driving a *poda-poda* somewhere in Freetown doesn't sit well with me.

Dad never told anyone about those first few years in New York City, not even his mother and sisters, when they reunited as adults in Santo Domingo.

Dad's father Ismael may have contributed to him being such a bastard of a father to me, and may have been a conduit for why he was so hell-bent on becoming someone other than who he is. While he avoids talking about my childhood altogether, unless it's a gentler, kinder version, perhaps this is Dad's way of giving me insight into where our beef stems from. Where sympathy and empathy collide may be what truth and reconciliation feel like for other people. Maybe this is what I'm starting to feel—at once informed and heartbroken by the image of Dad sleeping in a subway as a child. I feel like something greater ensured my own survival. More importantly, this protective energy enabled me to learn a valuable lesson from my parents: what kind of mother not to be.

I ask Dad if he thinks being a caul bearer helped him survive the streets. "I don't know, maybe," he says. "*Something* was on my side, with me." Yes. I *over*stand where Dad is coming from. We don't talk about Ismael again.

• • • •

Just as I start wracking my brain about how to get to Morocco with the hope of retracing the probable footsteps of Dad's paternal ancestors, a freelance assignment falls in my lap.

It doesn't matter that the TerminEditor who hooks me up with the gig is about as pleasant to deal with as drinking a forty-ounce bottle of toxic waste. The assignment, covering a world music festival in Morocco, enables me to cut through the red tape of acquiring permission to film and roam around the kingdom freely. For a few days in Rabat, I'll be able to traverse a decent stretch of the country. From the instant I accept the gig, I start praying to and thanking the ancestral forces that made it all happen.

Back at our Dominican joint, Dad and I are communicating in the only way we know how: with bitter sarcasm.

"*Lissen,* don't get kidnapped in that Arab country," he says, mostly joking. "You know how *dose* people are."

"Shit, Dad, so you not only hate being Dominican but now also partially Berber?" I say. "Why don't you come with me to Morocco?"

"Maybe," he says, "if you come back alive first, then next time."

Now what?

First things first. By the time I come back from Morocco, Family Tree DNA should have Dad's and my mitochondrial DNA results from the lab. I know Rocío's side of the family better than my father's, but I can't guess in which direction the results will point us just by looking at her or her mother. I haven't seen Rocío in fifteen years or spoken to her over the phone in almost a decade. And before that, when I did sporadically see her as a child, she switched up her looks almost every single time, reflecting the flavor of whichever guy she was with. I cannot begin to imagine what she may look like today.

I have to think this one through. Reaching out to her may result in some valuable jewels about the family that my grandmother, in her eighties, may shy away from passing down. Talking to Rocío could also unearth some potentially shattering or disappointing information about our familial history. I don't know. Either way, I have to weigh the cons against the lesser ones and keep it real with myself. Am I ready to look this woman, who represents everything I despise, squarely in the eye?

I have never bought in to the idea that blood is thicker than water. Love and respect are meant to be earned from our children, our spouses, our families, and our friends. My relationship with Rocío, or lack thereof, has reinforced that notion. Connecting to my birth mother may do little more than inject unnecessary drama into my already chaotic life. Besides, I can't assume Rocío will want to have anything to do with me.

I'm packing for Morocco, trying to figure out the easiest way to find Rocío without sucking my grandmother or uncle Antonio into it.

"How about Facebook?" Sacha jokes.

"I don't think so, but whatever, I'll try it," I say.

I log on and do a search on Rocío's name. There she is. Her profile is public, and the picture is from a time when I sort of knew her. Her wall is full of biblical quotes and shout-outs to her children. I come across a current photo; she now looks over a decade older than her fiftysomething years. In another photo, she poses in matching outfits with her grown children. Their smiles are as wide and antiseptic as they were in that newspaper photo I found at her Boston crib in the late '80s, the last time we were all together under one roof. The image is so cloying that I may slip into a diabetic coma if I stare at it any longer.

I'm discouraged at first. I still feel nothing for this woman. I thought somehow that extending an olive branch to my ancestors would result in an awakening inside me for her. It hasn't. Is there something wrong with *me*?

There's a Moroccan saying: "A teacher will arrive when the student is ready." I'm not sure who the teacher and student are in this equation, but that may explain why Rocío was so easy to find: because I am ready, or maybe because she is.

I write her a short note before jetting to the airport with my travel companion and camerawoman Lisa. I plant a kiss on my kid and husband and throw my Ellegua headstone into my tote bag for safe traveling.

It's a sacred ritual. Travel challenges mental hoarders of stress and other useless shit to declutter. No magazine article or movie or book can embody what it's like to make the journey, to arrive in a new place and taste the food, to smell the air, and to see and hear the ebb and flow of life. To me, travel is more valuable than any stupid piece of bling money can buy.

I probably won't read it, but I buy the travel guide, the one with the most striking cover I can find—the one with a tall man dressed in a brilliant indigo *gandora* with his head wrapped in a faded yellow turban and matching leather *babouches*, standing in front of these enormous golden doors embossed with intricate shapes. I go as far as packing the book. Even if I don't crack it open until I'm on the plane ride back home to New York City, I can use whatever I miss doing or seeing as justification to come back.

What I do need is a map, which I cop from Chakib at the tourism board in midtown Manhattan, where I go for suggestions on routing my trip to the country of my dad's direct paternal ancestors.

"I want to watch the sun rise in the Sahara, like somebody must have in my father's father's line. I want to lay eyes on my distant cousins, the Imazighen, living on the Atlas Mountains. I'd like to visit Fez, and drive up the Atlantic coast to Tangier. I want to look at the south of Spain from the tip of Africa," I say. "I want to bond with her rather than just walk all over her."

"Oh, you will definitely see a lot of Maroc," he says. "You may even end up wanting to send for your family and never return."

CHAPTER THIRTEEN

Tripping in Morocco

The world is a book, and those who do
not travel read only a page.

—SAINT AUGUSTINE, AMAZIGH SAINT

WE MEET OUR GUIDE, ADNANE, AT MOHAMMED V INTERNATIONAL
Airport in Casablanca. I look familiar to him, he says. He looks familiar to me, too, but there's no way I could have met him before. Adnane's
never been out of the country, and this is my first time in Morocco. The
closest I've come to this place is Andalusia, about a three-hour boat
ride from Tangier, up north.

"You know, when God made us, He made forty versions of every
single being and then scattered them around the world," Adnane says.
"This is how we are all connected." The "me" he knows, Adnane says, lives
relatively close by, about a three-hour drive east of Rabat, where we're
headed on our way to the imperial city of Fez.

"I believe you, because a dozen of you live in New York City, and
at least half of them drive Seaman taxicabs." I say. If Adnane took
off his djellaba and wore jeans and a button-down shirt, he could be
from a variety of Caribbean and tropical South American countries,

including the Dominican Republic. "You look Garifuna, too. Brazilian, Cuban—you have many brothers scattered around the world. At *least* forty."

He shoots me a puzzled look. "What is a seaman? Does he work on a boat?" asks Adnane.

"No, not exactly," I explain. "They guide people by car to wherever they want to go in the city. Every single one I've met in over fifteen years has come from my country."

"The United States?" asks Adnane.

He makes a good point. Depending on whom I'm talking to back home, I vacillate between what comes before and after the hyphen that identifies me. Most times, when I travel abroad, it's a different story. Before President Barack Obama took office, I preferred to unload our burdensome distinction as the world's imperial bogeymen and women by dumping the "-American" part of who I am. The hyphen has taken on an umbilical quality. I claimed being solely Dominican at times of convenience, like during former POTUS George Bush *numero* two's reign. After a while I got tired of being asked "Wow, are all you Americans as stupid as your president Bush?" for the millionth time. The ascension of Barack Obama gave us a tight face-lift abroad, especially in those first few months during his short-lived honeymoon period.

"I'm dominiyorkian," I say, "a transnational who isn't all the way American or Dominican but travels between both worlds."

"Ah, I see."

"An American-Latino, yes, now I see," he says. "Okay sister, welcome, Insha'Allah, we will begin our journey."

Adnane says something in Moroccan Arabic, or Darija, to our driver, Mounir, who looks much younger than his nineteen years, with a clean-shaven baby face and bashful countenance. He rarely makes eye contact. Mounir nods at Adnane, and we set off for the capital city of Rabat, a two-hour drive north of Casablanca.

It's a good thing we're leaving. The frantic energy and stench of gasoline, similar to that in São Paulo and Santo Domingo, is overwhelming. It feels like I'm wearing a blanket of soot and oil on my face, hands, and hair. Imagine wrapping your lips around the tailpipe of a bus and inhaling the fumes into your body as hard as you can. That's what breathing in downtown Casablanca feels like at first.

I roll up my window and look out at the familiar faces of men and women walking together, some dressed in hijabs and djellabas, and others like hip Parisians in tailored black clothing, skinny jeans, and big curly hair. It feels like we're driving down a more beautiful (albeit grimy) version of Steinway Street in Astoria, Queens. Globalization by way of McDonald's and KFC has captured the hearts, the minds, and from what I can see through the window, the growing bellies of the folks here.

We arrive in Rabat, the French-decreed capital and current political center of the country, and are greeted by a beautiful woman from the tourism board dressed in a black tank top and blazer with a pair of tight-fitting jeans and open-toed stilettos. Amina has thick raven hair that brushes a few inches below her shoulders. Her matching smoky eye makeup accentuates her awesome feline eyes. She's wearing translucent powder several shades too light over a thick layer of ghostly face cream.

I learn in the first few minutes of meeting Amina that she loves salsa music and dancing (yes!), anything French (I can dig that), riding shotgun (always, to our extreme vexation), swank (after long rides with her, I welcome that), and European toilets (will prove to be an annoyance outside of Rabat). She's prone to regular outbursts and crying fits, which is kind of weird. Later, I'll have to make up a story about my camerawoman Lisa being on some kind of crazy American medication that makes her snap, in order to make Amina stop sobbing when the delivery of my homegirl's Bronx accent scares the shit out of her. All I want to do is connect to one set of Dad's paternal ancestors, and here I am, stuck like Krazy Glue to a hysterical tour guide. And yet, it's worth the drama because we're two women traveling with film equipment, something you must be careful doing in the kingdom. It's not like either of us is Richard Bangs, Rick Steves, or some other random white dude rocking safari jackets and khakis.

• • •

Today Rabat is a relatively quiet, almost dull seaside city with a population of just over two million. If its ancient walls could testify, the roar would be so deafening that one would find it almost unbearable. Its origins lay in the eighth century BC, when Romans and Phoenicians settled around the estuary of the Oued Bou Regreg River in today's Chellah. When the Roman Empire fell into decay and subsequently split, the Imazighen turned the former settlement into a *ribat,* a fortress-monastery.

When the Almohads came to town in the twelfth century, the *ribat* was transformed into a Kasbah, or citadel, and used as a strategic jumping-off place to reconquer Andalusia. Under Yacoub al-Mansour, the southern Spanish territory was briefly brought under Muslim rule. Rabat enjoyed its new position as an imperial city and flourished during those days, which lasted until al-Mansour's death in 1199. After that, the city fell again into relative decay.

That changed in the 1600s, when Andalusian Moors fleeing the Spanish Inquisition settled south of the Kasbah, establishing a city called Bou Regreg. At once, on the east side of the river, a motley crew of Christian renegades, Moorish and Imazighen pirates, and a group of multinational adventure seekers settled in Salé. For the next three hundred and some years, "Sallee Rovers," or corsairs, tormented coastal communities on both the Atlantic and the Mediterranean, roving as far as the shores of the United States, looking for Spanish gold, and southern England to capture Christians as slaves. In those days, Rabat made Times Square in the 1970s and '80s look like Disneyland.

I wonder if any of my paternal ancestors got caught up in this mess before finding their way to the Caribbean and, ultimately, modern-day Dominican Republic. The past is buried deep within the ground in Rabat, although the ancient walls in the old city are still standing, painted in electrifying variations of royal blue that make the winding roads look like streamlets of shallow ocean water. Because it almost overwhelms the senses, Rabat is a fitting place to start the journey toward the Sahara Desert, through the Atlas Mountains, and then the northwesternmost tip of the African continent, in Tangier. From there, I'll be able to see, weather permitting, the southernmost tip of Spain, where another chapter of my family history likely began.

On our way out of Rabat en route to the imperial city of Fez, a familiar sound compels me to ask Adnane to stop our black minivan in its tracks. "What *is* this music?" I ask him. "Who are those men marching down the street?

"It's spiritual Islamic music. They are Sufi practitioners, the Aissawa from Meknes," he says.

The music is familiar. I'm told the singers are chanting Islamic prayers to the polyrhythmic beat. One of the men, swaying front to back with his spiritual brothers, looks as if he is moments away from going into a trance, induced by the music. At the head of the procession is a man who looks like a close relative to Dad, dressed in a black-and-white-striped djellaba. He's obviously the master of ceremonies or, as his Afro-Cuban Lucumí or Santeria counterpart would be called, an *akpon*, leading the way. A group of men follow, dressed in red and white hats with matching outfits carrying flags in vibrant hues of turquoise, emerald green, blood orange, and bright mustard. Behind them is a man balancing a bronze vessel atop a tray on his head, almost identical to what I've seen at a festival on Rockaway Beach celebrating the Yoruba sea goddess Yemaya. The parallels don't stop there. Both Gnawa and Santeria music can be traced to sub-Saharan Africa and slavery.

I follow the procession to the park, where a woman dressed in hijab lets go of her daughter's hand and falls into a spirit possession, wailing something I don't understand and dancing around the singers. The other people in the park are not taken aback. This relationship with God is socially acceptable here.

The woman's feverish movements, the widening of her eyes, and her trancelike state are behaviors I've seen before at a *bembé*, a spiritual drumming, in a Brooklyn basement. As the *akpon* chanted religious songs dedicated to the orishas, or Yoruba deities, the initiated priests dancing in front of the sacred drums fell into trances that were almost identical to that of the woman in the park. My world is getting smaller.

We jump in the car and head toward Fez, making stops to play musical chairs in the back of the truck as Amina takes naps in the passenger seat. We are hoping to make it to Fez before night falls.

We make a pit stop right outside the city at one of the best-preserved sites in the kingdom: Volubilis. Most Moroccan sites can make anyone feel like they've stepped into a gigantic replica of the Metropolitan Museum of Art. The Volubilis ruins are a breathtaking frame of what was once a Mauritanian capital founded in the third century BC. We hop out of the truck to find the last family walking out of the makeshift front gate. A petite woman with dark wavy hair tucked underneath a dark scarf, accompanied by her husband, mother-in-law, and kids, is the day's last visitor. She walks over to me and offers her hand, asking me in Darija and then English, "Where are you from?"

I tell her, "New York City and the Dominican Republic."

She gives me a once-over. I'm not showing any of my tattoos. I'm wearing a pair of loose-fitting jeans and an embellished long-sleeved rust-colored tunic.

"I thought you were Moroccan," she says. I go on to tell her about my ancestral DNA exploits and Dad's link to this part of the world. She's read about the science on the Internet, she says.

"I feel at home here," I say to her. "I wish to come back alone and experience more of the country—maybe attend a Sufi mystic ceremony."

"Insha'Allah, I hope to run into you again, sister," she says, shaking my hand. "I would like to have you over for tea at our home." The woman slips into the driver's seat of her car and leaves with her family.

Adnane is able to sweet-talk the security guards into letting us in for a few minutes to walk around the site and retrace the oldest footsteps in the country, aside from the Sahara, as the sun gradually sets above us.

• • •

By the time we pull into the hotel's driveway in Fez, it's almost pitch black outside. Lisa and I are disheveled, starving, and sore from taking turns riding on the hump in the middle of the backseat. Amina awakens refreshed from another nap and places a phone call on her cell, presumably to the hotel's manager. Adnane, who is based in this dreamy city of about one million, slips into the night with Mounir.

We enter the lobby of the hotel. I look over at Lisa, who is likely thinking exactly what I am: Did riding the hump in the backseat of the truck finally kill us on the way to Fez and transport us into another dimension akin to heaven, if there's such a thing? The air is pungent with the smell of rosewater, sweet almond cookies, and tagine. My stomach rumbles. I try not to look around too much. The colorful tiles, the ornate chandeliers; everything is exquisite, almost overwhelming. "You welcome," says a gorgeous young woman with a strong accent. Several people have told me that Fassi women are considered the country's most elegant, prolific cooks, and sought-after wives. I hear it's because they are also known to be lighter-skinned and therefore more beautiful than other Moroccan women. The colonial white-is-right mentality is pervasive even here, in Eden.

"Where are we?" I ask.

"Welcome to Palais Jamaï," says a woman who I assume is the hotel's manager.

Though rolling with Amina has literally been a pain in the ass, at the end of the day, it's been worth the hell ride it took to get here.

The only thing more beautiful than this place in the evening is the view of Fez in the morning from my balcony. It feels almost like I'm floating on a fat meringue cloud overlooking the medina. If Aphrodite chills at home in Cyprus for most of the year, then Fez must be the goddess's playground. To my left, I can see the roof of al-Karaouine, the first and oldest functioning university in the world, and below that, exquisite Andalusian-style gardens.

After a breakfast of strong coffee, sweet mint tea, local pastries, and fruit, we meet Adnane and our driver in the hotel lobby and head over to the medina of Fès el-Balim in the old part of the city. While Fez's foundation dates back to the ninth century AD, the thousands of Andalusian Moors who fled Spain during the *Reconquista* cultivated its character. Today this city is the spiritual and cultural center of the country. The medina is also the largest living Islamic medieval city on the planet, and quite possibly the most immense refugee camp for stray cats.

There's something about the culture of the marketplace that excites me. The frenetic vibe of the medina makes me feel more at ease than I do strolling in the tranquility of, say, a street in Rabat. I see old men on donkeys yelling into cell phones and women clustered in groups rushing in and out of the gate. Children shouting in French, German, and Spanish, looking for work as unofficial guides, compete with elderly homeless women for whatever dirhams tourists can spare. The scent of fresh bread, herbs, and cat urine drift through the air from every winding road, as do sounds of American and Moroccan hip-hop.

The hip-hop of Morocco—where Casablanca is akin to the Bronx—is crazy fresh. While graffiti art isn't as popular as it was in New York City back in the day and, more recently, in Paris and Amsterdam, every other branch is fully represented here. The music, rapped in Darija and in French, sounds really dope, and the lyrics reflect what's going on with the country's young people. The content—I'm told by rapper Masta Flow and my favorite local hip-hop producer, DJ Van—ranges from tolerance, police corruption, respecting women, and other sociopolitical issues to partying and spirituality. In Fez, the medina is where it's at.

While looking through the bootleg hip-hop CDs at a stall in one of the many winding streets I won't commit to memory, a fortune teller dressed in a black burqa steps to me. Her eyes are aquamarine, and the parts of her face I can make out are a dark brown. Her hands are painted in an intricate pattern with what looks like dried henna. The woman says something in Darija I don't understand. I motion to Adnane, talking to a man nearby. I ask him to translate discreetly, hoping that no one else in our scattered crew notices, especially not Amina, who's shopping nearby. She's starting to make us all feel like we're rolling with an FBI agent and not a rep from the tourism board.

"She says she wants to give you information, but for free," says Adnane, "and that she's seen you before in Ouarzazate."

"Sure, I understand," I say, eager to hear what she has to say.

"You are from here. Your soul, that is," she says to Adnane, who translates. "And this will certainly not be the last time I see you. You may want to bring your father here someday, the man born with good fortune," she says. Adnane is puzzled. I understand. Dad, the caul bearer whose luck I'm not sure has found him yet.

She takes my hand and traces the lines of my palm with her thick index finger. "An ancestor, one who left not so long ago, may come back soon and—"

"What's going on here?" asks Amina, carrying a bag with a belly-dancing outfit and other goodies. "Is she begging for money?"

"No, she is asking if I want henna. It's nothing, let's go. Thank you, sister," I say to the woman through Adnane. "Next time we meet, maybe I will have something to offer you." The woman disappears into the crowd.

"It's time to head out to the Sahara," Amina says. "We don't want to be on the mountain at night."

I'm almost sad to leave Fez, a city I feel kinship with. However, after Bennett mentioned Dad's probable link to the Imazighen, I'm eager to get started on the long drive through the Atlas Mountains, where clusters of these ancient people live in virtual isolation.

They say that Atlas was a Greek god before he became a North African mountain chain extending through Morocco, Algeria, and Tunisia. Atlas was, as you might imagine, a gigantic specimen, a Titan constantly beefing with other freakishly large creatures roaming the Mediterranean at the time. After clashing with the wrong Titan, Atlas decided to hide along the African shoreline. When he laid his head down to take a nap, his head rested in Tunisia, and his feet burrowed in Morocco. Even during the months when it snowed on parts of him, he found comfort in the warmth of the desert. He made himself so comfortable in that position that he never awoke from his slumber, eventually morphing into a mountain range.

Atlas can be a scary god, especially for people afraid of heights like I am. We zip up narrow winding roads past other cars and trucks. Along the way, we stop for Mounir to rest and say his prayers. Water up here is scarce, and the living conditions are, by Western standards, so minimal that I doubt many people could wrap their heads around it. We see very old women with a series of tattoos on their faces, loaded down with large bushels of wood and branches, accompanied by goats. The sun and wind have turned their faces and hands into leather. I'm too intimidated to stop and talk. I'm afraid I'll contaminate them like a Western explorer would a newly discovered nation living deep in the Amazonian rain forest.

A small Amazigh girl who bears a striking resemblance to Djali is playing by herself in front of her tiny home. Her nearest neighbor must be miles away, in one of the insular communities we can see dotting the arid patches of land on this side of Atlas. The girl runs up to our truck and asks if we have anything to spare. Her smile reveals decaying teeth, but her large dark eyes and the wild curly hair framing her pretty face are arresting. She is quite something, and we all scurry to see what we can give her—water, dirhams, gum, aspirin, and sweet dates. I ask her through Adnane what she sees for herself in the future.

"If I am lucky, I will find a husband who will take care of me."

I wish she'd said something different, but patriarchy is as prevalent around the world as racism and xenophobia are. We can't hide from it, not even here.

What feels like hours and hours later, we arrive at a Vegas-style über-cheesy hotel in Erfoud, not far from the Merzouga Dunes. Thank the gods that we're here just for a few hours, to eat and shower before heading to the desert.

We are deliriously tired from the trip, but no matter, it's the Sahara or bust. Plus, we don't want to see this place during the day. We change, shower, and meet downstairs in the lobby in one hour. I'm determined to lay my eyes on a stretch of the planet where I'm certain some male ancestor of Dad's, at some point in his life, journeyed across on camel or on foot. I want to see what he saw at least once in this life. I sort of wish Dad were here.

My New York City instincts are starting to kick in. I'm paranoid. "Are Mounir and Adnane so sick of us that they're going to whack us right here, wherever *here* is?" I ask Lisa.

"I know, girl, right?" she says, "Not for nothin', but I'm thinking the same shit."

It's darker here than any place I've ever been. It's darker than driving through the thick bush in Sierra Leone. It's darker than driving through a *campo* or mountain range in the middle of the night in D.R. It's so dark, I can't see my hands in front of me. I can only feel.

"If we're going to go out, we might as well go out together," I whisper sort of jokingly.

"Don't fuck around like that," Lisa snaps.

There are no streetlights dotting the path we're taking to Merzouga. I'm afraid we may run over somebody along the way. We're driving fast, making wrong turns down streets that all look the same: dark.

"It's nothing, sister, we were just a little lost," says Adnane. "Mr. Mounir has never been here before." To my surprise, neither has Amina.

"Are you sure you're not trying to whack us?" I say, laughing nervously.

"What is *this*? Whack?" Adnane responds, laughing.

Minutes later, I feel like we're driving on top of an ocean, swaying from side to side, undulating to the rhythm of whatever is underneath us. At first it's a little disorienting. Mounir turns on the headlights, revealing a hideous crew of desert rats tagging along, jumping from side to side like kangaroos. This goes on for another twenty minutes.

"*Here* is the desert," Adnane says. It feels as if we've parked atop a sinkhole.

"That's it. Goodbye, Lisa," I say. We erupt in laughter, tipsy from a cocktail of nervous energy and delirious exhaustion.

A man dressed in a radiant blue caftan-style top with matching pants and a white turban appears like a ghost before us. I can only make out the outline of his body. It's so dark I don't want to get out of the car for fear I'll drown in the sand, but I do. I'm told to sit down on something I'm assuming is a camel. Slowly, the large animal rises to its feet, and I'm hoisted at least ten feet into the air. For some strange reason, I'm not scared of the dark anymore. I submit to it.

As we make our way across the sand dunes, the sun gradually begins to ascend above us. I can hear drunken Spanish tourists howling in the distance in Castilian Spanish. I can make out the outline of a couple hopping up and down, clinking beer bottles. A few others are rolling around atop a large rug. We move as far away as we can from the group, our camels traversing thin strips of sand that threaten to swallow us whole.

The sun is looming above us as the moon, directly behind us, sets. In the single cheesiest instant of my life so far, my eyes begin to well. I blurt out the first thing that comes to mind: "Oh, this place looks like God's own personal art gallery." Lisa doesn't respond. Come to think of it, maybe God is a He after all, because only a cruel force would create something this beautiful and make it inaccessible to most people. It's not easy to get here. Nor is it cheap.

Lisa's eyes are wet, like mine. We say nothing for a while. Mounir, exhausted from driving so many hours without much of a break, is sleeping on the rug next to us. Adnane, who's been here before, is talking softly to the local tour guides nearby. The only loud voice I hear is coming from Amina, wearing a huge straw hat and black Jackie O. sunglasses. She's complaining about the sun and applying another layer of SPF 50 to her face so vigorously that she's missing what's going on around her. Maybe I'm exhausted from the lack of sleep, or perhaps I'm on the verge of heatstroke, but Amina is growing on me. She's like a physical manifestation of Eshu, the mischievous Nigerian trickster god who owns every crossroad in the world. When bored or provoked, he's known to play jokes on his children and inject a little irony into life's mix.

There are no words that could do this moment just justice. More than anything, this place feels familiar. I bury my hands in the hot sand and think about the embodiment of memory or, more specifically, our natural ability to carry the past in our bodies and minds. Individually, every grain of sand brushing against my hands represents a story, an experience, and a block for me to build upon for the next generation. I quietly thank this ancestor of mine for surviving the trip so that I could one day return.

"Pull. Over! Pull *over* to the side of the street," yells the police officer during our first few moments in Tangier. He noticed the tip of Lisa's camera peeking out from the back window. He begins to yell as if we've been caught with kilos of *cocaína* rather than a video camera. Thinking about having to replace a smashed or confiscated Sony EX3 camera, and losing footage in the process, freaking nauseates me.

"Oh shit, what the fuck?" says Lisa.

"What the hell did we do?" I ask Adnane.

"No worries. You are *welcome*. I will take care of this." Adnane jumps out of the car and begins to reason with the cop. There is something about him that can make the biggest asshole smile. Had the man lived in the States, he would have had a promising future as a diplomat or a hip-hop exec.

The two begin to laugh, and Adnane asks Amina to come out and introduce herself, which she does.

The *brigade touristique,* or the tourist police—the *tourist* police is *this* gully—walks over to the driver's seat and shakes Mounir's hand. Then he walks over to shake both of ours.

"You welcome," he says, smiling, in broken English. "I am to sorry for scaring you, *please,* enjoy your time here." I don't answer but offer him a forced smile, thinking of how this scenario would have played out had I not been with Adnane.

Tangier has always been the international crossroad of the world, if not one of its most seamy. Everyone has had a piece of her. Greek traders and Phoenicians were the first to settle here. The latter fashion plates introduced the djellaba to the country. The Imazighen, Morocco's oldest inhabitants, and Arabs have maintained a long-term presence, and the city was passed back and forth for centuries between Portugal, England, and Spain. When France and Spain began carving the country up like a turkey in the 1920s, Tangier was made an international free zone with all kinds of tax breaks and incentives making it the place to be. This is what attracted a bevy of artists, writers, thrill seekers, and sexual misfits. Tangier became a place where the living was cheap, inspiration was everywhere you looked, and young boys were available to fuck at a dime a dozen—all desirable prerequisites for living *la vida* expat.

Fast-forward to recent times. The current king sees the city's potential and nurses Tangier back to health. Let's not get it twisted, though— addicts sailing in from Andalusia are tweaking on all kinds of *drogas*, and there are enough prostitutes here to film a Moroccan edition of *Pimps Up, Ho's Down.*

Nevertheless, Tangier is a charming city with inspiring grit. Like the rest of the country's cities, this one is divided into an old medina and a Ville Nouvelle. This is a city where you can see the Atlantic on your left and the Mediterranean on your right in one sweeping motion. The southernmost point of Spain is only seventeen miles away from the Cape Spartel lighthouse. I'm ultimately here to connect the dots and see where one story likely ended for my father's own personal Adam before another one began over in Spain.

It's so clear today I can make out the silhouette of Andalusia across the strait from my rickety white plastic chair. We're at the coolest open-air café on the planet, Café Hafa, with plastic bags full of chicken sandwiches and greasy french fries. Decades ago, we might have caught the Rolling Stones and Paul Bowles smoking hashish in any one of these stadium seats. We may have seen Henri Matisse, Samuel Beckett, the Beatles, William Burroughs, just about anyone who epitomized cool, sipping mint tea and creating art inspired by their surroundings.

Today the café is packed with men talking shop and playing back-gammon, and groups of schoolgirls in and out of hijab, doing home-work. We order rounds of strong coffee and sweet mint tea for our crew. "Please keep them coming," I say to our waiter.

I'm just beginning to soak in the last several whirlwind weeks here. I think back to the fortune teller I met back in Fez. Something tells me she's right. I'll be back.

CHAPTER FOURTEEN

Running the *Fukú* Down

Being a mother is an attitude, not a biological relation.

—ROBERT HEINLEIN, *HAVE SPACE SUIT—WILL TRAVEL*

BACK HOME, I FIND A MESSAGE FROM ROCÍO SITTING IN MY Facebook inbox. Half of me hoped she hadn't responded. The other half wasn't sure she'd care about our mitochondrial DNA or our direct maternal ancestors' origins.

It turns out our haplogroup is L3d, sub-Saharan African. When sifting through the results of ancestral DNA tests, it's not out of the ordinary to find matches across dozens of countries, with varying percentages of likely origins. However, that isn't the case with us here. Within our haplogroup, every single match pointed to a pinprick of a place, located on the westernmost tip of Africa that's easy to overlook. Bordered by Senegal in the north, Guinea on the south and east, and the Atlantic Ocean on the west, modern-day Guinea-Bissau is one of the smallest countries on the continent.

When I find out that our Supreme Matriarch is West African, things begin to make perfect sense. A chill runs down my spine. I will never meet this woman Rocío and I descend from in this world, but

I've already encountered her in my dreams. She is *la africana,* who in different scenarios has jumped in to save me like a guardian angel. She is the same *africana* whose face I've never seen but whose body—thick legs, a tall frame, and large healing breasts, sometimes dressed like a pauper and other times in elegant long multicolored ruffled dresses— I've known since I was a little girl.

I imagine the woman we descend from is someone who had a *fukú* put on her by a jilted lover, a jealous woman or a diviner to whom she may not have paid a debt. I can see it clearly, how this curse between mothers and their firstborn daughters may have started with her. I broke that *maldición* by breaking away from my own mother and unloading the baggage I would have otherwise inherited.

The *fukú* may have had origins in a marketplace in precolonial Guinea-Bissau when it was a part of the kingdom of Gabon, a territory of the Mali Empire, areas of which endured until the eighteenth century. Or it may have happened during the Portuguese invasion when parts of the region became Portuguese Guinea, known as the Slave Coast, in honor of its most booming economic activity.

This would be a more likely scenario: My maternal ancestor's mother or grandmother made a detour into Europe first, finding herself in the Kingdom of Castile where she had one or more children, including a daughter from whom the women in my family descend. And that daughter, known as a Black ladino, was reared as a Christianized African. In 1510, seven years after the first African slaves were forced onto the Spanish colony in present-day Dominican Republic, the first sizable shipment of Black ladinos arrived on the island. Perhaps L3d, *la africana,* was one of them. Or she may have migrated to the island from present-day Haiti.

All the above scenarios are possible because there are many roads, some indirect, that bridge the African continent to both sides of Hispaniola. The one thing I know for sure is that had the transatlantic slave trade not happened, I would have never existed.

In fact, the eastern side of Hispaniola was the first place in the New World to import African slaves to work the sugar mills and tend to their hypocritical Christian masters' needs. Like their European counterparts, the Spanish were ill equipped to live in the tropics and thought manual labor was beneath them. They couldn't realize their New World dreams for themselves even after they confiscated the land and drove down the numbers of the island's Indigenous inhabitants by slavery, genocide, and disease. The genetic evidence of Columbus's effect on human migration to the island is still there, on the bodies and in the essence of Dominican people.

Maybe the melodrama, the moment our First Mother, if you will, was damned, played itself out on a cobblestone street in the colonial district of Santo Domingo, the first permanent European settlement in the New World that still exists today.

I've had this recurring dream several times: An angry voice is screaming in a barely recognizable creolized Spanish. I can't explain why I understand what's being said, but I do. "From this day on, the women in your family, living and not yet born, will break from one another in total repulsion."

I can see *la africana* only from the back, this time dressed in gaudy Spanish clothes that seem too heavy for the tropics. She slowly walks up a hill, trying her best to shrug off the *fukú* as superstition, powerless words from an archaic hater. And yet something in her knows better. I sense that she feels uneasy. The same gods who kept her from succumbing on her journey to the New World, regardless of whether or not she acknowledged them, were fickle and sometimes irrational.

The curse followed us here to another land. When I gave birth to my daughter, I had to confront the *fukú* for fear it would present itself in our relationship. My desire to slay the curse is why I worked so hard to earn my daughter's love and respect from the first moment I held her in my arms. It is the reason why I checked my ego and accepted

Dad's offer to help me break the first link shackling my spirit—my less than ideal choices in men—so I could direct my energy to mother my daughter in a loving environment.

I remember looking at my newborn, sitting in an infant car seat as I packed the last of my shit, and saying to her: "Listen kid, it's just you and me now, so let's help each other out. Always be honest with me, and show me how to be the mother and father I never had. I'll make a mess of things sometimes, and I'm sorry in advance, but I'll try. My word is bond."

Djali, a hair over six months, may have been smiling at me or just gassy, but I started feeling better. The guides Casimiro identified in Maria's apartment lifted me up and, with that, hooked me up with a new set of *cojones*. I worked through my postpartum depression by taking the pressure off myself to be perfect, and praying to my spirit guides to continue propping me up when I was too exhausted to stand on my own. The *fukú* was starting to reverse itself. I could feel it. For breaking that first link, the universe rewarded me with a beautiful and smart daughter, a fine career, and someone to love, you know, in *that* way.

I'm tempted to delete Rocío's email and pretend I never reached out to her in the first place. I clearly remember the last time I saw her, though it feels like a lifetime ago. We were at Antonio's house in up-state New York. He orchestrated the whole thing. My grandparents, who had recently relocated from Santo Domingo, came over. Rocío flew in from Florida, accompanied by a man she'd recently married. I was months shy of turning twenty-two, and pregnant. I thought this was an ideal time to connect with Rocío. It was my duty, I felt, to foster a relationship with this woman, though I hardly knew her. Not doing so, I thought in my hormonally imbalanced mind, would somehow negatively affect my relationship with my own unborn.

I didn't recognize her when I first saw her at the train station. Rocío's thick dark mane was cut into a dreadfully layered strawberry-blond Dorothy Hamill bob. She was curvaceous, wore hazel contacts, and had ditched the Bostonian accent. Just by looking at her, I guessed that Rocío's new husband was either white or Latino with a European phenotype.

On the drive to my uncle's house, Rocío didn't ask how I was doing. She never inquired about my pregnancy like the rest of the family did. Rather, Antonio and I were made to sit through a long wedding video starring Rocío, dressed in a virginal white gown, and a groom wearing a dim-witted expression plastered across his face.

"Is your husband lobotomized?" I asked.

Rocío laughed. She was too enraptured by the telenovela unfolding before us to listen to me. Their video featured many close-ups of the new bride staring deeply into her current love's eyes with an intensity that rivaled that of José Luis "El Puma" Rodríguez.

"Come and meet my man," Rocío said to me.

We walked to the picnic table, where my grandfather was already sitting with him. Rocío's new husband sat hunched over on a bench, avoiding eye contact with everyone at the table. We found out, after prodding him, that he'd been born in Cuba and ended up in Miami several years earlier because of a lottery.

"What did you do in Cuba?" Antonio asked.

"Oh, I used to cut the balls off of goats," he replied in a Cuban accent, still avoiding eye contact. Antonio smiled, thinking the guy was joking. He wasn't. Dude didn't crack a smile. I wondered if this weirdo was one of the people I'd read about whom Fidel Castro, known to have flooded the States with mental patients and criminals, had rigged the lotto for.

Rocío interrupted. "What do you think of *my* papi?" she asked me.

I said nothing, concentrating on not breaking out into laughter.

"What do you care what she thinks of your papi?" Mama snapped. "She doesn't give a shit."

"*Oh*, Mama," Rocío said, chuckling, "you are *so* tough."

"I have to go to the bathroom," the groom blurted out. He was visibly uncomfortable, almost squirming in his seat.

"Papi," Rocío said, "let me go with you. Okay, *mi querido*?" They disappeared for almost an hour.

"I wonder if she's going to literally wipe his ass," Antonio said. "He looks like he'd need the help."

Papa excused himself for a nap. He never returned to the table or left his room for the rest of the weekend.

I left without saying goodbye. Several months later, Papa died.

Rocío and I spoke once more, when she called me the week following 9/11. I sat on my bed, staring vacantly at the cable box and counting the minutes it would take this time for the conversation to go from her miserable life to how awfully Dad treated her when they were together. She went on and on, and I, zoning out, said nothing. Maybe I was exhausted, but a rush of sympathy for her washed over me about fifteen minutes or so into her soliloquy. My birth mother was so fettered by her past that she couldn't ask, not even this time, how I was doing.

Then I felt nothing.

I stare at my inbox. I like not knowing Rocío's number or her address. I'm just as happy that she doesn't have mine. However, after discovering Dad's results so far I'm curious to contact her and see what I can mine that will give me clues about our ancestry. I'm also interested in whether she'll live up to the hyped-up stereotype that all of us Dominicans, here and on the island, vehemently reject and deny, deny, deny . . . our Blackness.

I open the email. My first impulse is to throw up in my mouth, but I don't. Rocío starts the letter with "my beloved firstborn daughter," which irks the hell out of me. This isn't one of those reality shows about the reunion of a mother and the daughter she gave up for adoption at birth because she was too young or too broke to take care of her.

I can't believe what I'm reading. The molasses-sweet prose— granted, it may have read less dulcet had it been written in her first language—is making my gums hurt. She sounds delusional. I can't help but think that she missed her calling as a romance novelist or a telenovela screenwriter. "I consider myself blessed for you to address yourself to me even if it is at the autumn of life, just before winter approaches and memories and life are far gone . . . A trip to roads long ago walked . . . a visit to moments not yet gone . . . memories frozen that enable us to grow . . ."

"What did your mother say?" Sacha asks.

"A mother isn't the person who births you; it's the person who rears you and shows you love," I bark, immediately regretting it. "I'm sorry, man, it's just annoying."

"Well, are you going to interview her, or did she say no?"

"I can't tell if she's saying yes or if she's telling me that she's dying of something. It's cheesier than Velveeta and as authentic."

I respond to Rocío's email with the formality I'd accord any stranger, even on Facebook: "Thank you, kindly, for your note . . . I will make plans . . . Best . . ."

Over the years, I've maintained a sporadic, mostly textual relationship with one of Rocío's daughters. Michelle has always fascinated me because she stood out, even more than Giselle, from the rest of Rocío's litter. I swore that Michelle was a Chinese boy when I first met her as a toddler in Boston, and when I was told she wasn't, I argued the fact with her mother. She favors her father physically more than her other kids do, and she has Rocío's Asiatic eyes. I imagine they came from that ancestor on Mama's father's paternal line. Mama and Antonio have told me the same story with no variations about this man who originally came from a land they referred to as Indochina, modern-day Vietnam. Supposedly, three brothers left the country seeking adventure. One ended up in India, the other was lost at sea, and one landed on the north coast of the Dominican Republic.

Michelle first contacted me after she turned eighteen, then again after becoming a wife and mother grappling with her own identity. She wanted to visit New York City for a breather, and I played host.

When we met after all those years, I still felt no spark or a familial bond. Nothing magical happened, and the feeling was mutual.

"Raquel, really, it's all fucking good," she said in a straightforward, husky voice. "It is what it is, and *it's* beyond us."

I think I would like Michelle more had she not been related to me through Rocío. She is a blunt, no-bullshit woman who spent part of her adolescence living with foster parents—I don't know how that happened, considering she lived in the same town as both Rocío and her father.

I text her: "I need a favor."

"I'll pick you up at the airport and drive you wherever you need to go," Michelle responds almost immediately.

"It's going to be weird," I write back. "Glad I'm only staying in Orlando for two days and then heading to D.R."

"Yeah, that's why I want to fucking be there, dude," Michelle replies. "It's going to be so freaking weird."

I almost miss my flight. I lag at the boxing gym, doing extra rounds of the heavy bag and mitts, extra crunches, extra everything with Coach Sanchez until my arms feel like they'll fall off if I try to lift them over my head. I'm one of the last people to board the American Airlines flight. On the plane, I try to think about everything but my imminent meeting with Rocío. Instead, I sketch out a plan for my forthcoming trip to Santo Domingo that's totally ridiculous, because there's no such thing as planning for Santo Domingo.

We make a smooth landing at Orlando's International Airport. I'm hoping it's a good omen that all will go well over the next forty-eight hours. I take my time walking out to meet Michelle.

I can't remember a time when there was peace between Rocío and me, even during the periods of my life with Dad and Alice when she made brief appearances. It's as if she dropped in only to prove to the men in her life, maybe even to herself, that she had a child whom she gave a shit about and who gave a shit about her. We both failed miserably at pretending. I wonder what, if anything, will change.

Orlando is rather depressing. A blanket of fat clouds and gray skies follow me for the next two days.

"It was gorgeous and hot before you came, and funny enough, it'll be nice the day after tomorrow, when you leave," says Michelle.

"Yes, it figures," I say. "Does Rocío know you're picking me up?"

"Yeah, she's called like a million times—she's anxious."

"Okay, let's do this."

"Yes, let's," says Michelle. "I wonder if my mom's going to be in denial or if she's going to insist you meet the new guy. You know, I heard she told Giselle that her dad was French Polynesian and not from Haiti."

"That craziness sounds about right. The guy was a monster, but still, French Polynesian? Hysterical," I say.

"Listen, if it means anything at all, Mom is a wonderful grandmother to my daughter," Michelle says. "I think she spoils her to make up for the past, you know?"

"It doesn't really matter to me, but I do understand your mother trying to make up for the past." I stare out the window. "My father treats Djali like I think he wishes he treated me when I was a kid."

"Well, I can't wait to hear about where this maternal ancestor of ours came from," Michelle says. "You know, during one of Mom's spells of delusion, she started looking, out of the blue, into getting the twins bar mitzvahed. Then she just let it go. Weird, right?"

"Yo, have you ever heard of a *fukú*?" I ask Michelle.

After what seems like too short a ride, we pull into Rocío's driveway.

Michelle enters the house first, positioning herself as if she has floor seats to an NBA final. I walk in slowly behind her.

There's a tiny woman standing in front of me sporting an eggplant-colored velvet sweatsuit. I can tell by the way she squints at me through her thick glasses that she barely recognizes me.

"*'Ello*, Raquel." She smiles nervously, leaning in to embrace me with her miniature arms. "How *ar'* you?" Her voice is still soft and monotone. I lean in as if greeting an acquaintance who grew up with my mother rather than the woman who bore me.

I'm underwhelmed, but I won't tell her that. I had hoped, at the bottom of the well, that I'd feel something magical. But I feel nothing for this stranger in front of me, *nada*, except maybe a little compassion. Rocío isn't carrying her genetic familial history only within her; a few new chapters are etched across her face like battle scars.

"I'm fine," I say. "How are you?"

Rocío looks as if life itself has been an emotionally and physically abusive partner. She is missing teeth, a genetic flaw inherited from her father's side of the family. Her hair is dyed a reddish brown, covering the silver stands that started sprouting on her head when she was still in her teens.

I follow her a few feet into the crowded living room. Rocío has a huge leather sectional wrapped around two walls. I saw the same one in the Brooklyn apartment of Biggie Smalls and his former wife, Faith Evans, when I interviewed her there in the '90s. Rocío's is black with animal-print pillows, and Biggie's was dark teal-meets-money-green. A collection of lighthouses adorns a table to my right. Above them on the wall are porcelain macaws and other tropical birds. Real and fake plants are everywhere, and a large indoor water fountain sits at the edge of a hallway leading to one of three bedrooms. I feel like I'm back in the Costa Rican rain forest but without the sensation of sitting in the lap of Mother Nature.

The tchotchkes compete with the wall in front of me; it's cluttered with photos of the five children she had after me, their children, and other family members I've never met.

Everything sparkles. Perhaps the exhaustion of cleaning every ornament in this room is preventing Rocío from unwrapping a shitload of exercise and dance DVDs stacked next to the TV set.

I haven't heard a thing she's whispered since I sat down. "Excuse me, can you repeat that?" I ask her.

"Yes, I try to be transparent, which I have never been with you, unfortunately," she lisps. "With your first child, you know, you make mistakes that, later on, you look back and you say, 'Oh my God, how *could* I ever?'"

"I never thought I'd see the day when you admit to anything—"

"I became a woman in the States, and when I had my first child, and I was going through a lot of stuff like leaving the old, you know, the country for the first time."

This is the first of many times Rocío will refer to me, that first child, in the third person. It's as if she's talking about the black baby doll sitting on the miniature chocolate suede chair that I'm assuming belongs to Michelle's daughter.

"I lost my identity in the marriage with your father. You are somebody that you don't know—"

"I know myself," I say.

"*I* am somebody that you don't know."

"Oh, *you're* somebody, yes, I don't know you."

"Yes, *you* don't know *me.*"

"Yes, that was by your design," I say. "Today, honestly, I'm glad things worked out the way they did, or I would not be the person and mom I've become. And I don't think I'm dissing you in your own home by stating that."

"No, *no, no, no,* as a matter of fact, I have a lot to ask for—forgiveness," Rocío says. The edges of her eyes are wet. "Because I was *not* a good mother to you."

Speaking of mothers, I try to broach the subject of our mitochondrial DNA results with Rocío and Michelle. All the women on our maternal line, as well as their daughters and sons, share a haplogroup. We all descend from one woman who lived some twenty-six generations or so ago.

"I want to know—now," Michelle says. Like me, she doesn't do mush.

"Our First Woman, the female we all descend from, is West African. Through my sample, we were able to discern that all of our matches point to the region where Guinea-Bissau is located."

"Wow, that's cool," Michelle says. "I've never heard of Guinea-Bissau."

"Yes, it's intriguing," Rocío says. "We are so mixed, Dominicans and other Hispanics, so I don't know why that *tyrano* used to kill Haitians when they crossed the border."

"Yeah, especially since the dictator was reportedly part Haitian," I respond.

"Do you want to go to that place someday—Guinea-Bissau?" Michelle asks me.

"I thought of going, but my instinct tells me just not now every time. And then there's this thing, this curse I think we have, that prevents me—"

Rocío's eyes widen. She's ditched the light contacts somewhere along the road to now, and is back to rocking her natural brown eyes. "What do you mean—a *fukú*?"

"Yes, between mothers and at least their eldest daughters."

"I think it's with all mothers and daughters," Michelle says. "Besides, Mom, you have three firstborn daughters with different men."

Rocío ignores Michelle. "My mother and I didn't have a good relationship growing up. I thought I was adopted."

"I wish I were adopted, but then again, maybe I chose this path," I say.

I tell Rocío and Michelle about the woman in my dreams whom I've always somehow felt related to, as if she's a spiritual guide or guardian of sorts. Rocío looks at me like she's listening to a horror story.

"You know, I've had similar dreams throughout the years," she says, "but I thought it was some *brujería* that Haitian whose name I won't say put on me to terrorize me even in my sleep."

"I don't think that was *brujería*, Rocío," I say. "I think there are other ways to look at it—this could be seen as insight. Many different cultures of people around the world believe in the power of dreams."

"So, you know, Jim is in the room down the hall, and he wants to meet you," says Rocío, just when I thought we were getting somewhere.

Jim is Rocío's latest tragedy, or boyfriend. He's a quadriplegic. I'm told the man resting in the room at the end of the hallway is a Hershey, Pennsylvania, native and former truck driver who lived in a trailer park before fate brought him to this house. One day while driving his Ford Explorer after trucking for hours, Jim dozed off and crashed, and was pinned underneath a wheel. His spine shattered into pieces, and he was left totally paralyzed except for some mobility in his arms. I'm not sure how Rocío met him or how he ended up in the room down the hall and not with his own family, but she claims it was love that brought them together. Rocío has always loved fixing broken men, and I guess this guy is no different.

"I'm not interested in ever meeting another one of your boyfriends or husbands. It's not what I came here for," I say.

"He really helps me more than any man I've known, and he doesn't expect anything from me in return."

"Rocío, he cannot move. He can't walk away from you."

"But he is *different*," she says. Her eyes are wet again.

"Different from whom? Different from the awkward Cuban goat castrator? The Mexican closeted gay dude I kind of wished I met just because? The Dominican *jodedor*-looking guy who's the reason why I don't want to learn how to drive and I'm terrified of cars that go faster than forty miles an hour? I know he must be different from our Haitian Lord Voldemort—at least *this* guy can't beat the shit out of anybody. He can't move."

"I'm sorry I put my child in harm's way, but I was not myself in California." Pause. "I was so scared," Rocío says.

"Are you referring to me?" I ask.

Rocío holds on to each one of her elbows with the opposite hand, rubbing them as if she's cold. She changes the subject. "I've always wanted to be a writer, to write my memoirs. I always wanted to travel."

"You can still do that. You only *look* older than you really are," I say. We break into laughter. Tears are running down Rocío's cheeks. She excuses herself to go to the bathroom before coming back and asking me her first direct question; I no longer exist in the third person.

"So, Raquel, what can we do to make things right from now on? Or are we going to live in the past?"

"Well, I'm not a born-again anything, so I do look back. It's what lets me know where I'm going, and it reminds me what I've learned in order to get here."

"So what is your verdict?"

"The verdict is still out," I say. I don't know how to tell her what my intuition is screaming into my ear, which is to run in the other direction as fast and far as I can. I decide to tell her a different truth. "I can tell you that I have no hatred for you or resentment. My wish for you is that you start taking care of yourself and focus on the kids hanging on *that* wall."

Rocío sàys nothing. She excuses herself to turn Jim over, which she has to do every couple of hours. "Are you sure you can't come back here for a few minutes? He really wants to meet you."

"No. No, thank you."

Rocío walks down the hall. "I think now is a good time to go," I whisper to Michelle. She agrees.

We slip out the front door and quietly walk to the driveway. I can see Rocío through the French-style windows of her bedroom. She looks beaten down and almost depressed as she preps her boyfriend to turn him over. I can see his emaciated body from the waist down.

Their codependent relationship works: Rocío and Jim reflect each other. What he is on the outside—immobile, wounded, and perhaps, unwanted—is likely what Rocío feels on the inside. I sit in the passenger seat of Michelle's silver Nissan Altima and watch my birth mother labor through the routine she's confined herself to for years now. I think this may be the last time we see each other in this lifetime.

"At first I was nervous about the situation escalating into a fight or something," Michelle says on the way to the hotel. "But it wasn't that bad at all. It was more like you two were acquaintances from long ago—a lot of heavy words were exchanged with no real chemistry from either side."

"You're right," I say. Rocío and her kids and I aren't close. And so life must go on, like it has before, but with more understanding. "I don't know if I'll bother telling her what her direct paternal origin is when that cousin you introduced me to on Facebook, the one from one of Papa's affairs before Mama, takes the Y-DNA test."

"Why didn't Uncle Antonio do it?" Michelle asks.

"To be honest, I think he just doesn't want to have anything to do with Papa. Who could blame him?" I reply. "But our cousin didn't hesitate and took the test as soon as I sent it to him. We don't stay in contact, either."

Antonio was the second person after Dad who agreed to take the test when I approached him about it months ago. However, when the Y-DNA kit arrived, he freaked out and disappeared for weeks. When

I caught Antonio on the phone, he said, "Why are you bothering me? Go fuck yourself."

"But what did I do?" I responded. "If you changed your mind, you should just have told me."

"I don't have time for your bullshit," he said, followed by "Don't call me anymore," to which I obliged.

For some, excavating the past isn't an adventure, it's more akin to tearing a Band-Aid off an open wound. Still, I didn't have time to wait and see whether he'd change his mind. Papa's spirit, or Michelle's know-how, led me down another, less dramatic avenue.

I am now halfway through my yearlong journey.

CHAPTER FIFTEEN

Flash of the Spirit

> You kept us caged in / Destroyed our culture and
> said that you civilized us / Raped our women and
> when we were born you despised us . . .
>
> —Immortal Technique, "The Third World"

I FIRST GOT INTO THE HABIT OF ARRIVING AT THE AIRPORT OVER
three hours ahead of schedule when Djali was a toddler. At four, she
became my travel buddy. If she didn't have school now, Djali would
have been standing on this long line next to me, rolling her eyes at this
all too familiar sight. As always, I'm stuck behind a family of seven
traveling with fifteen plastic-wrapped suitcases, a brood of screaming children to regulate, and impatient men in tow. This is par for
the course when heading anywhere in the Caribbean, but for some
reason, the drama is always super-sized when Santo Domingo is the
final destination.

By the time I arrive at the gate, I'm spent, and looking forward to
relaxing on this huge steel bird that'll drop me off in paradise in a matter of hours. A middle-aged woman, accompanied by an elderly man,
sits down in front of me. She is dressed in skintight black slacks and a

matching button-down shirt. Her face is many shades lighter than her hands and neck. Her electric-blue eyeliner takes me back to a school lunchroom in Yonkers, where Socorro tried to convince me that it brought out the blue specks in her almost black eyes.

The lady starts talking to the woman next to her like I imagine Hipólito Mejia would his boys in private. She's homesick and deliriously happy to be going back. "I just hope, just pray," she says in *campesinaese*, "that I don't run into any filthy *maldito haitianos* invading *mi barrio*." If the woman kept her mouth shut she could have easily been mistaken for West African or, to her horror, Haitian.

The lady next to her says nothing. She halfway smiles and looks at me like she's thinking, *Ven acá loca, have you not seen yourself in the mirror lately? Has living in this country not shown you that you ain't white?*

I can't help but blurt out, while looking squarely in the lady's direction, "Wow, what a stupid woman" in the relatively small lounge area. "Sonia Pierre you ain't."

The woman pretends not to hear me, but the people around her do, and a handful smirk, except her traveling companion, who hisses and sucks his teeth at me. Still. The acknowledgment from the handful of my compatriots makes me feel better about going back to the old country. I may be a bit idealistic, but transcultural *latinoamericanos*—rooted in the States with a foot firmly planted in our parents' respective homelands—might be impacting how some of our elders are starting to think about racial identity.

As we board the plane, the woman's neighbor says to me in Spanglish, "I'm glad you said something to that horrible *estúpida. Lo odio cuando una cabróna ruidosa* makes all of us look like we're in *those* times." The woman tells me she lives in Washington Heights and was born in Salcedo, the birthplace of the Mirabal sisters. I think I'm safe to assume that "*those* times" refers to the decades spanning Rafael Trujillo's evildoing, or perhaps the propagation of his ideals by Joaquín Balaguer for years after he was snuffed out in 1961. Though it's been over a half-century since his death, Trujillo's self-loathing legacy still haunts the Dominican consciousness both here and in *la república*.

"I couldn't help myself, that kind of talk gets me heated and anxious about visiting the country," I say. "I don't want to get into stupid arguments over there."

"Don't allow your mind to be stuck in *those* times either and write everyone off, or you'll just be acting as backward as that woman with the ridiculous face," says the woman, sliding into her designated aisle so that I can pass. "No disrespect, *mi hija,* but some of the Americans *de tú generación* think you're above it all, but you're just as bad, with all that 'nigga this' and '*mi* nigga, *mi* nigga, *dímelo locó'—eso sí está bastante feo.*"

I hate to admit it, but she's right. With the fusillade of "*this* nigga, my nigga, *that* nigga, come on *nigga, tú 'ta pasao* nigga, yo *nigga,* nigga look *good,* that nigga *crazy*" you hear walking down my block—any block, playground, post office, supermarket, gas station, restaurant, in any Latino 'hood, really—you wouldn't be too far off to think the word could be translated to mean everything from "friend," "foe," "please," "egg sandwich," and "How does my hair look?" If Latino-American rappers from Cypress Hill to Fat Joe and Immortal Technique want to truly rep what the streets are saying, they simply aren't dropping enough n-bombs into their lyrics. Today, I'd be embarrassed by my nineteen-year-old self for thinking it was somehow cool and revolutionary, in a hip-hop context, to drop it so often.

I walk all the way down near to the last aisle and sink into my way-worse-than-coach window seat. I don't care that the stench from the bathroom is already overpowering due to the many kids who haven't been able to make it to the toilet in time and peeing on the floor instead. I don't care that the loud family with fifteen plastic-wrapped suitcases is sitting in the aisles next to and behind me. I won't bark, "Yo, my little egg sandwich, can you *please* stop kicking me?" at one of the little rugrats sitting directly behind me who will kick the shit out of my seat for the duration of the three-and-a-half-hour flight. I'm starting to feel too excited to be going back to the island to even think about bugging out.

Instead, I'll spend the time rereading an interesting bit of information I recently stumbled upon when researching Latino migration to New York City. I've walked by the plaque many times in Riverside

Park, recognizing him as the first merchant and non-Native inhabitant of color on the island, but I never gave this guy, Jan Rodrigues (also spelled Juan Rodriguez), a thought until now.

Although he was the first non-Indigenous resident to live in Manhattan, Jan Rodrigues is sort of a footnote in New York City history. There's currently not a wealth of information on him other than a short, albeit dramatic, narrative he was at the center of and a few mind-blowing biographical details.

Jan was born Juan Rodrigues in Santo Domingo—that's right, today's Dominican Republic—to a Portuguese father and an African mother. There are few details describing what Rodrigues looked like: "black," "mulatto," and "black Spaniard."

Rodrigues arrived on the island of modern-day Manhattan in June 1613 as a crew member on the Dutch explorer Thijs Volchertz Mossel's *Jonge Tobias*. When Mossel broke out to Amsterdam shortly thereafter, leaving Rodrigues behind, allegedly over some major beef, the sailor was given eighty hatchets, knives, a musket, and a sword. This payment suggests that he was either a former soldier or could have been given an advance on future services, a common practice by sea captains who left crew members behind.

That August, Captain Hendrick Christiansen steered his vessel, the *Fortuyn*, to shore and anchored in Lenapehoking. There, Christiansen met Rodrigues—he introduced himself as "a free man"—and immediately solicited his services as an interpreter with the local Rockaway Indians. Rodrigues ultimately facilitated a trade agreement between the Indigenous-Americans and Christiansen.

All was well until Captain Mossel returned on the *Jonge Tobias* in April of the following year. Vexed as hell by all accounts, he contributed a new adjective to describe Rodrigues in the annals of early New York City history: "black rascal." What ensued was like a scene out of *The Warriors*: Mossel, feeling too betrayed and distraught to go to fisticuffs with Rodrigues himself, sent his crew to jump him, leaving the Dominican man wounded. If not for the intervention of Christiansen's posse, Rodrigues's story likely would have ended right there and then.

Juan Rodrigues, the first freeman of mixed African and European descent to live in Manhattan (he was also the first recorded resident of Governors Island), the first Dominican, and the first person who was racially, ethnically, and culturally similar to modern-day Latinos, disappeared—on paper. There are no records of his death or any more dramas he may have costarred in. What we do know is that Rodrigues, like too many Dominican men before and after him, is said to have fathered several children with Indigenous Rockaway women.

Depending on whom you ask, Rodrigues could be painted as a shady opportunist or a shrewd businessman. What's arguably most interesting about the scant details of his life isn't what he did but how he went about doing things in Manhattan. His facility with the Indigenous-American language was a bonus. It was Rodrigues's trans-cultural skills that made him an exemplary settler because he managed to set up shop as a successful trader and eke out a comfortable life in Manhattan without slaughtering or displacing the island's original inhabitants, but by living peacefully among them.

My spirits aren't broken as much as they are frazzled once we land in Las Américas International Airport. I clap louder than anyone else in the ass-crack section of coach the instant the wheels touch down on the runway. *La familia* Saran Wrap have been screaming at one another since we took off about nothing in particular. The little girl sitting behind me doesn't miss a beat, kicking what feels like Wilfrido Vargas's merengue anthem *"El Baile del Perrito,"* on the back of my seat while we wait in the humid cabin for almost an hour for a gate to become available.

I turn on my iPhone and browse through the photos my grand-mother lent me to scan. There are several photos I've come across at different times over the years: Rocío and my aunt Paloma as children; Mama and Papa's wedding; me as a baby in Santo Domingo posing with Antonio, Paloma, my poodle Oliver, my grandparents, and my favorite toy, a Donald Duck mobile. A photo of a born-again virginal Rocío in a white wedding dress with poufy sleeves, gazing into the goat castrator's eyes on their wedding day, makes me laugh out loud every time I see it.

There are also photos I've never seen until recently. There's one of Rocío's maternal grandfather, a tobacco-colored impeccably dressed man with severely slanted eyes and a full head of neatly coiffed hair. There's a picture of a couple of Don Manuel's sisters, one whose features probably favor her father Elpidio's Haitian mother, holding a baby Rocío on her lap. I'd never seen a photo of Elpidio's mother but was told her last name was Durán and that she was either Haitian or half Haitian. Papa's mother, Emilia, a woman whose own mother was born in Puerto Rico, is as hard on the eyes as I remember her being in person. She is posing with her head covered and wearing clothes that hide her figure. There's an air of ice-cold prudishness about her that still makes me shiver.

There's a photo of an annoyed Don Manuel and a giddy teenage Rocío on the day of her wedding to Dad at Paraíso. Papa looks disgusted as he walks his firstborn down the makeshift aisle, surely regretting the day he allowed the esteemed doctor Antonio Zaglul to intervene on the couple's behalf. I'm told that the flower girl marching in front of them became a drug addict and died of an overdose when she grew up.

Then there's Casilda, Ismael's mother, Dad's paternal grandmother. I know so little about Dad's side of the family, and like him, I am mostly indifferent toward them. Casilda's photograph is the most striking out of the bunch because she's such a mystery, especially now that Dad told me she was a seer. Her hair is pulled back in a bun, showcasing a face that is somewhere between beautiful and handsome. The world is reflected in her features: epicanthic eye folds, a wide nose, and full, unsmiling lips. The photo looks like it was taken for official use; the rust from an old staple marks the upper right corner of the small sepia head shot. I am hoping to trace Casilda's direct maternal ancestry on this trip if her only living son, Dad's uncle Arquimedes, agrees to let me scrape his cheeks.

Making my way out of the terminal in Santo Domingo, I try not to look like a zombie as I pass the throngs of people waiting impatiently for family members and would-be theft victims. It's hard to tell who's who in the sea of smiling faces cheerfully waving by the exit.

The biggest mistake at this airport is to look or act like you don't know where you're going or whom you're meeting, even if you're of Dominican descent. An acquaintance from a local nongovernmental organization emailed me something I dismissed as hyperbole back home. I asked her why, after watching a news story on Spanish-language news, there are so many iron barriers enclosing homes in the capital. Why are people locking their homes from the inside, making sections of Santo Domingo look like gated Hasidic neighborhoods dotting Brooklyn. She wrote me back that Santo Domingo is almost like Miami in the 1970s and '80s, with cocaine cowboys running amok, fanning a rise in overall crime. The gates have become a part of life on this island. Yesterday's *conquistadores,* capitalists, and missionaries are today's drug lords, capitalists, and underpaid policemen, all profiteering off the misery they fuel.

My *paraíso,* it seems, has been riddled with bullets and gaping holes from Tony Montana's souped-up M16 assault rifle–grenade launcher. Yet I have learned to love this place over the years, for better and worse, almost as much as I did and do New York City since moving back in the '80s, bullet holes and all.

I nod and smile at folks waiting for family members. Dominicans carry within them the history of the island in their phenotypes as much as they do in their blood. I see a collage of pre-Columbian, African, and European history on their bodies though it's difficult for many of us to see ourselves as being more than different shades of white. Over the years, people have told me that there isn't such thing as a Taíno or African left in the Dominican Republic. They are right—there is no such thing as a pure *anyone* on the island, much less a pure Spaniard or European. The *fukú* many people here and the world over shoulder is a bad case of Stockholm syndrome for their colonial masters.

I look through the crowd for the driver I arranged to pick me up, a man named Lenin, whom I quiz before agreeing to leave the airport with him. Driving down El Malecón makes me feel like I'm back home—not my home, exactly, but a close relative or friend's home—

where there is an abundance of *confianza*. This is a place where magic happens but where I know better than to overstay my welcome.

This is how spirit works here if you allow intuition, or your *guías*, to lead the way. Less than two years ago, I came to Santo Domingo to partake in an international film festival. I didn't call the only person I knew in the city, my aunt Paloma, whom I'd lost contact with over the years. On our day off, I decided to hang out with my then-fiancé Sacha, in the city's Zona Colonial, a district where I lived with Rocío for a spell and went to grammar school.

I asked my assigned festival driver to drop Sacha and me anywhere near the Mercado Modelo, a large, mostly indoor market where one can buy an array of typical souvenirs, from mamajuana, amber and larimar jewelry, paintings, and carnival masks to love potions, tambora drums, and tambourines. Botanicas, or spiritual pharmacies, where people can buy whatever they're prescribed to appease the African gods and Indigenous spirits who still charge the land, line the back entrance of the *mercado*.

"*Por favor*, drop me off anywhere near Avenida Mella," I tell our driver.

"No, you don't want to go around there, even with that tall boyfriend of yours," he responded. This guy's job was to make sure I showed up on time to my scheduled panels and other mandatory events. Because I was *casi una dominicana*, almost a Dominican, he felt the area was too dangerous. He persisted. "There's nothing of quality here, and it's getting so dangerous, especially for foreigners."

I said nothing. Rather, I suppressed an overwhelming feeling to deck this guy and opened the door the next time he stopped, motioning for Sacha to follow me out of the car.

The street was, as it has always been, teeming with activity. Old men sat drinking *café*. Haitian men and children selling oranges and vendors harassing people to drop cash in their shops made the street challenging to navigate. Teenage guys and young men, dressed in jeans cinched below their asses in an array of bootleg urban clothing brands, gave the old streets the appearance of a hot summer day on Dyckman. Instead of yelling steady clips of "*mira, my nigga, yo, nigga, y que,* my nigga," the youngish toughs spent their time catcalling the mostly white American and European female tourists shopping in the area. "*Mira, ma-mi, mami, mami, ma-mi, MAMI, ay, que abusadora.*"

As stupid as these guys sounded, handfuls of women stopped to flirt and talk to them. They had their pick. Every taste, as mixed an array as one can find in a large box of chocolates, was represented on the streets: short and long, round and thin, dark to white chocolate, some fruity and others nutty. The potential pot of gold waiting on the other side of the rainbow inspired some to hop on the hanky-panky gravy train and get paid, a prospect to consider in a country where 21 percent of the young men between the ages of fifteen to twenty-four are unemployed.

We walked up the steps to the back entrance of the market. I stopped to ask a vendor if there'd been a surge in popularity of all things botanica, because I didn't remember seeing so many lining the steps of the *mercado*. Maybe I just hadn't paid attention.

"*Ay, mi hija,* I don't really know," said a vendor. "You should go to San Miguel, the first botanica to your left at the top of the stairs, and ask the owner—he and his brother are the *mercado's* largest suppliers of spiritual products."

Though pretty small, San Miguel was fly in comparison to the other spiritual bodegas in the area. An oil painting of the divine dragon slayer that once stood watch behind Maria and Casimiro's door, and others depicting Dominican life, lined the wall outside San Miguel. Even in the dim light, I could see that all the products were stacked meticulously.

The *collales,* or colored beads strung into a series of protective necklaces representing the different gods and spirits, glittered. Every *Chango Macho, Niño de Antocha, Virgen de la Altagracia,* and other saints were lined up like soldiers in formation. The lucky perfume and spiritual water labels faced the front and sparkled as if they had been dusted that morning. The smell of fresh herbs permeated the air.

The customer service wasn't nearly as good as the presentation. A woman wearing glasses, with long raven hair, sat eating lunch toward the back of the botanica, ignoring me as I tried making small talk. A short burnt caramel–complected man in slacks spoke loudly, even by Dominican standards, to someone at the other end.

"Is that the owner of this botanica?" I asked the woman.

"*Sí.*" She nodded. "He's on the phone with a sister-in-law who's very old."

I looked around the tiny store, giving myself two more minutes before promising Sacha we'd jet. As I nodded goodbye to the apathetic woman and started to leave, I caught a section of products labeled "Cepeda." I picked up a bottle of honey and told the woman, "My last name is also Cepeda."

"That's nice," she said. "My husband on the phone is a Cepeda." She went back to eating.

The man turned around, still on the phone, to change positions. I noticed he wore a mustache and a button-down green gingham shirt, a bit formal for botanica wear. His complexion was as dark as Dad's would be if he lived in the tropics. The man looked at me and smiled and put his call on hold. "*Hola,* do you want to buy that bottle of honey?"

"Yes, it would be great to take back home to New York as a *recuerdo,* because my last name is also Cepeda."

"Is that so?" he asked. "Are you visiting any Cepeda relatives here?"

"No, I don't know anyone on my dad's side here. I know they exist, but I grew up knowing more people on my mother's side, and most are living in the States now."

The man's face grew serious. He scanned me from head to toe. "Can I ask you a question? What's your father's name?" I tell him. "*Ay, mira eso,*" he told his wife. "I'm her father's uncle, and she's my great-niece." He turned to me. "Your father's father and I had the same father and were raised together."

"I'm talking to my sister-in-law, who just saw your father when she was in Nueva York," added the man, who hold me his name was Jorge. "Let me take you across the hall to Botanica St. Elias to meet your father's other uncle. He is maybe even younger than you are."

"This is so weird," I told Sacha as we headed across the hall. "In a city of more than two-point-two million people in a country about twice the size of New Hampshire, I meet *this* guy?"

"There are no coincidences, Raquel," said Jorge. *"Nos vemos pronto."* *Of course there aren't,* I thought. *There is only divine time.*

And this time will be no different.

I came to *la capital* with a long list of things to do while in town, which will have to be dramatically cut down because, well, I'm here.

Things don't get done in Santo Domingo on anybody's time. The traffic here rivals that of Calcutta and Mexico City, especially in the afternoon. What should be a six-minute car ride without traffic will take at least thirty on the narrow roadways, busting at the seams with *guaguas,* taxis, trucks, women barely holding on to newborn babies and small children on rickety *motoconchos,* and horse carts. On the way to the Zona Colonial, I see impossibly old women selling newspapers by the traffic lights under the unforgiving sun, and homeless Dominican and Dominican-Haitian kids, and Haitian children, many smuggled in scores by Haitian traffickers after the earthquake, peddling whatever, to make their daily quotas.

The cabdriver comes to a screeching halt on the charming Calle Las Mercedes. I stumble out of the car. I'm dizzy from inhaling toxic fumes and emotionally drained. As many forgotten children as I've seen and met across continents—the homeless, the sexually abused, those who have miraculously survived being set ablaze, the amputated, the starving, the hated—I have not yet come across a face that has been able to desensitize me. Somehow the bags I'm carrying become heavier with pessimism.

The streets are almost empty at lunchtime, when people retreat into restaurants and bodegas to eat. I rush toward the former residence of the country's twenty-second (twenty-fifth and twenty-sixth) president, Ulises Heureaux—it's now home to the *Academia Dominicana de la*

Historia—to visit its elusive director, Frank Moya Pons. Moya Pons has written more about the history of this island and the rest of the Caribbean than one can possibly read in a lifetime. If any person can steer me in the right direction, it is *El Maestro,* the man I affectionately call The Teacher.

I'm a few minutes late for our lunch meeting. "Excuse me," I ask a receptionist on the second floor, "is Dr. Moya Pons here? He's expecting me for lunch."

"Yes, he *was* expecting you a little earlier," she responds, barely looking up from the stacks of paperwork mounted on her large wooden desk. "He couldn't wait for you anymore. He's out to lunch. I will tell him you came by."

The one person in the entire country upon whom I don't want to make a bad impression has left the building, or rather, the dreamy two-story Spanish colonial mini-manse. ¡*Carajo!*

I stand by the entrance of the *academia* for a few minutes, looking down both sides of the street, trying to guess which route will take me longer to arrive at my great-uncle Jorge's botanica.

I want to spend a few hours lost in this district of ghosts, to share the narrow sidewalks with them and the tourists, the white- and blue-collar workers, the shoe shiners, stray dogs, and squatters who've bum-rushed entire buildings in the area. This colorful district is as complicated as it was when it was first established in 1498 by Bartolomé Colón, the younger brother of the New World's greatest Space Invader, after the epic failures that were La Isabela in 1494, and La Navidad in 1492 in modern-day Haiti. The third try to establish a city—this time erected on the southern coast of the island—proved a charm for Bartolomé and the European settlers. Originally coined La Nueva Isabela and later renamed Santo Domingo, the settlement, for the most part, jumped off. Today the area is called the Ciudad Colonial and, colloquially, La Zona.

Let me backtrack a bit.

There were human beings living on the island of Hispaniola, née Quisqueya, before Cristóbal Colón's arrival (to use the name *il italiano* answered to back then). The Indigenous people of Quisqueya and the surrounding islands had gradually made their way to the region in four waves from the Orinoco Delta, starting between 400 and 3000 BC.

The first group of migrants were nomadic people who made do living in natural shelters like caves, rivers, and inlets, subsisting on fish. The Andalusian-born chronicler and priest Bartolomé de las Casas—we will revisit him later—met some of them in the 1500s living in Punta Tiburón on the west side of the island, modern-day Haiti, and on the far west side of Cuba. He called them Ciboneys.

The second group were masterful ceramicists descending from the Arawaks, who still live in the tropical rain forests of South America. They eventually broke out and spread throughout parts of Hispaniola and Puerto Rico and most of the Lesser Antilles, absorbing and displacing the aforementioned wave of Amerindians. The Igneri, as they are traditionally known, were fishermen, farmers, and hunters.

The third group covered an extensive wave of Arawak-descended people from modern-day Venezuela and Guyana called the Taínos, meaning "noble" and "good" people. Their movement lasted about a thousand years, and they absorbed and eliminated some of their pre-Columbian predecessors. Taínos, who themselves were mixed with other Antillean groups of Amerindians, were masterful pharmacists, artists, and inventors. They learned how to strain cyanide from yucca to make a staple we eat on the island today, called cassava bread. They could hunt, farm, fish, and cure almost anything with their knowledge of herbs and nature. They built large canoes to travel between islands, developed biological warfare in the form of pepper gas, and contributed words to the Dominican and North American vocabulary we use today. If not for the Taínos, there would be no hammocks, or *hamacas,* to nap in after stuffing ourselves with barbecue, or *barbacoa.*

The last wave, the Caribs, were also descendants of the Arawak but differed from the Taínos in that they were already skilled and more developed navigators and hunters, wicked with the bow and arrow.

At the time of Colón's arrival, the Taínos were thriving in and controlling most of the Greater Antilles. They discovered the admiral and his crew on Christmas Eve 1492 after his flagship, the *Santa Maria,* ran aground on the northern coast of modern-day Haiti. Colón observed that some of the Taínos were rocking gold ornaments, which compelled him to leave behind the thirty-nine crewmen who couldn't fit on the two remaining smaller vessels, the *Pinta* and *Niña,* to construct a fort out of the remnants of the ship. Upon his return from Spain a year later, the admiral found that all of the men in his crew had been killed for raping the Indigenous women and killing some of the men. *So, what now?* Colón must have thought.

The admiral decided he would establish the formal American colony farther east from La Navidad, in modern-day Puerto Plata. He named the settlement La Isabela in January 1494, in honor of his Spanish patroness. Almost immediately after the establishment of the intended commercial outposts, all sorts of maladies plagued the settlers, causing illness and death. There was a shortage of labor, food, and medicine. To make matters worse, members of the Spanish lesser nobility started to bug the hell out when Colón suggested—in what one might consider a pre-Communist move—that everyone work without the distinction of social rank. Things went from bad to worse. Colón lost control, and his paranoia ultimately led to the unleashing of two violent military campaigns against the Taínos. Colón had high hopes of trying to make slaves out of the *indios* in order to appease the disgruntled capitalists up north. It's a good thing for future colonialists that the admiral kept hope alive.

The Taínos and Caribs were enemies, which made it fairly easy to divide and conquer them. There is a school of thought that persists about the Caribs raiding Taíno villages to feast on the flesh of Taíno men and enslave the women as cooks and concubines. While warring tribes across the globe have ritualistically tasted and eaten parts of their enemies, there's another, more plausible way to look at the picture. It's possible that the Taínos may have bloated the facts about their foes to the Spanish, who in turn never questioned them; they simply took note of the accounts without investigating whether they were true. This version of events could be used to justify the need to save the savage souls on the island to their hard-core Catholic masters on the throne back home. Whatever the case, it worked.

On December 20, 1503, the Spanish Crown legally sanctioned Indigenous slavery in the form of *encomiendas*—under the condition, naturally, that the slave masters would teach their captives the Catholic faith. It was a win-win situation. For being exemplary Catholics, the Spaniards on the island were rewarded with VIP passes to heaven and the free labor they desperately needed to extract gold from the mines and toil the colonial plantations. And the Taínos? They got to learn all about and, because of severely shortened life spans under Spanish rule, meet Jesus at the gates of heaven before their European masters.

The earliest days of contact (forced and otherwise) between the Spaniards and Taínos resulted in children with mixed destinies. Some were recognized by their Spanish parents and totally assimilated into European culture. Some moved back to Spain with their parents, and others blended in with the colonial communities across the island. The majority, however, maintained their mothers' inferior social status in the community.

Although the invasion of the island of Hispaniola was *the* American colonial springboard, what happened to the Taínos at the hands of the colonists is one of those ungodly narratives that played itself out over and over throughout the Caribbean and the Americas. One can substitute Columbus and the Taínos with any number of explorers and the people who had the misfortune of discovering them. On the island of Hispaniola, the effects were devastating.

During the first few decades of Spanish occupation, the numbers of Taínos decreased at a rapid-fire pace. They had no defenses against a laundry list of European diseases that included smallpox and the measles; some committed suicide rather than live as slaves; some died in combat, raging against the colonial machine; and countless others fled to the mountains, caves, and other hiding places beyond their enemies' reach. Some scholars estimate that the Taíno population, reaching upward of three million in Hispaniola, was wiped out in the first few decades of European occupation, with clusters surviving around the Caribbean.

The Spanish chroniclers and census takers may have gotten it all wrong. We need to revisit these numbers. As in the rest of the Americas, there was no way to account for the Taínos who revolted, escaped, and found ways to survive and resist European colonialism. Taínos contributed much more than cassava bread to the Dominican Republic: They left a genetic imprint, a footnote that reads, "We may not be living in huts or dressing in the traditional garb of our ancestors, but we're here, albeit in fragments."

In the 1950s, before ancestral DNA testing, researchers studied a fairly new popular Taíno settlement in the northeast, originally founded by Enrique, one of the last caciques of the colonial period. They saw high percentages of blood types found in Indigenous-Native-Americans: O positive, with no Rh-negative factor, like Dad. In the '70s, they studied dental records that proved Indigenous retention in the same village: shovel-shaped incisors in thirty-three out of seventy-four people, also characteristic of Native-Americans and their Asian ancestors.

In 2006 a national haplogroup-A mitochondrial DNA survey on the island examined hair root samples taken from sites throughout the Dominican Republic. The results indicated that the northern, central, and eastern regions of the country had the highest percentage of Amerindian ancestry. Hapologroups B and C obtained higher frequencies in the east, and one of only two samples taken in the west belonged to haplogroup A. When further analyses were conducted on the haplogroup A samples, nine lineages were identified in the Dominican Republic: three post-Columbian and six pre-Columbian.

Studies with healthier population samples should be undertaken because the Dominican Republic currently has a population of over ten million people. If more studies are done, more pre-Columbian history—silenced due to genocide by academia and European chroniclers—will reveal a rich and diverse narrative.

I find my great-uncle Jorge helping a customer at his botanica San Miguel. It's a shame I can't collect a DNA sample from him; Jorge and Dad's father had different mothers. Before I left, Dad told me that his father's oldest full brother, Arquimedes, was still alive, so I packed a mitochondrial DNA kit, hoping to trace my grandfather Ismael's direct maternal ancestry. Dad and Jorge tell me that Arquimedes's greatest asset is his photographic memory: he could recall dates and details of events as if they had happened earlier in the day.

Jorge offers me a cold *cerveza* and a seat. "I was told you were coming back to interview Arquimedes," he says, "but is there anything I can help you with?"

"Yes, I want to know how you got into the African and Indigenous spiritual business. Why are you even interested in it?"

"There are things in our blood that are just naturally passed down to us, whether we want to recognize them or not."

"Like what?"

"How do I tell you?" he says. "Here we are Catholics because we believe in God. We are believers of the spirits, too, but we don't put *fukú* or throw *brujería* on anybody. We sell things like any pharmacy would." Jorge pauses to help a woman looking for an herb associated with *La Virgen de la Altagracia*. He continues, "God gave everyone gifts, and because of genetics, many men and women in our father's line have been given the ability to see things, to transmit spirits and such."

"I've heard stories—"

Jorge excuses himself to help a woman looking for herbs she can wash with in order to conceive.

My stomach churns. Until now, the few people I've met on Dad's side have been zealously staunch church ladies, the kind of killjoys who made Dana Carvey's *Saturday Night Live* Church Lady come across like Mary Magdalene when she was tricking. I remember one summer when my aunt Esperanza asked her son's friend, "Are you the son of the devil?" with unnerving calm. "Because we know that his children are left-handed." I almost choked on pizza crust as the boy sat there, speechless and confused.

Years later, Esperanza and Rebecca—I had just met Rebecca, Ercilia's daughter from the next man—asked if I thought gay people would go to hell on Judgment Day.

"If I were God, I would send all the deadbeat dads to hell first, rather than a guy just because he is gay."

"*Ay, Dios mío que estas en el bendito cielo.*" Esperanza gasped, clenching her blouse as if she were about to have a nervous break-down. "I can't believe you would think such a thing."

I wonder what Ercilia and her daughters would say, watching Jorge carefully attend to one person after another looking for saints, special herbs, and prescriptions for all sorts of universal maladies like revers-ing bad luck, enticing a lover back, losing weight, or getting rid of a husband's mistress.

"On your father's father's side, we ride a different current," says Jorge.

I've heard different versions of the same story since I was a kid liv-ing in Paraíso. I was told that once upon a time, in a *barrio* not far from here, a man was accused of sexually assaulting a young child. He ran into someone from the Cepeda family who told him, "Listen, *if* you did commit this unjust crime against an innocent, you will lose the hand you used as a weapon." The man laughed and went on his way. Very soon thereafter, the alleged pedophile, a factory worker, lost his arm in an accident on the job.

"Is this true?" I ask Jorge.

"Oh yes," he says. "There are many stories like that out there about us."

"You know that my father also has religious fanatics in his family," I say.

"Sure, some people take after their mothers, and others somehow remember what's in their father's genes.

"Look at you, for instance. I can see that you were born and basi-cally raised over in that land, and still you walk with spirits, like part of your family does here," Jorge says. "I know you can see things."

CHAPTER SIXTEEN

She Who Walks
Behind Me

My guess is that it comes from the mother
or, at least, from her spirit.

—LEWIS HYDE, *THE GIFT*

BEFORE WE GET INTO THE SUBJECT OF "SEEING," JORGE EXCUSES
himself to help another customer fill a spiritual prescription. "*Por
favor, Doctor,* a bath to help me sweeten my aura for my husband," an
older woman says. Jorge takes her to his brother's botanica across the
way. The last time I was here, I noticed his brother had a wall full of
colorful baths for every ailment I could think of.

To kill time, I take out my iPhone and scroll through my texts and
inbox. I come across an automated email from Family Tree DNA, stating that a new result has been posted to my page. I follow the link to
find that Dad's mitochondrial DNA results have come back from the
lab. I sit on the wooden crate and stare at the link. I have no freaking
clue what to expect. This news will change everything. Maybe I'll finally be able to place Dad in Matanga after all, or perhaps I'll find out

that we are Jewish. If the latter turns out to be true, Dad—who wrongly associates whiteness with Jewishness—will hold it over my head for all eternity. I hold my breath and click on the link.

To my astonishment, I find out that Dad's direct maternal ancestors fall under haplogroup A. Ercilia's most recent ancestor was Indigenous, which in the Dominican Republic means Amerindian or Taíno. Dad has no matches in Family Tree DNA's database as of this printing. Despite what history has told us about their fate, the Indigenous islanders have managed to survive, like their European and African counterparts, in varying proportions.

La india. This woman has come up over and over again throughout my life. When I think about the notion of *una india,* an Amerindian or Indigenous-American spiritual guide illuminating my path, I'm not terribly surprised, but I didn't expect this guardian angel to come courtesy of Ercilia.

"*Mira, mi hija,*" an old woman sitting next to me on the A train once said, "*tu camina con una guerrera india.*" I was a teenager and didn't fully understand what she meant—I couldn't see anyone walking with or behind me, much less an Indigenous-American warrior. I smiled and brushed her off as crazy. *No one is walking with me—I'm sitting!*

Casimiro tried to explain what the lady meant by *guías espirituales,* or spiritual guides, when I mentioned what happened on the train to him. "These are *seres incorpóreos* that lead you out of the womb and remain with you all your life, guiding you," he said, "and some of these spirit beings can come in the form of one or more of your *antepasados,* your ancestors." I snapped, "Oh yeah? Well, tell *la india* to deliver me from Papi, then."

Years later, I was taking a stroll in East Harlem with my then-infant daughter. We went inside a popular botanica to buy incense and sage to burn in our apartment. The woman behind the counter walked over to me and said, "Oh, you're here for the *india* statue, right?" I told her I wasn't. "Well, then," said the woman, "you should strongly consider getting one to keep in your home. I think you owe it to your guide."

Again I dismissed it. I often took for granted the messages I received from the world as new age shit, rather than show our culture and belief systems any respect. Today it's all starting to make sense.

Maybe this is what Ercilia meant when she told me in my dream on that August day in Boston that things would start making sense someday. Perhaps those spirits, those ancestors, had something to do with my being here. In fact, I'm sure of it.

Jorge walks back in and sits on the crate next to mine. "*Sabes,* I'm also blessed with the gift of seeing," he says. "You see how we met, right? So is this not true?"

I wish I could sit here all afternoon and listen to Jorge opening one proverbial door after another, granting me access to parts of my self I've second-guessed most of my life. Soon people start lining up again to consult with the spiritual pharmacist. It's time for me to go. "I'll see you soon," I say. He doesn't respond.

The sun is starting to set in the Zona Colonial as I make my way to El Conde, the district's crowded thoroughfare, to catch a cab back toward Avenida Anacaona. I look up and see a family of squatters on the second floor of a colonial home. The mother has dark brown skin and thick braided hair. Her daughter, hanging wet laundry on the house's iron gates, has long straight hair and light-colored eyes, either hazel or green. Looking at the people walking past me on the streets and thinking back to the photographs I viewed on the plane—especially Casilda's—I'm left wanting to know more about where our ancestors came from.

Groups of very young women are starting their shifts on El Conde. They'll spend the rest of the evening walking up and down the *avenida* in tight jeans and high heels until some man, any man, rents them for the night or the duration of his stay on the island.

I sit and wait for a cab on a bench in Parque Colón, watching shoe shiners—all of whom are small children—fight for customers. Pigeons are shitting all over a bronze statue of the admiral pointing off to somewhere in the distance, as an Indigenous woman—presumably the female chieftain, Anacaona, hanged by the Spaniards in 1503—is frozen in time climbing up toward Columbus. Families are eating ice cream while their children play tag and taunt the stray dogs that are a fixture all over the Zona Colonial. I wonder if Dad's father ever played with him here, or in any park, at least once before throwing him out on the street.

I've been waiting all day to jump on Skype with Djali so I can break the mitochondrial news to Dad, who's staying at my place while I'm away.

"Hi, *dah'ling*, you're as sweet as a lemon," Dad says, "have I told you that?" Djali cracks up in the background.

"Talking to you is always a pleasure, Dad, like drinking a tall glass of vinegar."

"Wow, that is *so, so nice*," he responds.

"Dad, so, I received the results of your direct maternal ancestry today by email," I say. "You're not Jewish on your mother's side."

"*Oh*, really?" asks Dad. "Then what am I?"

"You came out to have a direct maternal ancestry that points to pre-Columbian *indios* on the island," I say.

Dad looks confused. "What do you mean, like *dose* Taínos?" he asks. "They were all killed—it was a *terrible* thing."

"This DNA stuff is proving that they still exist."

"There is no such thing as an Indian," Dad says, laughing. "Are you making these things up, or are you *crazy*?"

"There is no such thing as a pure Spaniard on the island, either, unless someone moved here from Madrid last week."

"I don't know, maybe I have Mongoloid blood," says Alice into the camera. She is blocking Dad from view.

"What does this have to do with you—*Jesus Christ*, Dad—" I yell.

"*Dah'ling*, please, it's not with *you*," he says, a decibel away from yelling at Alice.

"But I—" Alice says. "I'm just saying that Finns have high cheekbones and, and—"

I'm desperate. "Dad, Skype costs a lot of money to use," I lie. "Tell her to go somewhere." It works. "Dad, I'm hoping to see Arquimedes next week," I say. "I'm calling him next."

"Just don't embarrass me," he says. "You know how you can talk."

"Any woman who has an opinion embarrasses you."

"Oh, isn't that *nice,*" says Dad. "Just do *not* embarrass *me.*"

The phone rings once, twice, three times. The anticipation makes my knees buckle. I feel as uneasy as I did the day Maria made me walk up and down her hallway in a pair of her open-toed *tacónes.* She hoped that learning how to walk in high heels would make me more feminine. My wide feet busted out of every opening, making each step more painful than the last, and my knees tremble in agony.

This is what calling Arquimedes's home feels like. He is the closest living relative to the man who is likely responsible for Dad's own arrested development and wack parenting skills.

"Buenas," says the woman who answers the phone. I stop pacing back and forth in the living room and sink into the couch. The woman, part servant and part caretaker to Arquimedes and his elderly wife, passes the phone to the Mrs.

"We've been expecting your call," the Mrs. says, flatly. "Your father told us something about an interview." I feel like I'm talking to a secretary and not a relative. The truth is, I deserve nothing more. Arquimedes's daughter lived up the block from Dad, and I never visited or committed her name to memory. For years, the fact that she was Dad's relative was enough to turn me off. That said, I felt lucky that Dad's uncle would agree to an interview.

"Yes, *sí, sí, señora,* I will come to you," I yell into the receiver as loudly as Jorge did back when I first met him at his botanica. I stare at Casilda's photo as the Mrs. talks about her last visit to New York City a few months ago. *La africana* never revealed her face in my dreams before, but there's something about Casilda's photo that evokes her teflon spirit. For some reason I can't explain, I'm drawn to Dad's grandmother. "Yes, so we will expect to see you then," the Mrs. says after we settle on a date and time for me to visit the couple in Santiago, where they recently retired, and then I jump off the phone.

I think back to the afternoon Dad gave me Casilda's photo.

"I'm telling *you*—my grandmo'ther *say* right before I left, *days* before, 'Something *bery,* bery *bad* is going to happen to *you,* but *you will not* die from it, but it will be like something you will not see coming,' " Dad said. "And I knew when things got *bery bad* that I wouldn't *be* killed *and* I would not die during *that* time." Dad never told his grandmother what happened. I wonder where she received that prescient information. If her feelings were so strong, why did she let Dad leave in the first place? Perhaps to Casilda, destiny was fixed, regardless of whether she saw the shit before it hit the fan.

I'm reminded of a dream I had while I was still at St. Thaddeus that I believe saved my life. In it, a shiny black truck emerges from the ground on Seaman Avenue, leaving a large gaping hole in its wake. I turn around to find the truck driving slowly behind me. I veer into the woods, and the truck trails behind. I run into the middle of the street, and the monster truck follows. Nobody can hear me scream or cry for help. No matter which way I turn, the truck emerges like a bully and stops me in my tracks. A tall, thin mahogany-hued man dressed in a shiny black suit and top hat steps out of the truck. The man has long curly black hair pulled into a ponytail. He turns to me and says, "Get into the truck, Raquel."

I run as fast as I can to Mighty Burger, on the corner of 207th and Broadway, and tell a woman working behind the counter that a creepy man and his truck are following me. The man drives his truck by the eatery, stopping to smile and wave at me. I can hear what he's thinking: "I'll see you again real soon."

I was so shaken that I awoke almost drowning in my own sweat. After that dream, I was on alert for months, taking note of who was walking and driving beside me on the desolate streets. I looked both ways before crossing and shuddered every time I saw a black truck.

Then it happened. I was late, rushing down Seaman Avenue with my headphones on, in a rap-induced daze. I felt safer because the sun had started to shine earlier in the day, so I let my guard down. The only real sign that winter was still here was a trace of gray and yellow snow melting on the wet sidewalk.

I noticed a black car that looked like a jitney cab driving slowly alongside me. It sped ahead, then stopped at the red light on the corner. It was the same street where the black truck of my dream had torn through the ground. The driver stepped out of the car. He was dressed in black from his fedora to his shoes. He peered at me and pointed at the passenger seat next to him.

"Leave me alone, you fucking pervert," I yelled at the man. "I knew you were coming."

The man smiled. My legs felt like they would give out. He got back into his car and drove circles around every street I walked on: Cooper, 207th, Tenth Avenue, 204th . . . He drove by St. Thaddeus. I don't think I've ever been as happy to be in school as I was that morning.

I knew better than to tell the police. And Dad never seemed to give a shit about anything I told him that didn't have to do with tennis. One afternoon after practice, I was sitting on a bench by the flagpole next to the baseball field. A middle-aged bald white guy wearing a tank top and short running shorts hissed at me from above. I looked up to find a very small man looking down at me. When he was sure I was watching, he began stroking the bright red balls exposed from the side of his shorts. I started yelling, "You dirty shit! Fucking pervert!," but he kept going until an older woman walked over and I pointed him out. The bald man bolted. I ran over to Dad to tell him what had happened, and he shushed me away. "I'm in the middle of a *game*," he said. "Get *outta* here!"

I wondered if the man in the black car was scoping me out in the park that summer and became convinced that nobody would notice if I vanished, or if it was just a freaky coincidence. Although I struggled with spiritual cynicism for most of my life, I couldn't ignore feeling that someone or something had sent me that warning in a dream.

Instinctively, I wrap my left hand tightly around my right as the cab-driver slows on Arzobispo Nouel in the Zona Colonial. I feel an infinite number of tiny needles piercing my hand, and my knuckles are tingling. We stop in front of Colegio Mahatma Gandhi. I'm early for my next meeting and ask the driver to drop me off here.

"Do you know someone who goes there?" he asks.

"I used to."

I walk through the gate slowly, rubbing my wet hands together. No kids are in school today. I don't know if they're out or on vacation.

"*Hola, señora,* do you mind if I take a quick walk around? I went to school here when I was little—"

"Just hurry." The woman doesn't smile back. She is as frigid as the folks I remember who taught and worked here. The building is decrepit, like the less frequented side streets around the Colonial Zone, sagging and cracking all over itself. The walls are sweating and the air is dank though the tiny classrooms are empty.

I've been in this room before. I can't remember learning a thing here, but the sound—the loud whack of a thick wooden ruler smashing against my small hands and knuckles—is echoing in my head.

"That is wrong!" I remember a teacher yelling. "Come up here and stick your hand out, *estúpida!*"

CRACK! CRACK! I wouldn't make noise, infuriating the teacher and making my classmates giggle.

"Oh, you're going to be defiant Raquelita?" the teacher said calmly, sweat pouring down her forehead like that of Ms. Mabel in Dad's building. CRACK! CRACK! CRACK! "How was that?"

I didn't let out a sound but felt my stomach burn and my temples throb. My right arm and shoulder were almost numb. I imagined this was what being shot in the arm with Rocío's .22—the one she kept in the kitchen back in California—would feel like.

The cruel woman, fueled by the giggling, didn't wait for the tears to well up; she continued to hit my hand in front of the class until I couldn't lift my arm anymore, until tears involuntarily streamed down my sweaty face. "*Diabla puta asquerosa,*" I whispered, with my back turned to her, "*monstruo.*" Like a set of falling dominoes, the class keeled over laughing.

"What did you say?" she yelled back.

"I said," the tears burning my skin, "you are a *puta asquerosa.*"

Rocío was called in and told I was a terrible student. My teacher said I lacked self-control and discipline, evident in the way I hurt my hand punching the concrete wall on the playground during a fit of anger.

Rocío smacked me across the face when we got back to our converted ground-floor apartment a couple of blocks down. I didn't bother explaining what really happened. To Rocío and the mean women who ran the school, I was *una fiera,* a wild girl who couldn't manage the easy task of being seen and not heard.

I'm back in front of the wall that I allegedly punched until my hand swelled and I couldn't feel it anymore. There are small red handprints with names like Josephina, Omar, Cesar, Lidio, and Antonio. I hope none of these kids have gotten hit with rulers.

I hurry out of Mahatma Gandhi and jump back into the cab. I don't want to be late for my lunch with a lady who probably knows more about Taíno history than just about anyone else on the island.

A tiny woman with cropped silver hair holds court across the street from Mesón de Luis, on the corner of El Conde and Hostos. I can see her in the lobby of the hotel from my seat at the busy eatery. Her tiny dog brushes up against her legs while she talks on the hotel's landline. At times she puts the call on hold to greet an endless stream of people, presumably American students and professors, spilling in and out of the lobby. Then the woman walks out through the double glass doors toward my table and sits down.

"I figured it was you," she says, smiling. "Let's order. Everything here is damn good."

Lynne Guitar, a Michigan-born anthropologist and historian, is one of the most notable documentarians of Taíno retention on the island. It doesn't sound controversial upon first read, but contesting almost anything written and accepted by the academia as gospel can start a revolution here.

Ancestral DNA studies have been particularly validating to Guitar because it's enhanced her work by giving scientific support to the historical documentation she's established.

"Too many people say that Dominicans are a European-African mix, but Dominicans are Indigenous-based, with an overlay of European and African," Guitar says. "We know for a fact that 98.7 percent of the Europeans who came here in the first thirty years were males, and they weren't celibate, even the priests. And so who did they make love with? Indigenous women."

I wouldn't call it making love, but nonetheless, the implication brought something up Bennett Greenspan tabled as a possibility for early Jewish and Moorish settlement on the island and throughout Latin America.

Fourteen ninety-two was a big year for intolerance in Spain. We already know they behaved savagely with the Indigenous people living on Quisqueya almost immediately after setting foot in modern-day Haiti. However, it was also the year that the last Moorish king, Boabdil, surrendered Granada to Ferdinand and Isabella. Soon thereafter, the Spanish monarchs signed the Alhambra Decree, expelling Jews unless they converted to Roman Catholicism. As early as 1501, Muslims and *Moriscos* from Granada were persecuted and expelled if they didn't convert or, in the case of the latter, if their conversion was suspected of being a front. The oppression of Muslims and Jews in Spain lasted for centuries. Many did convert, disingenuously, after feeling the wrath of extremist Christian crusaders.

If crypto-Jews and Moors found themselves passing for Spanish Catholics after seeing so many of their people kicked out of Spain in 1492 and thereafter, we can be certain that some of them found themselves aboard the S.S. *Columbus.* It's possible some would have bonded with and married Indigenous women. After all, they had an enemy in common. In that case, Indigenous women may have gotten married in a Catholic church to these men and subsequently taught Judaism and Islam at home without understanding the difference. This is the only way, drinking from the same goblet of hate and resentment toward the Spaniards, that I could see "making love" make sense.

Many, if not most, of the Taínos were wiped out by Spanish disease, greed, and slavery. However, there's another reason why we should question the assumptions made in colonial accounts about how many Indigenous folks survived. As Guitar has documented, we don't know how many Amerindians lived on the island during the colonial times because the Spanish only counted the ones working on plantations for their census records. How could they have possibly accounted for the Taínos hiding in the mountains and caves across the island? For all we know, the Spanish chroniclers, reporting on scout's honor, may have fudged the actual numbers to justify the importation of African slaves to the island. Their actions have shown that it wasn't beneath them.

At any rate, "all the mothers were Indigenous women, and the progeny of this mix had the immunities against those invisible allies, those viruses and bacteria that the full-blooded Indigenous peoples did not have," says Guitar. "I tell Dominicans, 'You're *not* Spanish—be proud! You've got the best of three incredible races in you. The best of three roots makes for a very strong tree.'"

This is how the Indigenous, the African, and the European managed to survive extinction in the Dominican Republic and throughout Latin America. The mixing over centuries also explains the vast array of phenotypes and hair textures, the extreme polarities of experience that exist within the lives of a single family.

It's complicated, though, which roots—African, Indigenous, European, Arabic, and more—we choose to sow. A few days ago I met a young man of obvious mixed ancestry here in the colonial zone. He gushed that his Y-DNA test confirmed his direct paternal ancestors were English. Admittedly, he probably didn't realize how giddy he came across, exalting the European fragments of his self. Curious, I asked about his mitochondrial DNA results and whether he found any links to Africa or the Indigenous population in the country. His response was a flippant no. The thing is, he's hardly alone. On our respective journeys, there are also those individuals who embrace their Indigenous and African ancestry while emphatically denying their whiteness. There are others who embrace Taíno heritage while vehemently rejecting their African ancestry and vice versa. Claiming or at least acknowledging all sides, historically good and bad, isn't accepted in most cultural circles. Either way you slice it, we're all selling out some branch or branches.

In Puerto Rico, for instance, 80.5 percent of the population checked the "white" box on the 2000 census, a sharp increase from 1899, when the island became a U.S. territory and 61.8 percent chose "white." In 2010, 75.8 percent of the population of fewer than four million checked off "white," marking the first drop in over a century.

In the United States, it's just as *complicado*. Most Latinos across the country do not look like, say, their favorite euro-friendly *telenovela* stars, but over half of the approximately 50.5 million living in the United States identified themselves as white and no other race in the 2010 census. I think we may have been duped into believing that completely assimilating, even at the cost of suppressing parts of ourselves, is the key to success in America.

The issue may be that the census forms are just really, *really* confusing. Many Latinos view ethnicity not only in a cultural context but in a racial one as well. When asked if she's Black or white, my Ecuadorian-American *comadre* in New York City replies, "I'm Ecuadorian." The same can be said for Mexican-Americans, Dominican-Americans, Puerto Ricans, and so on. Therefore, when you read, "Hispanic origins are not races," it leaves many scratching their heads, like, "*¿Qué?* Say *what?*"

According to the 2010 census, about one third classified themselves as "Some Other Race" alone, as opposed to the 40 percent who classified themselves as "Other" in the 2000 census, the latter representing 95 percent of the 15.3 million of the folks who did so. In 2010 a tiny percentage of Latinos identified as being nonwhite alone—3 percent checked "Black," for example—and 6 percent of Latinos, including me, reported as being of multiple races.

In the future, as further ancestral DNA studies are done and the easy-to-use kits become more affordable in this sucky-ass economy, I suspect there will be a rise in the number of Latino-Americans reporting to be of multiple races. Perhaps finding out that we carry New World history in our genes will transcend racial checkboxes altogether and enable Latino-Americans to rethink what America is supposed to look like.

I pull up to Arquimedes's house after a two-and-a-half-hour bus ride from Santo Domingo. I wait for him in the receiving room at the front of the house for a few long minutes. I don't think I've ever been in a receiving room. I can see the Cepeda patriarch, his arms burned as brown as a tobacco leaf, gently rocking back and forth while reading a newspaper on his chair. A lot of planning went into this day. I bought an outfit back home just for this occasion: a matronly tent of a floral dress that covers my tattoos and knees. I don't want to risk the chance of coming off disrespectful by showing too much skin or accentuating my figure. I'll donate the dress as soon as I get back home.

The Mrs. greets me first. I immediately recognize her from the neighborhood back home. She must have been a beauty when she and Arquimedes first met. Time has been kind to her attractive seventy-something-year-old face. *"Bienvenida,"* she says in a slightly tremulous voice. "We just moved here because it's easier to manage." She makes one excuse after another for a mess that doesn't exist in this tidy home.

"Gracias, señora," I reply. I'm really embarrassed for never stopping to greet her back home. I promise myself that today is the first day of the rest of my life. I'll start making amends with the universe by kissing this woman's ass for the duration of my stay. "Please, take all the time you need to get ready. I will sit right here until Don Arquimedes is ready to talk to me."

The Mrs. gets up and whispers something in her husband's ear.

"Hola, come in," Arquimedes says. His voice is gravelly, and his Dominican accent is mad heavy. "Funny, you're not as dark as I thought you'd be, not for a Cepeda."

I don't know how to respond to the man without being a smart-ass. "Thank you for agreeing to talk to me about my father's family," I say, smiling nervously.

Arquimedes looks like his mother and nothing like his green-eyed brother Ismael or Dad. "You and your father may be the lightest people I've seen in our entire family," he says. I smile, thinking of how I'm going to explain and convince him to give me some of his deoxyribonucleic acid.

A morbidly obese little boy with a really big butt runs out of a room in the back. His complexion is dark and smooth, like polished obsidian. His hair is cropped into a short 'fro.

"Is that boy your caregiver's son?" I ask the Mrs., trying to make small talk. The lady shoots me *mal de ojo* from the kitchen.

"No, he's our daughter's son," Arquimedes says.

His daughter walks in a few minutes later from work. She is shorter than her parents and exactly the same complexion as me, except her hair is fried straight, courtesy of a *desrizado*. "This is my nephew's daughter from New York," Arquimedes says, introducing me. She looks at my voice recorder and smiles, retreating into the back room never to be seen again.

"Let's begin, shall we?" I ask. I don't notice just how bad my Spanish has gotten until I press myself to be proper. I struggle to say *usted* instead of *tú*, the customary way of addressing older people, and all the other words that have gotten mauled when put through the American grinder. I wish I could speak our dialect as well as I could read it and speak it when I was a kid. I feel off-kilter, somehow a bit less Dominican.

Arquimedes sits in a large wooden chair by the hallway and says nothing for a few minutes. He's wearing the same distant expression Dad did when he revisited his past, though this old man doesn't look blue. For Arquimedes, evoking the past is clearly a bittersweet journey, a pleasant throw he can drape around himself on those rare cold nights on the island. "Oh yes, let's begin," he says, halfway smiling.

"What can you tell me about the Cepedas?" I ask.

"Well, my grandfather Juan Cepeda was not as black as, say, an African but very dark *indio*." Before that, Arquimedes says, "he used the last name Marmolejo until he got married in 1927." Turns out his father had not legally recognized him, so he had to drop his paternal surname. "To confuse matters," Arquimedes says, "my father, Apolinar, traded in *his* mother's, Emilia Jimenez Moya's, paternal surname, Jimenez, for his dad's new matrilineal surname, Cepeda." My head is spinning as I try to keep up with it all. Ismael also used the last name Jimenez because he was born before his parents were officially married.

Apolinar Cepeda married Casilda Romano, and together they had ten kids. Like way too many Dominican men, he was a *mujeriego*, fathering an additional eight children with different women. Casilda used her mother Natividad's last name, which was Romano. Arquimedes rocks back and forth a bit before settling into a position that makes him look regal, like a king on a throne. "My mother's mother was a very tall and very dark woman from nearby La Torre, with hair in between *bueno y malo.*" Casilda's father, whose last name was also Jimenez, left Natividad and their children for another woman. Arquimedes never met him.

Before becoming a housewife, Casilda—who was raised in an El Seibo *campo* out east—cultivated tobacco in her *conuco,* a Taíno word that means a small plot of land. After having kids with Apolinar, she resettled to Santo Domingo so the kids could receive a city education.

Do you remember Ercilia? I ask. "I barely knew her, but the limited time I was around her, she was quiet and sad."

A glassy-eyed middle-aged man appears from the hallway, stomach first, and stands next to Arquimedes. The guy looks like him but with less hair and more weight. He stands there next to his father for several minutes, listening and making sucking noises with his teeth. He doesn't say a word, just stares at his mother, then father, then me. He does not smile.

Arquimedes, still rocking back and forth in his chair, continues. "I met Ercilia on April 6, 1944, at 85 Barahona Street in the Villa Francisca section of Santo Domingo—I should say Ciudad Trujillo, because the city was named after that *tyrano* back then." He looks out the back window. "I remember my sister Felicia and I were interrogated for three days straight by the regime for our anti-Trujillo activities. I didn't think we'd get out, but thanks to a family friend, Cucho Alvarez, we did, and our lives were spared."

When Arquimedes met Ercilia, she and Ismael were recently married with a newborn daughter and my one-year-old father, both born on the same national holiday, February 27. Even back then Ercilia's religious fervor and passive demeanor were as intense as when I met her decades later.

Arquimedes's description of Ercilia's parents is nothing like how Rocío's side of the family painted them. Ercilia's mother was described as being "very black" and her father as "very white" by Antonio and Mama. Arquimedes's account is quite different. "Ercilia's mother, last name Prandis [or Brandis]—she claimed her father's male ancestors were English—was originally from Baní and had a golden-brown complexion and average looks," he says. "And Don Pedro, a musician originally from San Pedro de Macorís, was darker than his wife."

I wonder if he knows anything about Ercilia possibly being adopted.

"Ariel, that's my nephew's daughter, you know her," Arquimedes tells his son, still standing silently next to him. Ariel, I'm told, is a doctor. He gives me a once-over before extending his hand.

"Hello, I'm your father's cousin," he says, lowering his voice. "I saw you in a magazine here a while ago. You look a lot better in the paper than in person." I doubt the Mrs. or Don Arquimedes heard him. Arquimedes is looking off, surely traveling back through his mind's eye to some another time. Much like the Mrs., his face is still handsome. I can't believe that this fat balding man or the short obese woman in the back room could be their progeny. No one says anything. The caregiver, making lunch in the kitchen, smiles.

I think back to the Dalai Lama quote I had up on my refrigerator for years, which read in part: "We cannot learn real patience and tolerance from a guru or a friend. They can be practiced only when we come in contact with someone who creates unpleasant experiences."

I decide not to respond to the son. "Thank you," I reply, smiling.

He raises his voice, presumably so his parents could catch what he was saying. "It's good what you're doing, asking about those times," he says.

I turn my attention back to Arquimedes. The Mrs. sits close by in a rocking chair. I don't notice when Ariel leaves.

"Did you ever hear that Ercilia was adopted?" I ask. "She has always maintained that she was."

"Yes, I heard the same thing," he says. "I heard she was of Arabic ancestry and lived in San Pedro de Macorís in an extremely poor family who eventually gave her to a well-off family. It was a resounding rumor, to say the least."

"Speaking of Arabic ancestry, after I had Dad's direct paternal ancestry tested for my project, the results came back being Arabic or, more likely, Berber," I say.

Arquimedes laughs. "Well, I guess one never knows, but I have to accept it, because science proved it."

"*Señor*, I'm interested in finding out some more information about the ancestral origins of your mother's mother's side of the family," I say. I take out the test and assure him and the Mrs. that no blood will be shed in the process.

"We're Dominican," he says, "but I'm happy to give you a sample if there are no needles involved."

"Two more things," I say. "How did Ismael lose his fortune by the time he came to New York City, and how did he die?"

Ismael's weakness was women. He loved them more than life itself, more than the children whom he shipped off to his mom after remarrying and having a new set of children with the next woman, Fulana. He loved women even more than money and his spiritual gifts.

Nobody knows what exactly happened between Ercilia and Ismael—he never talked about it—but when Fulana stepped into the picture, Ismael lost his head. "He began obsessing over her schedule, her every move, until losing his fortune to bad business," Arquimedes says. "They moved to New York City, where he lost everything—including Fulana, to a younger man." After that, Ismael began drinking.

When their divorce was final, Ismael moved back to the Dominican Republic to live with Arquimedes. "Fulana is my *comadre*," he says.

"Is?" I ask. "Does that mean she's still alive?"

"Yes, she still lives on Long Island, and you know, Fulana was never easy and isn't, but—"

"I hear she was wicked to Dad and his sisters," I say.

"I don't know. We have distance between us, she's always been nice to us and—"

"I'm almost positive Fulana named one of her daughters Raquel, too," says the Mrs.

My heart races. This bitch is why Dad suffered so much as a kid and, in turn, repeated the cycle with me.

"What happened to him here?" I ask.

"He fell in love with a really ugly *negrita* from our town, Los Pe-
laderos, who was our live-in help. They had a kid together who moved
to the States."

I'm dumbfounded.

"He became obsessed with her, too. One night they had a terrible
fight, and he woke up the next morning *grave* with high blood pressure. It never went down, and he died within a few days," says Arquimedes. "My brother died of a broken heart."

I catch a late bus back to *la capital* after politely turning down an offer
to spend the night in Santiago. Had the elderly couple been alone, I
would have probably stayed and listened to Arquimedes tell stories
about his clan for as long as he could.

CHAPTER SEVENTEEN

Paradise Gone

> Until lions have their historians, the tales of the
> hunt shall always glorify the hunters.
>
> —AFRICAN PROVERB

"LISTEN, RAQUELITA, IF WE ARE GOING TO TALK ABOUT OUR AN-
cestors, I want to explain something to your first, something about
your mother," says Paloma in her white pickup truck. "I just don't want
you to harbor hatred for her, because it's cancerous for you, spiritually
and physically."

Paloma looks like a thicker, silver-haired version of her older sister.
Today Paloma is a Taoist and devout student of Chinese medicine,
which might be the reason why she's so calm and coolheaded. The
aunt I knew as a little girl was as wild as the howl of a laugh that spilled
out of her like a volcano. I clearly remember stalking her as a little girl
in Paraíso. I waited for her outside the bathroom, where she'd appear
with her dark locks twisted and pinned up and her face lathered with
all sorts of homemade beauty masks, as if she needed to be any more
magnificent than she already was. Her fucked-up teeth only added
whimsy to her stunning looks.

"I do not hate Rocío. I don't really feel anything for her," I tell Paloma. "I have to tell you she and Dad are two reasons why I prefer ancestral DNA testing over genealogy—history is easier to digest than people who consistently challenge you to stay in character by creating, as the Dalai Lama says, 'unpleasant experiences.'" I recount my trip to Santiago and meeting Ariel as an example of my efforts to keep a cool head. Paloma lets out her roar of a laugh. Her eyes slant almost completely shut, which would not have scared me had she not been driving so fast down the streets of Santo Domingo.

"*Ay, Dios,* Raquelita," she says, still laughing and trying to catch her breath. "So, what do you have to tell me about our maternal ancestry? Those tests are becoming quite popular here, especially with people finding out they are Jewish, but also so many other things."

I tell Paloma we descend from West Africa on our direct maternal line, in a country now called Guinea-Bissau. Paloma smiles. "I think it's great, and I'm not surprised, though I thought we'd be Taínos," she says. "So, how did Mama take that *noticias?*"

"She laughed," I say. "Mama doesn't believe in any of it." I ask Paloma what she knows about her father's side.

"On Papa's paternal side, I don't know where his grandfather's male ancestors ultimately came from—maybe it was Spain—but I do know his grandmother was from Haiti and had the last name Durán." The Mancebo clan hails from Neiba, a town close to the Haitian border on the southwestern side of island, so that makes sense.

I've enlisted the help of a local genealogy and ancestral DNA enthusiast to help me navigate the extremely tricky terrain of Dominican genealogy. Arquimedes's account of the Cepeda clan's flip-flopping surnames sent the red flag up higher than the towers dotting the streets.

Paloma tells me that my maternal grandmother's grandfather, Dr. Jose Dolores Valdez, was a celebrated figure in his town of San Juan de la Maguana, a historical Taíno stronghold located in the west, near Haiti. Dr. Dolores Valdez was one of San Juan de la Maguana's first doctors and pharmacists and, in 1885, was elected into the town's government. Back then, official appointments were traditionally given to highly respected people in the community. It's amazing that *el doctor* found time to accomplish anything, much less manage to procreate at least fifty-two children with a rainbow coalition of women.

The picture said it all: The black-and-white one Mama gave me was of an older Dr. Dolores Valdez. The Vietnamese folklore passed down through generations in my *abuela*'s family could be bought just by looking at his brown face, almond-shaped eyes, and high cheekbones. He looks African, with an Asian varnish. Looking at his picture reminds me of something Lynne Guitar said to me at lunch when I asked her what Taínos looked like.

"Based upon their skulls . . . think of a modern-day Vietnamese, and that's what the Taínos look like . . . They had skin the color of a lion, [a] golden color, high cheekbones, almond eyes, straight black hair—small but very, very well built and strong." That's only the second time I've ever heard the word "Vietnamese" on this island.

Paloma pulls up in front of a large apartment building in a neighborhood that doesn't look familiar to me.

"That building to your right is on the land where Paraíso once stood," Paloma says.

I get out of the truck. I stand in front of a large structure stabbing the sky and look as far up as the sun will allow. This is holy ground for me, the place that brought me so much happiness as a child, where I discovered the world on a globe in Papa's study. I remember feeling that pieces of me were scattered around the world; I belonged to her, Mother Earth. Papa's globe was one giant *teta* feeding my chubby self with rousing curiosity.

Almost every night after dinner, Papa and I would take walks around this neighborhood. Sometimes he talked about his brother, a conductor and musician who traveled the world and lived in Italy for a time before coming back to become a founding director of Escuela Nacional de Bellas Artes. He told me stories of being a shoe-shine boy as a child, of being dirt-poor, of being self-made. Sometimes Papa mentioned something about his father's mother, *una haitiana*. "We are all related on this island," he said. "Only the ignorant hate their neighbors."

I remember sitting between my grandfather and his friend in the living room as they talked politics with the intensity of a bickering couple for what, to my young ears, felt like weeks. When he tried to make a point, *vicepresidente* Jacobo Majluta's knee shook so hard that I'd jump on his lap for the ride. Don Majluta's timepiece was so large and shiny that the reflection temporarily blinded me when I stared at it. Papa wasn't nearly as passionate, but I could tell he enjoyed his friend's company.

Not all was kosher in paradise. This is the stretch of land where my parents were married. This is where Rocío totally fucked up her life by leaving school and a comfortable situation for my father and an exhaustive list of other worthless men. This is where she forced me to leave the only stable family I had known, to live with her on Arzobispo Portes in the Zona Colonial before I leaped out of one nightmare and arrived in another with Dad and Alice in New York City.

"Do you remember the garden toward the back of the house where I played with my little pet rabbits?" I ask my aunt. "Whatever happened to them?"

"Of course I do," she says. "They were multiplying so fast, Mama had to hand them over to the caretaker of a piece of property she was trying to develop."

"Let me guess—"

"Yes, he started getting fat, and the rabbits started disappearing. I think they fed the whole *barrio* until most of them were gone, and you know, Mama, even as tough as she was, without Papa to intervene, lost control. He didn't want the land."

"That's sick shit," I say, imagining my bunnies being slaughtered.

Maybe it's for the best that Paraíso, as lovely as it looked from the outside, is gone. *"Bueno."* I turn and look at Paloma. "That's that, then, let's go."

"I'd like to know more about our African history here," she says, driving us to her house for lunch. "We've had such a long relationship with that part of the world, but I honestly haven't put much thought into it until now."

I understand where Paloma is coming from. Dominican Republic's centuries-old ties to Africa have been forgotten, revised, and as in the States, rarely taught. Still, the history of Africa in the Americas is a fascinating one, and somewhere along the line, the narrative runs through my veins.

In July 1502, just nine years after a shipwrecked Columbus was discovered on the western side of the island, Santo Domingo's governor, Nicolás de Ovando, made a move that would forever impact our gene pool. With the Catholic blessing of the ruling Spanish monarchs, he brought Spanish-speaking slaves of African descent to the island.

Bartolomé de las Casas, the first ordained priest in the Americas, accompanied Ovando to Hispaniola in 1502. The "Protector of the Indians" participated in raids and owned Taíno slaves, repenting after recognizing that they possessed human souls. He suggested that Africans be brought en masse to Santo Domingo and other Spanish colonies as replacements only to backpedal. While he wrestled with his spirit over the moral dilemma of Indigenous and African slavery, de las Casas himself owned slaves until 1544. By that time there was nothing he could do to stop the oars of the transatlantic slave trade from rowing.

Ovando and, arguably, de las Casas played a major role in what would become a genetic circumstance of the Columbus effect on Hispaniola, which is why, five hundred years later, we can see gradations of brown on the faces of her population. The *conquistador* led the way for other greedy Spaniards—like Hernán Cortés and Diego Velázquez de Cuéllar, for example—to realize their own American dreams.

The *conquistadores* would have to contend with the captives' own New American Dream: freedom. Marronage and slave rebellions became a way of life on the island of Hispaniola and throughout the rest of the Caribbean long before the slave trade made its way to North America.

Those first *negro* ladino slaves who landed in modern-day Dominican Republic—thought to be more cultured because they were Christianized—ran away as soon as they set foot on the island and were never recaptured. Later, between 1515 and 1518, the Spanish plantation owners moved to bring in *negros bozales,* or slaves directly from the African continent. They feared importing more *negros* ladinos because they spoke the same language and would be better able to organize and rebel. Alas, obtaining slaves directly from Africa didn't work out well for the *conquistadores,* either.

The earliest slaves imported directly from Africa came mainly by way of the Cape Verde Islands. These men and women were gathered from all over the West African region known as Upper Guinea, the territories between today's Senegal and Sierra Leone, including modern-day Guinea-Bissau. Many of these *negros bozales,* like the Hispanicized ladinos who escaped soon after arriving in 1502, would not bow down so willingly to serve the colonists.

The Wolof people of Senegal, literate and exceptionally shrewd merchants and traders back home, were reputed to be more defiant than other tribes known to the Spanish. The colonists on the island learned firsthand just how rebellious they were when, in December 1522, a group of Wolof slaves revolted on the sugar plantation of Diego Columbus, son of the discovered, and his partner, Melchor de Castro. The insurrection was quickly squashed and resulted in the severe punishment of several captured African freedom fighters. Others escaped into the mountains, never to be heard from again. This first slave rebellion in the Americas set off other insurrections for centuries to come on Hispaniola and throughout the Caribbean.

The number of runaways increased as many Africans joined communities of Taíno rebels led by the cacique Enrique, also known as Enriquillo. Since 1519, they had been warring with the Spanish, sneaking onto plantations at night to steal cattle and liberate other enslaved Indigenous and African peoples. While the news of Enrique's victories and steadfast resistance spread and inspired other uprisings, his story ultimately went out with a whimper.

The Taíno chief signed a pact with the island's colonists in 1533 in which he was granted amnesty and his followers their freedom in exchange for helping the Spanish recapture runaway African slaves on the island, estimated between two to seven thousand. Unfortunately, Chief Enrique wasn't the only sellout on Hispaniola. Throughout Spain's military campaign to recapture former slaves on the island, several captured African leaders negotiated their lives in return for betraying their own people. Regardless of how much they tried, it's clear that the hunters ultimately failed to suppress the hunted. I see fluctuating degrees of Africa living on in the bodies, hair textures, and faces of the people Paloma and I drive by on the streets.

"That's all really interesting," Paloma says. I notice that most billboards around town are of blond-haired and blue-eyed adults and babies, hawking everything from cell phones to hair products. Those ads are in stark contrast to the locals—Afro- and mixed-raced Dominicans make up nearly 90 percent of the population—and the billboards featuring brown-skinned presidential hopefuls are so badly photoshopped that they look like smiling corpses.

While some of us have gotten drunk off the white-is-all-right-flavored Kool-Aid, like the *dominicana* back at the Delta gate in New York City and my high school classmate Socorro, we are hardly the only diasporic souls who need to check ourselves. While it feels almost too easy to dismiss the entire community as self-loathing on the surface, especially when viewed through the filter of our own American racial paradigms, the bleaching of Black Dominican consciousness isn't as skin-deep as one might think.

The Dominican Republic became self-governing on February 27, 1844, after twenty-two years of unification under a Haitian-controlled government and before slavery was abolished in the Spanish Caribbean and the rest of the Caribbean was decolonized. As the emerging republic attempted to establish itself, the racial category of the people immediately became a grave issue for the Western powers that were. At the time, the slaveholding United States needed to find a way to conceive of Dominicans as other than Black in order for them, Spain, and France to recognize *la república* as an independent nation. In a report to then president John Tyler, U.S. Secretary of State John C. Calhoun suggested that recognizing the Dominican Republic as an independent nation would help America prevent "the further spread of negro influence in the West Indies."

A commercial agent named John Hogan was sent by Calhoun to assess the racial constructs of the eastern side of the island. By any means necessary, his mission was to find a way to justify the claim that most of the country's population was somehow *white.* And he did. Hogan's explanation for whatever degree of blackness existed in *la república* had nothing to do with the fact that the island had been inhabited by slaves, free men and women, *indios,* afro-*indios, mestizos,* and other mixed-race people for over three centuries. Whatever blackness existed in the east, maintained the United States, was the fault of our insatiable Haitian neighbors, who forced themselves on Dominican men and women through the use of sexual violence.

Like scores of American statesmen, journalists, and travel writers throughout the nineteenth century, Hogan would go on to paint Dominicans as white in *relation* to Haitians. Whiteness became assigned to the people, as did a pliant and unthreatening view of the Dominican personality. Haitians were predictably painted as barbaric and savage Africans. How dare they jack their own independence before their French colonial masters decided it was time to grant it to them? Worse, how would news of a successful rebellion, if spread, impact the hearts and minds of African slaves throughout the rest of the Americas?

The United States created further division between both sides of the island with negrophobic travel narratives that were at their most prolific around the first U.S. occupation of the island, from 1916 to 1924. In turn, these accounts were lapped up by the Dominican ruling class and reincorporated into the nation's own writings about identity. At the bottom of the white-supremacist well lay America's interest in becoming the Dominican Republic's new economic and political masters. And this freedom was something that the island's elite were, for the most part, jonesing to give away like the neighborhood *puta.*

Still, African retention reveals itself in ways that we may not even think about, such as the polyrhythms of our local music, like merengue and bachata and gaga, and in our foods. I remember my first lunch in Ghana of what we would call *moro* (dirty rice), *maduros* (fried sweet plantain), and fish marinated with familiar spices. If I'd closed my eyes, I could have been transported to any Caribbean Latino restaurant in Nueva York or in the Dominican Republic.

Phenotypically, African retention exists on the faces of important figures who have held on to political roles throughout the country's history, perhaps most notably General Gregorio Luperón. About twenty years after independence from Spain, the country's ruling class moved to annex the Dominican Republic to their former colonial masters. An Afro- or mixed-race general Luperón—he's been described as both—became a fierce protector of the republic's sovereignty and waged a guerrilla war against Spain from 1863 to 1865. The War of Restoration, as it was called, is commemorated as a national holiday every August 16.

African retention is also preserved in our cultural memory; the stuff exists in our DNA. The way we speak, our tonal language, is a residual circumstance of the presence here and codependent relationship between Africans and Indigenous people. The latter contributed at least thirty-two hundred words to our lexicon.

Then there's religion. Most Dominicans, like my great-uncle, classify themselves as Catholic. And like most things in the country, Catholicism is *cortado,* or cut, with African and Indigenous-based religious expressions. Back in the day, Dominican state-funded propaganda rejected any kinds of so-called pagan or animistic forms of worship, passing them off as Haitian. Finding that citizens were commemorating the War of Restoration by engaging in Dominican voodoo, the Trujillo regime passed Law 391 in September 1943. Dominicans caught practicing any kind of *perceived* African spiritual expression in the republic were fined up to five hundred pesos plus up to a year in prison. After Trujillo, his loyal bitch-boy Joaquín Balaguer kept the negrophobic torch lit for another thirty-plus years, until the end of his third term as president in 1996.

One of the major consequences of the first U.S. occupation of the Dominican Republic was the rise of the former thief, pimp, and snitch Rafael Trujillo. Made up to the nines and wearing skin-lightening makeup, Trujillo became the Caribbean republic's most zealous proponent of all that is Eurocentric, despite his own partial Haitian ancestry. Back then, he spread white supremacy faster than Peter Popoff could "supernatural debt relief" on BET. Just seven years into his reign, the führer sanctioned the killing of twenty thousand Haitian civilians by shibboleth. How did he determine who was Haitian as opposed to Dominican on the borderland? Soldiers would hold up a piece of *perejil,* or parsley, and ask, "What *is* this?" It all came down to the R in *perejil.* In Kreyól, pronouncing the R is challenging, so the answer sounded something like *pewejil.* This how Trujillo sanctioned the violent death of thousands of Haitian men, women, and children during what became known as the Parsley Massacre.

As a public relations move following the Haitian massacre, motivated by his effort to whiten the Dominican race, the führer encouraged European immigration, particularly that of Eastern European Jews fleeing Nazi Germany. He also encouraged those on the losing side of the Spanish Civil War to emigrate to the island.

Despite the West, Trujillo, Balaguer, and our own ruling class, Dominicans have, perhaps intrinsically, managed to resist disremembering their African ancestry rather than forgetting it. Despite our own miseducation across Latin America and the United States about our history, we can't deny these demonized parts of our makeup. Doing so would come at the cost of denying our entire selves.

"I'm curious, Paloma," I tell my aunt over lunch of spaghetti and *maduros.* "Are there are any slave records or documents around town?"

"That's a good question for *el doctor* Moya Pons," she says, chuckling. "Raquelita, are you sure we are talking about the same Frank Moya Pons?" Maybe it's hard for her to believe I'd be cool with someone so respected in Dominican society because of the way I wear what Dad calls my *pajonaso:* untrained, wild, and worse, not fried straight.

Paloma and I have essentially become strangers. I haven't seen her much since I moved to Nueva York with Dad and Alice. I've never spoken to my aunt about life in New York, about Maria or the other women who've stood in her sister's place as my mother. I didn't think she or Rocío's side of the family wanted to know.

Today I'm getting to know her all over again, wearing the blemish of being Rocío's daughter like a huge zit on the tip of my nose.

"That's the cool thing about the U.S.—you can roll and rock with all sorts of people despite the *pajon*," I tell Paloma on the way back to my temporary home in Santo Domingo, a comfortable small bedroom in the apartment of a friend of a friend.

"Just please, Raquelita, *te lo súplico*, don't go anywhere near the Zona Colonial," she says. "It's too dangerous for *americanos*. Meet him somewhere else."

There we go again.

Today I will not be late for my meeting with Frank Moya Pons at Calle Las Mercedes in la zona. I leave hours before our meeting, enough time to grab breakfast and stop by Arzobispo Portes. I stand in front of the two-story slate-colored Spanish colonial structure and peer into one of the small windows to find that several flimsy walls have divided the large *apartamento* where Rocío once sent me to hell.

I wonder who lived in the building before I did, back in the days when colonists, African and Taíno slaves, and free people walked the streets of this, the first American city in the New World. There are no signs or plaques commemorating anyone of import who may have lived or visited Rocío's dwelling. Still, the energy—something the locals probably take for granted—is far out and undeniable. It emanates from every relatively ancient cobblestone, modest structure, colorful colonial, and over-the-top baroque church in this section of Santo Domingo. Like the Pelourinho district in Salvador da Bahia, Brazil, Santo Domingo is imbued with electricity. It's as if the stones have been charged and given life through bloodshed. Contrasting that spirit with the woman squatting in the middle of an already narrow path, taking a shit as a steady flow of people walk by her on this hot and muggy day, is surreal.

Our old apartment is mostly dark inside, but I can make out garbage strewn about the floor and a wicker rocking chair in the middle of the living room. I have two memories of Rocío here. The first is of her writing something on a huge blackboard in the large open space that was our living room and talking to a few dozen teenagers or adults sitting at school desks in front of her. The second is of her sitting on her bed, yelling that I was a traitor and wishing me bad luck before throwing me out of her house, bellowing, "Go to hell with your father, *maldita!*"

What was confusing to me as a child now makes perfect sense. It hits me like a ton of cobblestones: Rocío broke the *fukú* by putting me out with the day's trash. If it weren't for her setting me free, I may still be a caged bird today, holding my own daughter captive on a shit-laden perch. I am suddenly overcome with a feeling of gratitude toward Rocío.

As I start walking, a young woman extends her hand from one of the more beautifully restored apartments across the street and hands me a card. Her young son, a *caramelito* with piercing hazel eyes, nods hello.

"*Oye, amiga,*" she says. "I'm the real estate agent for some properties in the neighborhood." The woman, married to an Italian man, is a recent transplant to the city from Cuba. She points to the building across the street. The apartment I lived in on the first floor was just put up for sale.

"I saw you looking into the window from my window," she says. "Maybe you would like to take a look inside?"

"No, *no gracias,*" I respond. "It's not really what I'm looking for."

"Take my card, and maybe when you're ready, it'll still be here for you."

I find *El Maestro* sitting at the far end of an enormous air-conditioned office, reading email and finishing a paper he'll present at Harvard later in the month. Frank Moya Pons's enormous desk is overflowing with stacks of papers on one side and books on the other. He comes around from behind his desk to greet me. I try to imagine how he keeps his long-sleeve button-down shirt and slacks wrinkle-free. I find myself weirdly intimidated by his cool and collected swagger.

"*Hola, señora,* finally, we meet *here,*" he says, leaning in to shake my hand. Subtext: *Nice of you to prance in on time.* The man, possibly in his early sixties, speaks deliberately, not wasting any words on frivolity. He clearly lives in his head, one that contains enormous quantity of information about Dominican and Caribbean history.

"*Maestro,* what a fresh baller office." Subtext: *I'm so ashamed I missed you last time. Your awesomeness makes me feel like I showed up late to the Oval Office. Excuse me while I pick my face up from the floor.*

"Please sit down and let me know how I can be of service," he says.

"I wanted to know, how hard is it to uncover your roots here?"

"The Dominican Republic has suffered one historical calamity after another in the form of fires," Moya Pons says. I was afraid he was going to say that. He cites examples. For instance, in Santiago, records were burned in 1863 during the War of Restoration. When our neighbors to the west invaded in 1805, records disappeared. In January and February 1586, the English pirate and slaver Francis Drake burned Santo Domingo's earliest colonial records. The genealogical *tragedias* go on and on, inserting themselves like a Greek chorus throughout the island's history, with two consistent themes: *invadere et destruere,* invasion and destruction.

"So now that we are confirming through science that we're mixed-race," I ask Moya Pons, "how can we find our Indigenous and African ancestors in this country?"

"Only by ancestral DNA, not by records, because with the exception of the city of Santo Domingo, none, no other city in this country, has slave records," he says. Moya Pons hands me a small soft-cover book, *Libro de bautismos de esclavos: 1636–1670,* a volume of slave records that include baptisms. "These are the only records that refer to the slave population that you can consult."

"It's interesting how you can research your colonial and *alleged* colonial roots here with relative ease, despite how sticky the surname situation can be, but the African and Indigenous records are about numbers, not people," I say, less surprised than bummed.

"It's very difficult for you to relate a twentieth- or twenty-first-century person with a sixteenth-century slave [because] the records were quantitative, and later on you can find those records in some *haciendas* from sugar mills, for example . . . which are not common, either," says Moya Pons. "I would say it would be practically impossible, but maybe possible in the city of Santo Domingo, only by tremendous effort and great luck, to connect with one of those slaves baptized at the Cathedral of Santo Domingo in, say, 1650 with a Dominican family in the year 2000."

I trace the edges of the book with my index finger and say a little prayer to the patron saint of impossibilities, Santa Rita. In my case, discovering and connecting to my Indigenous and African roots is just one area in which ancestral DNA testing succeeds where genealogy cannot. Last names don't mean much here because we inherit our names from our fathers (in theory), and because names were sometimes given to Indigenous and African slaves who were baptized by their captors, while others were not. Last names in that case won't reveal ancestral origins, as I've seen with my own mitochondrial DNA results, Dad's, and perhaps Casilda's.

There's something else we need to consider: how people classify *us* in the United States. Looking at the race section on birth and death records is about as reliable as looking at the race section on census records and even, say, New York's sex-offender database, where phenotypically Black and mixed-race child molesters who have Spanish surnames are often listed as Hispanic and white. In death, the race and other particulars of two of my grandparents were wrongly recorded. Let's say Dad's mother wasn't adopted. By all accounts, the woman and man who raised her have been described as both Black and white and *indio* and Black. In death, her race was listed as white, entombing her true identity for evermore. Ercilia's case is hardly anomalous, making the search for our ancestral origins all the more challenging.

I'm reminded of what a fortune teller once told me years ago back home in New York. It's enough to give our ancestors light, or acknowledgment, when we cannot pinpoint exactly who they were in life. The intention is what matters. And that light elucidates their path back, enabling them to walk with, behind, and for us when life makes us fall flat on our asses.

Moya Pons and I decide to continue the conversation over lunch at a nearby Italian restaurant. A few minutes in, a well-known doctor walks in, wearing a polo shirt and cargo shorts. Because of his preppie clothes, I think he's a Black-American tourist until he walks over and greets Moya Pons in Dominican Spanish.

"You see that guy who just said hello to me?" he asks me after the man leaves.

"Don't tell me—*he's* white here?"

"In the U.S., you remember the one-drop rule—that one sixteenth of Black blood makes you Black?" he says. "Here, it's completely the reverse—one sixteenth of white blood makes you white, or at least non-Black."

"And has money bought him whiteness?" I ask.

"Yes."

"Look at a place like Brazil, where there are almost two hundred and fifty racial classifications. Can we contend with those numbers?"

"No, *no*, I don't think so. Dominicans are less sensitive to those racial classifications, and in my perception, those classifications we use here are more descriptive than an instrument for imposing social stratification on certain people," says Moya Pons. "I will not claim that this is a sort of racial democracy, but I will say that this is a very open society in racial terms."

I'd like to agree with Moya Pons, but I think about all the smiling corpses plastered on billboards around town. Then I think about Sammy Sosa and the Skin Lightening Creamgate of 2009. I saw it coming. I first met him over ten years before, at an after-party for a Hurricane George relief concert in La Romana. I was in town to interview Shakira for a music magazine. Later, in 2008 I saw a richer and more famous Sosa looking ridiculous with a conked hairdo, light blue contacts, and an ill-fitting suit. It was only a matter of time before he'd go all the way and bleach his skin. It would have been sadly hilarious had Sosa not planned to market and hawk the facial cosmetic to the Latino community worldwide.

I ask Moya Pons about any colonial ties to the Arab world that may explain Dad's paternal ancestry.

"There were Arabs who came from countries like Syria, Palestine, and Lebanon in the late nineteenth and early twentieth centuries," says Moya Pons.

"But before that, don't we have a connection to the Arab world?"

"Yes, there is a connection, but there weren't many Arabs coming during Columbus's time, unless they already became Hispanicized and, willingly or not, Christian . . . For certain there were some."

The surname Marmolejo comes to mind. I discover that the name originated in southern Spain, in the province of Jaén, not far from Seville. The word Jaén is believed to have derived from the old Arab word describing a place of rest on a caravan route, and indeed the city was used as a place of respite for armies moving from one main city to another during the Moorish occupation of Spain. Had we used our rightful surname—whatever that means today—Dad's direct paternal results would have surprised me less. This place, Jaén, is now on my list of places to visit, to connect to, to see what, if anything, awaits me. Something usually does.

Moya Pons is a fascinating person. Like Paloma, I'm trying to understand why such a difficult person to pinpoint would give me the time of day. I quietly thank the universe.

"A woman with the last name Cepeda taught me how to read when I was three years old," he says, on the car ride back.

I'll take that. I guess everything does end up working itself out.

It's time to go. The driver loads my bag into the trunk, and we start toward the airport. A few minutes in, I say, "Lenny, can you please stop for a second so I can inhale the fresh air of the Malecón before getting on that plane." He stops and looks at me like I'm crazy, but I don't care. I get out of the car and say a prayer of thanks to the Taíno spirit mother of the waters, Atabey, and her West African sister, the ocean goddess Yemaya. I'm grateful to be going home armed with more understanding and carrying lighter bags.

CHAPTER EIGHTEEN

Becoming Latina

New York taught me everything. New York City is everything.

—ADAM "AD-ROCK" HOROVITZ, BEASTIE BOYS

I CAN SEE THE LIGHTS DOTTING THE EARTH BELOW AS WE START descending over New York City. I didn't realize just how homesick I was until now. When the pilot says, "Clear for landing," signaling that we're minutes away from JFK, I start to experience a warm maudlin feeling. I imagine that one of those cars below contains Sacha and Djali, racing to pick me up from the airport. I'm already craving the freshly baked strawberry cake with vanilla frosting that Djali has baked to celebrate my return. I can almost smell it, cooling atop the kitchen counter, from up here. We'll talk for hours, working our way through the entire cake, distributing gifts and catching up on everything I missed over the last month. It won't be until tomorrow morning, when I hear the voice of my favorite anchor, Pat Kiernan, hip me to the local news, that I will feel totally home. When I look around the cabin at the other passengers fighting to catch a glimpse out the window, it's apparent that I'm not the only one who thinks these are the longest five minutes ever.

The mother-and-daughter pair sitting in my aisle have already unfastened their seat belts and fixed their hands in position to clap and holler the moment we land. The mom is dressed like a teenager, in a skintight red Rocawear sweatsuit with her *chichones* peeking out from her midsection and three-inch black boots. She takes a Bible out of the Ecko satchel tucked under the seat in front of her and clasps it to her chest, mumbling a prayer of some sort. Her daughter, dressed in a matching outfit, rolls her eyes. *"Ay, mami, ni' pa' tanto,"* she murmurs. "Look out the window, we're almost here!"

"Cállate, muchacha, before I slap you in the mouth," her mother snaps back. "You never know—*te olvidaste de* Flight 587 already?"

When we land, the applause and variations of *"¡Ay, Dios mío, Gracias!* Thank you, *Jesús, Maria y la Virgen de la Altagracia!"* are loud and melodramatic. As I always do, I join in the spirited clapping and fist pumping, but I'm clapping for different reasons: I didn't have to sit surrounded by *la familia* Saran Wrap, screaming and kicking the back of my seat.

I make my way down the filthy aisle of the plane, with one side of my headphones pushed back, and thank the flight attendants and captain, forcing smiles onto their visibly exhausted faces, before I exit. I'm starting to feel blissful as I make my way toward baggage claim and out the double doors to the pickup area.

The Dominican Republic is my holy land, my Mecca. It's equal parts archaeological site and ancestral shrine, a place where I can go to get centered when I start feeling off-kilter. While America will always, I think, feel foreign to me, New York City is my home. This is where I can construct my own identity freely and reject labels imposed on me. My foundation may be *por allá,* but my self is firmly rooted here.

I can see Sacha and Djali's car in the pickup area. My daughter's face is pressed against the window, looking in both directions for me. I imagine this is what Julie Andrews felt like when she frolicked through green Austrian pastures singing "The Sound of Music."

There's another email from Family Tree DNA with the results of Rocío's father Don Manuel's direct paternal ancestry. I expected to find a European ancestor on several paternal lines but assumed Spain would reign supreme. Alas, it hasn't, not yet. "Well, kid, we found out that your grandfather's direct paternal ancestry is either English or Irish. We can't say exactly which one."

What would Arizona governor Jan Brewer, the Birthers, and a growing laundry list of conservative Republicans say if they learned that many Latinos (me included) are mixed with European blood *because* of the thing they fear more than, say, another four years with President Barack Obama: illegal immigration.

And how about that old white lady from Azle, Texas, who placed a HISPANICS KEEP OUT sign on her property and justified her actions to a CNN reporter when asked if she found the sign offensive: "Well, you know, I don't care. I'm upset about them coming over here illegally, too. We think this is our privilege as an American to protect our property." Protecting "our property" from what? *Really?*

My own genetic and spiritual revelations have made me think about what exactly makes a U.S. citizen American. What does that *look* like as opposed to the face of an "illegal"? I always thought the face of America looked like the original people who settled here. They came after crossing the Bering Land Bridge from Asia, and according to their own indigenous religious creation myths, they've been here since time immemorial. Whichever philosophy we subscribe to, it's clear that Indigenous-Americans and Mexicans were here first.

Latinos are prototypical New Americans, the products of European immigration, colonialism, and slavery. What this journey has driven home for me is that being Latino means being from everywhere, and that is exactly what America is supposed to be about.

"So why is it either-or and not one or the other?" I ask Bennett.

"Your cousin's closest match in the system is to an Irishman, but he also has twenty-three out of twenty-five matches with an Englishman and one with a guy from Wales," he says. "Therefore, the honest thing is to say that he's from Northwestern Europe—not talking France. England, Scotland, or Ireland."

Great, there may be a shipwrecked pirate in *la familia*. Or maybe a British soldier who somehow survived and crossed the border into

Neiba from nearby Haiti during the revolution. Or worse, there's a possibility that this European man was a slaver. Whoever he was, his history will always be stitched with mine as a record of how the Americas were formed.

Against my better judgment, I exchange texts with Rocío a few more times during the year. They are as our communication has always been: super-sporadic and bordering on nonsensical. "Hi! Are you ok? I haven't heard from you in a while . . ." she texts, to which I reply, "I'm sorry, but when have we ever stayed in touch, ever, in decades?"

Every exchange is as grating as the last. In one, she reports that everything is okay with her boyfriend; in another, her granddaughter is sleeping over; in another, her chocolate Labrador gave birth to a litter, and she wants to know if I'm interested in adopting one of the puppies. Her texts show me how little she's changed. It doesn't matter that I told her I didn't care to hear about any more of her boyfriends. It doesn't matter that I told her several times that I travel too much to take care of a dog. Nothing matters to Rocío but Rocío.

I decide to text her that I have new ancestral DNA results.

Rocío responds by telling me, yet again, that she's always wanted to write a book about her life. She segues into tangents about how she's been victimized by everyone around her. Nobody understands her. Nobody sympathizes except her latest beau. She never expresses interest in her father's direct paternal ancestry.

I'm ambivalent. I respect Rocío for admitting that she was a less than desirable parent, something Dad has never been able to do, much less Alice. I forgive Rocío. And yet I can't force myself to feel something more for Rocío and her sob stories than fleeting compassion. I feel way more compassion for the casualties she's left in the wake of her failed relationships with men: her other children.

I arrive a few minutes early to find Jorge Estevez in one of the classrooms at the Smithsonian's National Museum of the American Indian in Manhattan, where he's coordinated educational workshops for almost two decades. I'm shocked. Jorge is not the constipated deadpan I expected. He's wearing a short ponytail covered by a black Yankees cap with the bill to the back, blue jeans, and a black-and-white-striped button-down polo shirt covering his large biceps. Estevez—a self-professed Taíno, he insists I call him Jorge—isn't overly zealous as much as he is passionate.

Today he's giving a run-through of a paper on a messianic figure from San Juan de la Maguana named Liborio Mateo Ledesma he's presenting in Washington, D.C., to another employee. Jorge delivers his gospel with the confidence of a rapper, mixing anecdotes with history. He smiles when he knows he's dropping science, revealing a set of shovel teeth and a Mongolian birthmark on his chestnut-colored face, two physical Indigenous characteristics. Whether he's talking to a coworker or, as I'll see later, presenting artifacts to dozens of visitors in the museum's rotunda, the message is the same: Taínos are victims of genocide by paper. "*Paper?* Why paper?" someone will ask, to which Jorge will reply, "Because they are still here with us." He is living proof.

The subject of identity in our community is such a complex issue that sometimes the only way to talk about it is through anecdotes. Here's one of many Jorge will share with me, usually told in one or two long breaths. This one is about a young Dominican-American woman who visited the museum, claiming there were no Taínos left on the island.

"So, my boss says to her, 'Oh, *really,* because one of my employees is Taíno from the Dominican Republic,' so naturally, she wanted to meet me. The first question she asked was, 'How did *you* know that you were Taíno?' And I replied, 'Well, let me ask you, how did you know that you were Dominican? Did your parents sit you down one day [and tell you]? You come to your identity because of the cultural icons, the conversation . . . the intimate knowledge of the culture. Nobody has to tell you you're Dominican, but you kind of realize very young and unconsciously that you're Dominican, and that's what you are.'"

Jorge pauses to take a call, and then picks up where he left off without missing a beat. "Taínos themselves were mixed with other nations, the by-products of thousands of years of mixing and absorption," he says. "If, by magic, you could take the Indian out of all things Dominican—be it language, genes, culture and customs, place-names, etc.—we would not be the same Dominicans. You can mix African and white in any combination, but Taíno is what makes us uniquely Dominican." Someone could argue that if you take out the African or European, we would not be the same Dominicans, either. "But guess what," he says. "We would still be indigenous [to the island]." The same could be said for Latinos throughout the Americas.

"When the DNA studies and results were first divulged, the historians right away claimed, 'Oh no, this is from Indians that they brought from outside.' But most of the Indians that were brought to the Caribbean from North and South America and the Bahamas were male. And if you look at most of the logs of the slaves that were being transported . . . the majority of them were male."

All of the DNA studies performed in the Dominican Republic and the rest of the Caribbean have been mitochondrial in nature, tracing direct maternal ancestry. "And most of the findings have shown local mutations that don't exist elsewhere," Jorge says. "Therefore, the academic arguments are baseless."

"How about those people—and there are many—who say that if you recognize your Taíno ancestry or express a connection to it, you're just denying your Blackness?" I ask.

Jorge pauses, scanning his mental Rolodex for which personal anecdote to cull from. "I got into a discussion with a self-identified Afro-Dominican woman from New York who said that I was basically saying I was Indian because I didn't want to be Black, which to me was very funny, because on my mother's father's side, we have Haitian ancestry. There is nothing prejudiced about us, but there is a difference between having blood of something and how you connected . . . so for somebody to tell me that, it's like, 'You don't know who I am.'"

Then there are people who don't find Amerindian or Indigenous DNA, which doesn't necessarily mean they aren't connected, at least spiritually. For one, they may not have tested the right line yet. "Right, and it's happening to a lot of people," Jorge says. "I have always told them that the connection to the Taíno is linguistic, spiritual, cultural, and biological. You could have all four, or you could only have one, but no matter who you are, if you're from the Caribbean, you're connected to the Taíno."

Jorge, eyeing the tattoos on my arms and wrist, turns the table on the interviewer and asks me a question: "Did you get that ink before or after your father's mitochondrial results came in?"

"Way before," I say, tracing the image of Atabey on my right inner wrist. "I've been told all my life that I walked with *una india,* and I've felt her physical presence all these years, so I see these tattoos as my spiritual armor."

"Spiritual armor, spiritual armor," he repeats, smiling. "It makes perfect sense."

The last results are in from Family Tree DNA, containing the direct maternal ancestry of Dad's paternal grandmother, Casilda. I want to see Dad's face when I reveal what I've just learned.

"Dad, meet me and Djali at the restaurant."

"Did you find out that I have a kid out *there* somewhere?"

"No," I respond, "I wouldn't traumatize someone else with that knowledge."

When we arrive at the restaurant, I ask him, "Have you ever met Casilda's mother or anyone else in her family?"

"I told you, I *don'* know too much of that stuff."

"Okay, well, her haplogroup is L1c1 and—"

"What does that mean? Is he Finnish?" Alice asks. "I have a feeling he—"

"Come on, *dah'ling,* chill *out,*" Dad yells. Alice laughs.

"So Casilda's direct maternal ancestry is in Central Africa."

Dad looks away, smiling. "I knew you wouldn't stop until you placed me in Matanga," he says, laughing, "but you know, I find *all* this *berry* interesting. I guess it's true, *somos una mescolanza.*"

"What happened to you when I was gone?"

"Come on, chill out," he says. When Dad learns a new phrase, he runs miles and miles with it. "Let *me* live."

I say nothing back. Our relationship, as delicate as it is, is better now than it ever was. It's going to be decisively up to me to keep the eggshell from cracking.

It never fails. Every time I write about Latino-American identity, I receive a flood of emails and comments from folks all over the country who are ripe for introspection and who have wondered about their ancestry. Many have been mistaken for other ethnic groups and are often at odds with their parents and grandparents on the issue of race. Other readers have expressed disbelief about how misinformed mainstream America is on the diversity of Spanish-speaking people, considering how long we've been here. Aside from the racism one expects from anonymous postings online, many non-Latinos have expressed a desire to know more about what makes us *us*.

One Facebook user wrote that he was born in California and raised in Colombia to Basque parents; his maternal great-grandparents had roots in Germany. When he moved back to the American South, people were amazed that a person of European descent could claim Spanish as a first language. Another first-generation Dominican reader—let's call him Joselito—was "dumfounded" by the race question when he applied for a marriage license. "Here I am . . . with a lineage around the world," he wrote, one parent claiming European ancestry and the other Middle Eastern and African. When he checked all the boxes, his application was returned. He could choose only one box, he was told. Jeff from New Jersey often wondered what the words "Latino" and "Hispanic" meant. An Italian-American, he considered himself Latino. Was he wrong?

Other Latino-Americans around the country have embarked on their own genetic adventures.

Ken Rodriguez, a New York City–born and Miami-based software trainer, recorded quite a few familial names going back two hundred years. While he knew little about his father's ancestral origins, there were rumors of Jewish ancestry on his mother's side. Already a practicing Jew when he took the test, Ken was eager to confirm with science what his soul already knew.

"Concerning my Jewish ancestry, the rumors were confirmed. My maternal DNA is Semitic, originating in North Africa, with two confirmed Sephardic Jewish matches from two separate Jewish families," he tells me. "Also exciting were my grandfather's paternal results. He was a match for the Cohen Modal haplotype, meaning his direct ancestry was certainly Jewish and likely descends from the Jewish high priests who have a tradition of descending from Aaron, Moses's brother."

In addition, Ken found one Amerindian and two Western European ancestral lineages. "In my opinion the biggest misconception is that Hispanic is a race in the first place. Hispanic people are generally a mix of different racial backgrounds. You can be White, Black, Asian, Amerindian, Jewish, and still be Hispanic," he says, echoing a sentiment of many Latino-Americans. "What unites us is the Hispanic culture, not our race."

Leo Toro, a Puerto Rican–born and Brooklyn-bred architect, was always curious about his ancestral lineage despite knowing his immediate family history. His spirit compelled him to take an ancestral DNA test. "I always suspected that my lineage traveled through and around the Middle East—difficult to explain something like that, really," he says. "But even as a child as young as eight, I wanted to go 'back to Egypt,' and indeed when I traveled there a few years ago, I joked that I was home." Leo always knew that Puerto Ricans were racially mixed and culturally diverse. "But now I know that I also have DNA that traveled past Asia over frozen land bridges to North America. It's a testament to the human condition, simply amazing." And empowering.

I'm at dinner with a dear friend, a santero from Queens. He sees something I do not.

"Raquel, you are lighting the path to your ancestors so brightly with this project of yours that one of them—maybe even one of your spiritual guides—may manifest in the form of a baby."

"A *what*?" I ask, shocked. Shortly after I suffered a miscarriage last year, my biological clock ran out of batteries. I started to feel like my baby-making days were pretty much over. The desire to change diapers now that my daughter was almost fifteen wasn't at the top of my list. Plus, I'd been training every morning at the boxing gym and sparring regularly, hoping to land a fight in the masters' division. "Yeah, I don't think so," I say, ordering another coconut mojito.

"Some of our spiritual guides are from our previous incarnations," my friend says, "and family *eguns*, or ancestors, are supposed to incarnate within the same family. It just may happen for you."

Months after that dinner, after being falsely diagnosed with "probable fibroids," I find out I'm pregnant. In fact, I'm in the second trimester, although I haven't had a single symptom. Sacha, who's been at the gym training with me all these months, is initially stupefied, and Djali, slightly disgusted. I'm hopeful that the idea of a new brother or sister will grow on her.

I wonder who this little person who chose me as a vessel is. I hope he or she won't be as disappointed as I was with my choice in parents. My pregnancy makes me rethink the Kabbalistic concept of *gilgul neshamot*, or the cycling of souls, a term Bennett introduced me to earlier this year.

Maybe it's about time I consult a rabbi.

Thanks to the juice of a Hasidic hip-hop executive, I find myself sitting across from Rabbi Rav DovBer Pinson in his elegant Brooklyn dining room.

Rabbi Pinson is like the Rakim of *gilgul neshamot*; he wrote the book on the subject. He's a world-renowned spiritual teacher and the head of the Kabbalistic IYYUN Center for Jewish Spirituality in Brooklyn. I feel lucky that he made the time, albeit at midnight on a Sunday, to talk to me. I piqued his curiosity when I explained, via email, my unlikely path to self-discovery, and that something had compelled me to seek him out.

Rabbi Pinson doesn't have too much time, so we get right into it. "How exactly does *gilgul neshamot* work?" I ask.

"The construct means every life we live is a new manifestation of a new reality. A new spiritual constitution arises and a very particular genetic code. The body that we possess throughout life is a direct reflection of our soul, which means our spiritual type," the rabbi says. "And there is a consistency between the spiritual self, our soul, and the physical self, which is our manifestation."

Part of the process of *gilgul neshamot* is that every single person has a specific soul purpose consistent with his or her body. The body is the vehicle, or the medium through which we achieve our perfection, our *tikkun.* "Once we achieve our *tikkun*," Rabbi Pinson says, "that part of our soul leaves the body understanding that its next stage is to develop the other areas."

Can this reincarnation of the Jewish soul be applied to other cultures and spiritual schools of thought?

"I believe that it's true cross-culturally," Rabbi Pinson says.

To my surprise, I learn that some Kabbalistic texts speak about the soul choosing to enter into a particular set of parents, family, and environment. We can even come back in clans where our children may have been our parents in a past life, and our parents, our siblings. Even our friends and close associates can reincarnate in subsequent lives to work something out.

Naturally, I'm happy to claim all the wonderful things I've experienced in life as kismet. And naturally, I can't believe that I intentionally chose Rocío and Dad as parents. Has every misstep and failure in life, the human suffering my eyes have recorded, all the *mierda* led me to this instant? The short answer is yes, of course. "Therefore, the fact that you were born to Dominican parents means something," Rabbi Pinson says. "There's something that you have to contribute to that culture or to articulate in some way—ignoring that would be denying a part of who you are."

Even the juncture in history and the zeitgeist we live in is something we choose, setting the scene for the spiritual fodder we need to grow and achieve deeper elevation of our souls. In each cycle, we carry traces of memory, including cultural traits. The things that come to us easily, our propensities, are carried on a deep subconscious level into our next life. There are no coincidences.

It's as if he's reading my mind, anticipating my questions before I ask them. He reiterates something I've learned from the Dalai Lama. "And with that said, our adversaries are really our guides," he says. "It works both ways, we're always there to teach and to be taught."

It's one o'clock in the morning, and Rabbi Pinson has to get back to work, but I can't leave without getting his feedback on the marriage of science and mysticism as a road to self-discovery. My transnational identity may have been formed when I was a child growing up in New York City and Santo Domingo, but it was enhanced because of the synthesis between *logos* and *mythos*, science and mysticism. The science of ancestral DNA testing, combined with the mostly unsolicited spiritual information I've received in North and West Africa, Europe, the Caribbean, South America, and the United States, from all sorts of people from every imaginable walk of life, has been reaffirming.

"I believe that's the future," Rabbi Pinson says. He thinks science will arrive at a place where we can realize there's one fundamental force in the whole universe regardless of what we, as children of world, may call it. Like many of the seers and mystics I've met throughout my life so far, and people who've embarked on their own genetic and spiritual explorations, Rabbi Pinson believes that the union of the scientific and the *mythos* is a messianic vision.

"It's imminent," I say, scanning through the last twelve months. If not for this genetic adventure, I doubt the universe would have rewarded me with the insight, the confirmation, that despite the obstacles, the winding roads, and the bullshit, I'm walking in the right direction and with the right people. This thing I am feeling, I'm almost certain, is the closest I'll ever come to standing somewhere in between truth and reconciliation.

POSTSCRIPT

Always remember that you are absolutely
unique. Just like everyone else.

—MARGARET MEAD

THE GIRLS START TRICKLING IN AFTER SCHOOL, OTHERS FROM
home, some with their moms and siblings in tow. They look like me,
like my daughter and her friends, like any other kid in our communities. They giggle, talk about boy drama, the latest dance craze and
songs, and play the guessing game about the sex of my baby.

The walls at Life is Precious, a suicide prevention program located
in the Boogie Down Bronx, are covered with art. Some of the pieces
are brightly colored affirmations like BE YOUR DREAM. Art supplies are
strewn about the couch and community table. There are plastic bottles
of glitter, markers, letter stickers, and all sorts of things that enable
the girls here—all Latina-American teenagers—to express themselves.

Sabrina, a Honduran and Ecuadorian fifteen-year-old, places her
sketchbook on the table in front of me. It's the special one she usually
keeps at home because of its size and weight. The first several pages
feature self-portraits of her sitting under a fat rain cloud. Half of the
book features dark drawings, the kind I imagine someone into Goth
would sketch. The farther I get through the book, I can see the clouds

271

starting to lift, the mood of the drawings shifting dramatically, evincing a sense of hope. Sabrina tells me that her life changed when she started coming to Life is Precious. She no longer feels alone or, as she says, "like an invisible person."

Something about Sabrina's drawings reminds me of a set I saw on a wall several years ago at a tiny makeshift museum in Freetown, Sierra Leone. In a series of three simple self-portraits, a young boy sketched his life to date. The first drawing was of him and another boy playing in their village before the conflict. The second illustrated his playmate, now presumably a soldier, stabbing him in the head with a machete. His tears are drawn like huge raindrops pouring out of him. In the third and final sketch, the boy—whose brain, I was told, was severely damaged by the attack—shakes hands with the child who permanently injured him. Art was used in Sierra Leone, like it is here at the center, as a vehicle to exorcise the traumas experienced by life's youngest victims, the children we keep failing over and over again.

A cool three-dimensional mask superimposed with a Dominican flag is tacked up on a ledge in the office of my friend Beatriz Coronel, the center's program coordinator. One of the pieces stands out more than the others, but for all the wrong reasons. It's a self-portrait of a blond and blue-eyed white girl drawn by Priscilla, a Latina with a russet complexion and dark features.

It turns out that Latina teens across the country are so weighed down by emotional baggage that some don't have the energy to articulate the pain. Latina teens have the highest suicide rates in the country, far higher than their white and Black counterparts. The epicenter of this problem is right here in New York City, the most diverse city on the planet.

When I first came to the center to talk to the girls about careers in the media, Beatriz told me about the cultural and societal factors at play. "The stress of acculturating, Hispanic culture, socioeconomic stress, and discrimination are some of the issues," she said. The girls then shared their stories, some of which sounded all too familiar.

Many of the teens at the center were bullied by their white classmates for not being American enough, for being "illegal." Black-Americans bullied them because of their "Spanish-people accents" and for not fitting neatly into their ideal of what it means to be Black and American. When I told them about my own genetic adventure, some of the teens expressed a strong desire to investigate their own.

When all the girls are present, I begin.

"Sisters, we're gathered here today for me to reveal the results of the mitochondrial DNA tests you took a couple of months ago." Their mothers, most of whom are single, gave me permission to explore their maternal ancestry and document the process on film. Beatriz and I wanted to focus on the girls and their mothers, hoping the project would bring them closer and bridge the cultural divides of both generations.

The girls are anxious, giggling and guessing one another's backgrounds. "I hope we're sisters," Maria says to me. "We are," I say. "There are aspects about the results that are going to bring us even closer."

Before I divulge the results, I need to make something clear to the girls. This is one aspect of who they are, and they're not getting their Latina cards revoked. "Whatever your results are, it doesn't make you less Ecuadorian, Honduran, Puerto Rican, Dominican, Mexican, Panamanian, or whatever you identify as," I say. "You can still rock your *boricua* flag on your tube socks, key ring, T-shirt, headband, book bag, and even attend the Puerto Rican Day Parade, Marisol." The girls laugh.

I explain that what the results may do is enhance who they are, maybe confirm something they felt intrinsically. *"Bueno,"* says one of the Mamis. "My grandmother told me we walk with *indias*, here and in Puerto Rico, but you know, that's just a spiritual thing." Mami provides the perfect segue. There's a thin line between who we are and what we feel we are.

"Mami, your direct maternal ancestors, as well as theirs," I say, referring to two other Puerto Rican girls in the room, "came back as Amerindian—that is, there is evidence that your maternal ancestors, after analysis, are indigenous to the island of Puerto Rico."

"What? You mean like the Taínos?"

"Yes."

"Oh my God, that is so cool, but my teacher said they all died," says one of the girls.

"Your maternal ancestor was a warrior. She found a way to survive, and I think maybe it's your mission to survive, too," I say. "Perhaps it was meant for you to get this information now, at this time of your life."

The girls are quiet, smiling, thinking.

The Honduran teen with the fresh portfolio has maternal ancestry in Meso-America, with a genetic match in Honduras and others in Central America. She isn't surprised. "Somehow I felt it."

"Beatriz, your mtDNA also came back as being indigenous to Ecuador, likely from the Incan empire," I say.

"I feel so proud, regardless of what else may come out if I test other people in my family," says Beatriz, "that the women in my family ultimately descend from a woman who endured Spanish colonialism."

There's a theme of survival emerging in the conversation.

"How about me?" asks a sixteen-year-old born to Dominican parents.

"Like me, you and your sister and the other *dominicana* sitting next to you, we have maternal origins in sub-Saharan Africa."

"Wow, *Africa*?" replies the sixteen-year-old. "That is so cool."

"And after receiving analysis on your results, we can say that your biblical Eve came from Lower Guinea, which today encompasses Nigeria and Cameroon." The sisters are smiling. The girl who drew herself as a blonde isn't.

"I wish I was something else, like Australian or Japanese," says Priscilla. "I don't want to be from Africa."

"But why?" asks one of the sisters.

Priscilla shrugs. "Can I get somebody else tested?"

"Sure, if you want to do it independently and your parents agree, but remember, this is just one aspect of your makeup."

"Well, I think we should have a party and celebrate," Marisol says. "We should celebrate the women we came from."

• • •

Several weeks later, I ask Beatriz how the girls are doing. I'm told they are going to create self-portraits reflecting their results.

"And how about *la dominicana*?" I ask.

"She had a hard time at first and goes through her moods," Beatriz says, "but then I overheard her say something really interesting. She and another girl were talking about—what *else*—hair."

The girls were arguing about the difference between "good" hair and *"pelo malo."* *La dominicana* said, "I don't have *bad* hair. It's just stronger than yours, unbreakable, like where I come from."

"I knew she'd come around," I say. "Our identities are a work in progress and really up to us and nobody else to ultimately define."

The fact that Priscilla is reflecting on what that means for her is all that really matters.

ACKNOWLEDGMENTS

It takes great effort to bring all things to life, this book included, and for this and more, I'm indebted to the following people for their respective roles as literary midwives.

My remarkable and wickedly cool agent, Ayesha Pande, embarked on this journey with me at the beginning and, years later, still walks with me, offering her unwavering support. My editor, Malaika Adero, gave me a home at Atria and committed herself from day one to realizing my vision, and I will be forever grateful to her and Judith Curr. I must acknowledge Jane Rosenman for rearranging her schedule to work with me on my final draft and for always being super-accommodating.

Family Tree DNA's Bennett Greenspan never ceases to amaze me with how he waxes poetic about all things related to ancestral DNA and migration, and how readily he made himself available to help me understand it all.

Explorer-in-residence at the *National Geographic Society* and geneticist Spencer Wells granted me an interview despite his whirlwind schedule, as did Southern Poverty Law Center's Mark Potok, and the historian and anthropologist Lynne Guitar. I will forever appreciate the magnanimous spiritual teacher Rav DovBer Pinson for taking the time to speak with me at his home, and Daniel Seliger for making the introduction. Two new—and, I hope, lifelong—friends were made somewhere along this journey: I admire Jorge Estevez's unyielding commitment to preserving the legacy of our Indigenous people on the island; and Frank Moya Pons for his kindness and willingness to bridge the generation gap even if we don't always speak the same language.

Beatriz Coronel is someone I hold in high regard for her friendship and for allowing me to play a small part in the important work she's doing at Life is Precious. I can't thank the program's founder, Dr. Rosa Gil, enough for identifying and doing something to empower and save the lives of many young Latina teens.

My friend Ambassador Julissa Reynoso took the time to read drafts of the manuscript while transitioning from the State Department to her new post in Uruguay. Michelle Maisto also made time to read pages and gave me useful feedback. Dominican genealogist Milciades Nuñez helped me unearth some nuggets about my family history. My generous friends Rita Sciarra and Rafael Juliá gave me a place to rest my head and space to write during my time in Santo Domingo. Sarah Edwards provided research assistance when her schedule allowed and always made time to gift me a kind word.

Speaking of which, I'd like to recognize and thank the following people for their support and words of encouragement: Henry and Kathleen Chalfant, Steve Zeitlin, Lisa Leveque, John "Jonone156" Perello and family, Tamara Warren, Lee Quiñones, Lorraine West, Joan Morgan, Kimberly Eisson Simmons, Gisella Baque, Michelle Jimenez, Melody Moezzi, Julia Rose, Anthony Perrone, Carmen Rodriguez, Ursula Williams, Andrew Kilgore, Jeff Mazzacano, Mauricio and A. J. Hernandez Anderson, Tracy Levenstein, Lisa Leone, Prince Paul, Cybel Martin, Lauri Lyons, Michael Dinwiddie, Mary Ann "Ladybug" Vieira, Margarita Guillermo, Fernando Ramirez, and Renato Rosaldo (for introducing me to Gloria Anzaldúa's work).

Todd Hunter at Atria provided much needed assistance, and art director Jeanne Lee and artist Thomas Ng get props for their work in designing the book's cover; Family Tree DNA's Max Blankfeld and Amy Whitman designed the discount coupon. Chakib Ghadouani of the Moroccan Tourism Board, Adnane Snoussi, and Mounir made my trip to Morocco one that I'll never forget.

The kind souls at Garden Café, especially Regina Christoforos, allowed me to sit and write all day for the price of a cappuccino or three. Because of the sanctuary that the Writers Room afforded me, I was able to read, think, and write in an ideal environment. Coach Moíses Sanchez—a befitting name, indeed—at Mendez Boxing pushed me to my physical limits and, at the end of every morning, made sure I left with the mental strength and inner peace I needed to work. Francisco Mendez showed me how boxing can do the body, the soul, and the mind plenty of good.

I'm grateful to all of my family members who granted me interviews, especially my maternal grandmother, and for my uncle whose blunt and razor-sharp sense of humor I partially relied on to reconstruct the earlier chapters of this joint.

My roller-coaster relationship with Dad was an impetus for this book, and he is the person to whom I'm most grateful, despite the past, because of the stories he entrusted me with and, more important, the love he shows my family every day. My stepmother, who always had a hand in raising Djali with me, stood by him all these years, and that couldn't have been easy: She deserves kudos.

My husband, Sacha Jenkins, and daughter, Djali, were patient and supportive during this process. Sacha, himself an accomplished writer and editor, read every draft and served as a sounding board. We both have love for and roots on the island of Hispaniola, Sacha in Haiti by way of Queens. We also love New York City and the hip-hop culture that reared us, all of which made for lively debates over which borough reigns supreme. Marceau, our son, waited one full week after I filed the book to arrive, and I can't thank him enough for that.

I couldn't have written this joint had life not happened the way it did and, as a result, drawn into my orbit the people you've met within these pages (and many more whom you did not). For that and more, I'm thankful to *all* of my ancestors, and the sprit guides who have led me here, to this very moment.

ANCESTRAL DNA TESTING:
NOW IT'S YOUR TURN

For more information about ancestral DNA testing, please visit FamilyTreeDna.com or call their Houston-based world headquarters at 713-868-1438.

FREQUENTLY ASKED QUESTIONS*

MtDNA (mitochondrial DNA)

What do I get when I test for the mtDNA at any of its levels?

Testing your mtDNA uncovers the deep ancestral origin of your direct maternal line (your mother, your mother's mother, etc.) and connects you with genetic cousins. Because your mtDNA has been passed on to you generation after generation by your direct maternal ancestors, it offers the most exact information possible for that line.

How do you perform mtDNA tests?

We perform mitochondrial DNA tests at Family Tree DNA by direct (Sanger) sequencing of both forward and reverse sequence values. We use test panels that return values for overlapping segments of the mtDNA. For mtDNA (HVR1) and mtDNAPlus (HVR1 and HVR2) tests, we perform an additional backbone haplogroup confirmation test. Specifically: HVR1: uses two panels plus one or more tests for haplogroup confirmation. HVR1 and HVR2: uses four panels plus

_____

*Reprinted with permission from Family Tree DNA.

one or more tests for haplogroup confirmation. MtDNA Full Genomic Sequence: uses ninety-six panels.

The results are reviewed by quality assurance, and any segment panel without a result or with a questionable result is rerun.

What are mitochondrial DNA haplogroups?

Haplogroups are genetic population groups, and mitochondrial haplogroups are composed of people who share a common ancestor on their direct maternal lineage. Your haplogroup tells you the branch on the mitochondrial tree of humanity to which you belong.

How are mitochondrial DNA haplogroups named? What are mtDNA macro-haplogroups? What are supergroups? Are they the same?

Mitochondrial DNA haplogroups are named according to their major branch with a capital letter. Subclades (branches) are then named with alternating numbers and letters; H, H1, H1a, H1a1, etc.

Macro-haplogroups (sometimes called supergroups) are the foundation for a number of other haplogroups. They represent older shared ancestors on the maternal tree. Macro-haplogroups link many of the more common haplogroups found today.

For example, haplogroup M is found throughout Eurasia and is especially common on the Indian subcontinent. Haplogroup M is considered a macro-haplogroup because it includes the haplogroups D, C, E, G, Q, and Z as subclades.

NOTE: Although mtDNA naming conventions are much like those for Y-chromosome DNA (Y-DNA), they are separate systems.

Don't we all go back to Africa?

Yes, all of our mitochondrial lineages trace back to a common ancestor who lived in Africa 100,000 to 150,000 years ago. Some lineages migrated out of Africa about 60,000 years ago, while others remained.

**This map shows each of the major (backbone)
maternal haplogroups' paths out of Africa.**

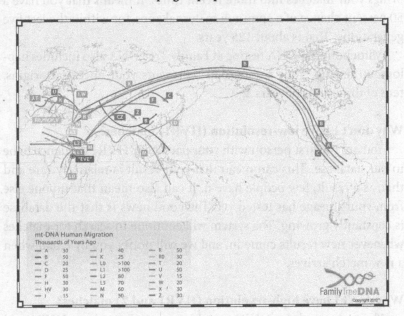

mt-DNA Human Migration
Thousands of Years Ago

— A	30	— J	40	— R	50
— B	50	— K	25	— R0	30
— C	20	— L0	>100	— T	20
— D	25	— L1	>100	— U	50
— F	50	— L2	80	— V	15
— H	30	— L3	70	— W	20
— HV	30	— M	60	— X	30
— I	15	— N	50	— Z	30

FamilyTreeDNA
Copyright 2012

The path that our ancestors took tells a story about human history. Testing your own and your relatives' DNA can help you understand both the diversity and commonalities of your part of the human story.

How many generations back does mitochondrial DNA testing trace?

Mitochondrial DNA testing covers both recent and distant generations.

To find connections in recent times, it is necessary to test multiple people who have suspected shared ancestry. This is done by careful examination of traditional genealogical records. Making connections with people in genealogical and historic interest groups can also be helpful.

Matching on HVR1 means that you have a 50 percent chance of a common maternal ancestor within the last fifty-two generations. That is about 1,300 years. Matching on HVR1 and HVR2 means that you have a 50 percent chance of a common maternal ancestor within the last twenty-eight generations. That is about seven hundred years.

Matching on the Mitochondrial DNA Full Genomic Sequence test brings your matches into more recent times. It means that you have a 50 percent chance of a common maternal ancestor within the last five generations. That is about 125 years.

Mitochondrial DNA testing at Family Tree DNA also includes haplogroup testing. Your haplogroup represents your ancestral origins, tens of thousands of years ago.

Why don't I have low-resolution (HVR1) matches?

You are the first person with your particular HVR1 sequence to be in our database. This can mean that your result is relatively rare and that, as a result, few people have it. It can also mean that no one else from your lineage has tested yet. The good news is that the database is constantly growing. The system will continue to search for matches whenever new results come in, and we will notify you by email when a new match arrives.

Why don't I have high-resolution (HVR1 and 2) matches?

If you do not have HVR1 matches, you will not have HVR1 and HVR2 combined matches. This is because anyone who is a high-resolution match has the same HVR1 result and is by definition also a low-resolution match. You will not have high-resolution matches if you have not tested your HVR2 region, or if none of your low-resolution matches have tested the HVR2 region. Your HVR1 matches who have tested HVR2 will have "(HVR2)" next to their names.

As our database grows, the system will continue to look for high-resolution matches for you, and we will send you a notification email when a matching result comes into our database.

Why do I have many mitochondrial DNA test matches?

There are some result haplotypes that show a high number of matches. There are two possible explanations.

Many people with the same results as your ancestors lived thousands or tens of thousands of years ago. The majority of their descendants carry their signature.

A more recent common ancestor—within the last one or two thousand years—with this haplotype had many daughters who in turn had many daughters and so on, leading to you having many distant cousins.

Increasing your testing level to the Mitochondrial DNA Full Genomic Sequence—the HVR1toMega or the HVR2toMega upgrade—will separate these two cases. This will allow you to focus on your relevant matches.

Why am I matching both men and women?

A mother passes on her mitochondrial DNA to both daughters and sons. Only daughters can pass it on to the next generation. Both men and women can take the mtDNA test. You will then match both men and women.

Y-DNA

What do I receive when I get tested for the Y-DNA at any of its levels?

Y-DNA testing can confirm your genealogical connections on your direct paternal lineage and expand your understanding of your deepest paternal ancestral origins. Because your Y DNA has been passed on generation after generation by your direct paternal ancestors, it offers the most exact information possible for this line.

How many generations does a Y-chromosome DNA (Y-DNA) STR test trace?

Y-chromosome DNA tests trace both recent and distant generations. The number of generations traced by a Y-chromosome DNA test depends on the type of test taken, short tandem repeat (STR) or single nucleotide polymorphism (SNP).

Where did my ancestors come from?

There are two places to look.

The first is your haplogroup, which is identified and described for you on the Y-DNA—Haplotree page of your myFTDNA account.

The second place to look is the Y-DNA—Ancestral Origins page of your myFTDNA account. We list the countries of origin reported to us by others who have test results that are the same as or similar to yours. This list does not represent places where your ancestors have been, so much as places where your Y-DNA signature can be found today. It can provide a guide to the possibilities of your ancestors' origins.

If you have few matches, this list will not be statistically representative. You will need to wait until more people who match your haplotype are added to the database. Several thousand people test at Family Tree DNA every month.

Don't we all go back to Africa?

Yes, all of our Y-chromosome lineages trace back to a common ancestor who lived in Africa about sixty thousand years ago. Some lineages migrated out of Africa; others remained.

This map shows each of the major (backbone) paternal haplogroups' paths out of Africa.

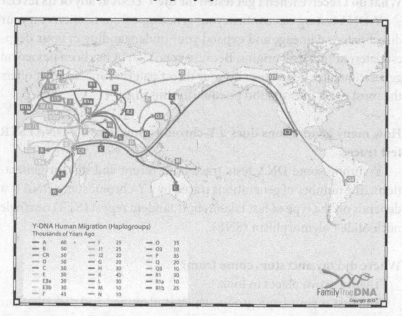

Y-DNA Human Migration (Haplogroups)
Thousands of Years Ago

A	60	I	25	O	35
B	50	J1	25	O3	10
CR	50	J2	20	P	35
D	50	G	20	Q	20
C	50	H	30	Q3	10
E	50	K	40	R1	30
E3a	20	L	30	R1a	10
E3b	30	M	10	R1b	25
F	45	N	10		

FamilyTreeDNA
Copyright 2012

The path that our ancestors took tells a story about human history. Testing your relatives' and your own DNA can help you understand both the diversity and commonalities of your part of the human story.

Ancestry

Can I test to determine if I have ancestry from one ethnic group, such as Native-American, Jewish, or African?

Yes. Our tests can tell you if you have ancestry from a population group.

Our Y-DNA tests trace the direct paternal line. This is your father's father's father. This is the best test when you want clear proof of ancestry on your direct paternal line.

Our mitochondrial DNA tests trace the direct maternal line. This is your mother's mother's mother. This is the best test when you want clear proof of ancestry on your direct maternal line.

How do I tell if I have Jewish ancestry on my direct maternal (mitochondrial DNA) line?

Judaism is a religion and not a genetic attribute that can be defined by a DNA mutation. However, because Jewish populations have been endogamous for much of their history, hints to your Jewish ancestry for your direct maternal lineage are provided by looking at the mtDNA—Ancestral Origins page in your myFTDNA account. Check the Comments column there. There are four possible situations:

1. You match only people who are Jewish. You will see in the Comments field Ashkenazim, Sephardim, and other historic branches. The answer here is a clear yes.
2. You match both Jews and non-Jews. The answer here is not clear. A higher level of testing—the Mitochondrial DNA Full Genomic Sequence test—will eliminate matches with one group or the other.

3. You match nobody of known Jewish origins. It is highly unlikely that you have Jewish origins on this line.
4. You do not have matches in our system. This is unlikely if you have Jewish origins.

How do I tell if I have Jewish ancestry on my direct paternal (Y-chromosome DNA) line?

Judaism is a religion and not an attribute definable by a DNA mutation, but we can give you hints about having Jewish ancestry by comparing your results against our database. Look on the Y-DNA—Ancestral Origins page to see whether the people you match have listed Jewish ancestry. Those in our Jewish database have a listing in the Comments column denoting Jewish ancestry. There are four situations when testing for Jewish ancestry. They are:

1. You match only people who are also Jewish on their direct paternal line. That is, the signature, or haplotype, matches only with people who have known Jewish ancestry. The answer in this case is clear.
2. Your haplotype matches both Jewish and non-Jewish lineages. The answer is not clear, and we cannot guess whether your personal lineage is Jewish.
3. You match no one of known Jewish origin. The answer is clear. You are unlikely to have Jewish origins on this lineage.
4. You have no matches in our system at all. That means we have never seen your specific results. We will know more about your ancestry when you start matching others.

I have a family tradition of Native-American ancestry. Is the Population Finder tool able to detect it?

The Population Finder program can detect a significant Native-American contribution to your genetic ancestry. If you have a 100 percent genetically pre-Columbian ancestor in your recent genealogy, Population Finder is highly likely to detect it.

For example, if your great-grandmother was 100 percent pre-

Columbian Native-American, Population Finder will detect your approximately 12.5 percent Native American ancestry.

Population Finder is also likely to detect Native-American ancestry that is a high percentage of a modern population. As another example, if all four of your grandparents have Native American ancestry from Mexico, your Population Finder results will reflect the amount of pre-Columbian ancestry within a normal range for those with Mexican heritage.

However, in the current release, the available reference populations limit the ability of the program to identify your specific ancestral group. It may also underdetect heritage that comes from a distinctive unrepresented group such as the Na-Dene.

Remember that you may have a Native-American ancestor but insufficient genetic heritage to be detected by a DNA test. This is due to the randomness of autosomal recombination.

Therefore, genetic testing can confirm your ancestry but not disprove it.

For more FAQs, visit FamilyTreeDNA.com.

DNA Test Kit Instructions

** Please Note**--Read this entire sheet before you begin your specimen collection. Scraping should be before eating or drinking, or at least an hour after eating and drinking. Avoid warm or hot fluids before scraping.

1. We have supplied 2 swab kits and collection tubes to insure accuracy.
2. The number on your tube should correspond to the number on your Release Form and the plastic bag.
3. With clean hands carefully open the plastic wrapper without damaging the scraper. Keep the plastic bag that has your kit number to put the tubes back after the collection.
4. Using one cheek scraper, scrape forcefully inside the cheek many times (about 60 seconds). A great scrape gives us a great sample! A weak scrape will yield less DNA and may cause several weeks delay.
5. Remove the small specimen tube marked with your kit number. Unscrew the top and gently push on the plunger at the top of the applicator stick, ejecting the scraper into the tube, just under the soapy solution. (Please do not jam the scraper to the bottom of the tube...it is difficult to retrieve)!
6. Remove the plastic applicator handle, leaving the scraper tip in the tube. Twist the cap onto the tube securely. The tube must be shut tightly to insure the quality of your sample. The tube with the scraper tip inside should be left at room temperature. However, it will not be harmed by winter or summer temperatures when sent by regular mail.
7. Wait 3-4 hours and repeat steps 4 to 6 for the second scraper and tube marked with your kit number.
8. Put the tubes inside the plastic bag that has your kit number and seal it. Insert the plastic bag and the release form in the self-addressed envelope provided, and send it back to Family Tree DNA via US Mail (postage within the US is $1.95). If payment has not yet been made, please make sure to write the Kit AND Invoice numbers on the check. This will ensure that payment is correctly assigned to your order.

SELECTED SOURCES AND
FURTHER READING

PREFACE

Sharon R. Ennis, Merarys Ríos-Vargas, and Nora G. Albert authored *The Hispanic Population: 2010* as part of "2010 Census Briefs" (May 2011; available online at: http://www.census.gov/prod/cen2010/briefs/c2010br-04.pdf).

To watch the full episode of *Haiti and the Dominican Republic: An Island Divided*, part of the PBS series *Black in Latin America* by Professor Henry Louis Gates, Jr., visit: http://www.pbs.org/wnet/black-in-latin-america/featured/haiti-the-dominican-republic-an-island-divided-watch-full-episode/165/. In the series, first aired in 2011, he covers other Latin-American territories, including Brazil, Cuba, Mexico, and Peru.

To read more about the passing of the mind-boggling "Dominican Republic Electoral Law Reform," first published on November 20, 2011, visit http://www.dominicantoday.com/dr/local/2011/11/11/41602/Legislation-eradicates-Dominican-Indians. I wonder if this ridiculous law will ripple throughout the rest of the Caribbean. The act of suppressing one's ancestry is not only oppressive but also hazardous to one's health. See, for example, the study "Differences in Albuminuria Between Hispanics and Whites: An Evaluation by Genetic Ancestry and Country of Origin: The Multi-Ethnic Study of Atherosclerosis" by Carmen A. Peralta, et al. *Cardiovascular Genetics*, 2010; 3: 240–247. (To access this paper online, go to: http://www.ncbi.nlm.nih.gov/pmc/articles/PMC2948758/pdf/nihms-229323.pdf.) Researchers found that higher European ancestry may be associated with lower levels of albuminuria, and that Native-American/Amerindian/Indigenous ancestry may be associated with higher levels of the protein among Latinos, depending on one's country of origin. "Since albuminuria is a known important risk factor for adverse cardiovascular events and kidney disease progression," states the paper, "our findings highlight the importance of recognizing the heterogeneity of Hispanic subgroups." The researchers observed that Latinos differ in their genetic ancestral component by country of origin. Of the Dominican folks tested, they found that 5 percent had Native-American ancestry and had the highest percentage of African ancestry of the participants tested, as well as European ancestry. To ignore *any* part of our ancestry is to disregard the genetic predispositions to certain diseases. Therefore, it hinders our ability to take necessary precautions. I'm just sayin'.

CHAPTER ONE: LOVE, AMERICAN-STYLE

I'll never forget the look on Dad's face when he found me reading a copy of Dr. Antonio Zaglul Elmudesi's *Mis 500 Locos* (Editora Taller, 2003), until I learned the role he played in Rocío's life, and later, in talking her parents into letting her marry Dad. In a way, I guess this man had something to do with my being here.

CHAPTER TWO: MEAN STREETS

The data I use is for Dominican-born people residing in the U.S, of which an overwhelming majority settled in Nueva York. Before 1990, the U.S. Census didn't identify Dominican as an ethnic group, lumping the numbers of Dominican-born people throughout the United States into one figure. The population estimates I used can be found on the chart "Population Change in the Dominican Republic," page 249, in *A Tale of Two Cities: Santo Domingo and New York* (Princeton, 2008) by Jesse Hoffnung-Garskof.

CHAPTER FOUR: UPTOWN '81

"God is smiling on you but he's frowning too / Because only God knows what you'll go through," rhymed by Melle Mel, is from a song titled "The Message," credited to Grandmaster Flash and the Furious Five and released in May 1982 on Sugar Hill Records. Check out a blurb about the origins of the song, which should have given propers to Melle Mel *and* Duke Bootee, the only people on the record. *Rolling Stone* features a blurb about the song's origins, available online at: http://www.rollingstone.com/music/lists/the-500-greatest-songs-of-all-time-20110407/grandmaster-flash-and-the-furious-five-the-message-19691231.

CHAPTER FIVE: AN AWAKENING

Bernhard Goetz, whom I occasionally still spot walking across Fourteenth Street not far from the train station where he shot four Black teens in 1984, was quite a polarizing figure until it became obvious that the guy was a colossal dick. Read Stanley Crouch's take, "The Joy of Goetz" (2003), in *New York* magazine at: http://nymag.com/nymetro/news/anniversary/35th/n_8601/. Incidentally, one of Goetz's victims, James Ramseur, died of a drug overdose and possible suicide on the twenty-seventh anniversary of the day he was shot, during the writing of this book.

To get an idea of what it was like riding New York City subways in the '80s, read Mark S. Feinman's "The New York City Transit Authority in the 1980s," available online at: http://www.nycsubway.org/articles/history-nycta1980s.html (the site is not affiliated with any official transit agency or provider, despite its name).

"The enemy could be their friend, guardian" are lyrics from Public Enemy's ferocious track "Don't Believe the Hype," from the groundbreaking album *It Takes a Nation of Millions to Hold Us Back,* released in 1988 on Def Jam Records.

CHAPTER SEVEN: *AVE MARIA, MORENA*

"She'll make the toughest homeboy / Fall deep in love" are lyrics from the song "Roni," off of Bobby Brown's "I'm A Grown-Ass Man" post–New Edition album, *Don't Be Cruel* (his debut solo album, *King of Stage,* is forgettable but came out before the aforementioned joint).

A little over two decades ago, a crew of Italian-American wild cowboys murdered Yusef Hawkins (also spelled Yusuf) in Bensonhurst. Read Sewell Chan's "The Death of Yusuf Hawkins, 20 Years Later," in the *New York Times,* available online at: http://cityroom.blogs.nytimes.com/2009/08/21/the-death-of-yusuf-hawkins -20-years-later/.

CHAPTER NINE: THERE'S NO OTHER PLACE . . .

I want to come and go as I please and continue to flow in hip-hop's inspired current without being questioned by someone who doesn't get it. I want to write like Robert Christgau and Joan Morgan and Greg Tate and Lisa Jones, all journalists whose contributions to *The Village Voice* replaced the played-out textbooks I barely cracked as a high school senior at the onset of the '90s. Nothing I read during this time hit me harder than Jones's *Voice* column "Skin Trade," parts of which she included and built on in her crazysexyfierce book *Bulletproof Diva* (Anchor, 1997). A couple of years later, Joan Morgan, who has since become a dear friend and colleague, released the groundbreaking *When Chickenheads Come Home to Roost: My Life as a Hip-Hop Feminist* (Simon & Schuster, 1999). Do a search on any of the aforementioned writers at www.villagevoice.com, and it'll be evident why I loved them so back in the day.

CHAPTER ELEVEN: TRUTH, RECONCILIATION, AND TIME MACHINES

I had the pleasure of interviewing geneticist Spencer Wells for an hour or so in the lobby at New York's Standard Hotel in the winter of 2011. I relied on the interview, as well as the information from his accessible book, titled *The Journey of Man: A Genetic Odyssey* (Random House Trade Paperbacks, 2004). Wells is currently the director of *National Geographic*'s Genographic Project, accessible online at: https:// genographic.nationalgeographic.com/.

Blaine Bettinger pens a popular blog called the Genetic Genealogist (www .thegeneticgenealogist.com.) I came across it after downloading his comprehensive eBooklet on Family Tree DNA's website, titled "I Have the Results of My Genetic Genealogy Test, Now What?" (Blaine T. Bettinger, Ph.D., 2008). If you're interested in reading the very latest news about the subject or embarking on your own genetic genealogy project, his blog is a must-bookmark. Bryan Sykes's *The Seven Daughters of Eve: The Science That Reveals Our Genetic Ancestry* (W. W. Norton & Company, 2002) is essential reading.

CHAPTER TWELVE: THINGS COME TOGETHER

More Arab- and Persian-descended Americans of my generation and younger are finding themselves in racial limbo, like their Latino counterparts. Helen Hatab Samhan contributed the chapter "Not Quite White: Race Classification and the Arab-American Experience" in the collection *Arabs in America: Building a New Future* (Temple University, 2000), which I'm told is an essential read on the subject. John Blake wrote a terrific piece about the issue for CNN called "Arab- and Persian-American Campaign: 'Check It Right' on Census" (2010), which can be found online at: http://articles.cnn.com/2010-04-01/us/census.check.it.right .campaign_1_arab-american-leaders-census-form-persian?_s=PM:US. Raja Abdulrahim wrote "Students Push UC to Expand Terms of Ethnic Identification" for the *Los Angeles Times* (2009), available online at: http://articles.latimes.com/2009/ mar/31/local/me-arab31.

CHAPTER THIRTEEN: TRIPPING IN MOROCCO

I enjoyed author and PBS host Richard Bang's *Quest for the Kasbah* (Open Road, 2009), from which I gleaned some of the historical information I used in this chapter.

I'm indebted to my travel guide, Adnane, and our trusted driver, Mounir, for all the history they shared with me about Morocco.

CHAPTER FOURTEEN: RUNNING THE *FUKÚ* DOWN

The anthology *Slaves, Subjects, and Subversives: Blacks in Colonial Latin America*, edited by Jane G. Landers and Barry M. Robinson (University of New Mexico Press, 2006), is a good source for information, including African slave laws in Hispaniola, the Senegambia region of West Africa—modern-day Guinea Bissau—and free African communities on the island. It is one of numerous sources that document Black ladinos. G. Aguirre Beltran's paper "The Rivers of Guinea," published in *The Journal of Negro History*, Vol. 31, 3:290–316 (1946), is essentially about the tribal origins of slaves in Mexico but has integral information about the Senegambia region and its relation to slaves in Santo Domingo.

"Do the Four Clades of the mtDNA Haplogroup L2 Evolve at Different Rates?," Antonio Torroni, et al. *J Hum Genet*, 2004; 69(6): 1348–1356. Full text is available online at: http://www.ncbi.nlm.nih.gov/pmc/articles/PMC1235545/citedby/makes mention of the L3 branch though focuses on the L2 haplogroup findings in 127 unrelated men from Santo Domingo and San Juan de la Maguana, Dominican Republic.

"Genetic Background of People in the Dominican Republic With or Without Obese Type 2 Diabetes Revealed by Mitochondrial DNA Polymorphism." Tajima A, et al. *J Hum Genet*, 2004; 49(9): 495–99. Available online at: http://www.ncbi .nlm.nih.gov/m/pubmed/15368103/.

CHAPTER FIFTEEN: FLASH OF THE SPIRIT
In true hip-hop fashion, I sampled the title of this chapter from my favorite Robert Farris Thompson book, *Flash of the Spirit: African & Afro-American Art & Philosophy* (Random House, 1983).

The late human rights activist and feminist Sonia Pierre fought for the rights of Haitians and Dominicans of Haitian descent on the island. She founded Movement of Dominican Women of Haitian Descent in the early 1980s. There's no room here to list all of her accomplishments and the work she's done for her community. To read more about her, watch videos, and read the latest news, visit: http://rfkcenter .org/sonia-pierre-4?lang=en.

I wrote an article for the *Village Voice* exploring the use of the N-word in the Latino hip-hop community and generation. The piece, "The N-Word Is Flourishing Among Generation Hip-Hop Latinos" (2008), can be viewed at: http:// www.villagevoice.com/2008-10-22/music/the-n-word-is-flourishing-among -generation-hip-hop-latinos/.

It was folklorist and City Lore founder Steve Zeitlin who first turned me on to Jan Rodrigues, also known as Juan Rodrigues. Zeitlin also introduced me to the author Steven H. Jaffe, who put me on to some sources. A number of books briefly tell Juan Rodrigues's story. One is Graham Russell Hodges's *Root & Branch: African Americans in New York and East Jersey, 1613–1863* (University of North Carolina Press, 1999), in which pages 6 and 7 are really good. Page 318 in *Unearthing Gotham: The Archaeology of New York City* (Yale University Press, 2001), coauthored by Anne-Marie Cantwell and Diana diZerega Wall, contains biographical information on Rodrigues. The book *Gotham: A History of New York City to 1898 (The History of New York City)* (Oxford University Press, USA, 2000), by Edwin G. Burrows and Mike Wallace, mentions Jan Rodrigues on page 19. *In the Shadow of Slavery: African Americans in New York City, 1626–1863* (University of Chicago Press, 2004), by Leslie M. Harris, mentions Rodrigues on pages 12 and 13. Simon Hart, *The Prehistory of the New Netherland Company: Amsterdam Notarial Records of the First Dutch Voyages* (City of Amsterdam Press, 1959), notes "the presence of the mulatto Jan Rodrigues, of San Domingo" on the island of Manhattan. Rodrigues's ethnicity has been taken away on occasion, including in Ira Berlin and Leslie Harris's *Slavery in New York* (The New Press, 2005), which just lists him as solely "Black" on page 34. The primary source from which all of Juan Rodrigues's biographical information is culled, the New Netherland Institute's Charles T. Gehring tells me, can be found in Simon Hart's *The Prehistory of the New Netherland Company, Amsterdam Notarial Records of the First Dutch Voyages to the Hudson* (City of Amsterdam, 1959). There's a plaque in Riverside Park recognizing Rodrigues as the first merchant and non-Native-American inhabitant of Manhattan.

The Columbian Exchange is mentioned in Charles Mann's epic *1493: Uncovering the New World Columbus Created* (Knopf, 2011), citing a term that historian Alfred W. Crosby coined to describe what happened to previously separated eco-systems after Columbus. On page 11, Mann writes about the dramatic impact that the Columbian Exchange had on humankind by citing Hispaniola, or modern-day Dominican Republic, as an example. *1493* is one of the sources I use for information on La Isabela in 1494 and La Navidad.

The term "hanky-panky," someone on the island hipped me to, is the Dominican equivalent of Jamaica's "rent-a-dread," in which local men rent themselves out to mostly white European and American tourists in exchange for romance and/or sex and attention.

The 21 percent unemployment rate for young men between the ages of fifteen to twenty-four comes from the CIA's World Factbook, available online at: https://www.cia.gov/library/publications/the-world-factbook/geos/dr.html.

The 1950s study I cited is from late researcher José de Jesús Alvarez Perelló's paper "La Mezcla de Razas en Santo Domingo y Los Factores Sanguineos (*EME EME*)," Vol. 2, No. 8 (Sept.–Oct. 1973).

Arlin Feliciano Vélez's paper *Genetic Prints of Amerindian Female Migrations Through Genetic Prints of Amerindian Female Migrations Through the Caribbean Revealed by Control Sequences from Dominican Haplogroup A Mitochondrial DNAs* (University of Puerto Rico, 2006) suggests the presence of nine lineages: six possibly Native and three of recent, probably post-Hispanic origin.

CHAPTER SIXTEEN: SHE WHO WALKS BEHIND ME

The material from Lynne Guitar's story comes mostly from my interview with her in 2011. At the time she was devoted to educating her students about Taíno history and to retention as director at the Council on International Educational Exchange (CIEE) at the Pontificia Universidad Católica Madre y Maestra, based in Santiago de los Caballeros. Her paper "Documenting the Myth of Taíno Extinction," in *Kacike: Journal of Caribbean Amerindian History and Anthropology* (2002), is required reading, as is "What *Really* Happened at Santo Cerro? Origin of the Legend of the *Virgin de las Mercedes*" in *Issues in Caribbean Amerindian Studies* (*Occasional Papers of the Caribbean Amerindian Centrelink*), Vol. 3 (2001–2002).

Dr. Fernando Luna Calderón wrote "Mitochondrial DNA in the Dominican Republic" in the *Kacike: The Journal of Caribbean Amerindian History and Anthropology* (2002) (online journal), special issue, Lynne Guitar, Ed., available online at: http://www.kacike.org/CalderonEnglish.pdf.

Elizabeth M. Grieco and Rachel C. Cassidy coauthored *Overview of Race and Hispanic Origin: 2000* as part of "2000 Census Briefs" (March 2001; available online at: http://www.census.gov/prod/2001pubs/c2kbr01-1.pdf).

CHAPTER SEVENTEEN: PARADISE GONE

Jacobo Majluta Azar was veep of the Dominican Republic from 1978 to 1982. He was president for forty-two days after Antonio Guzmán committed suicide.

Bartolomé de las Casas owned slaves until 1544, wrote David Brion Davis in *Inhuman Bondage: The Rise and Fall of Slavery in the New World* (Oxford University Press, 2008), pages 354–55.

Frank Moya Pons is inarguably a walking encyclopedia of Dominican and Caribbean history. He is the author of many books and papers on the subject. Here are a few of his writings I leaned on when sourcing Dominican history in this chapter: *The Dominican Republic: A National History* (New York: Hispaniola Books, 1995), *History of the Caribbean: Plantations, Trade, and War in the Atlantic World* (Princeton: Markus Wiener Publishers, 2007), and *La Otra Historia Dominicana* (Santo Domingo: Librería La Trinitaria, 2008). Moya Pons's paper "A Mulatto Nation: Notes on the Racial Evolution of the Dominican Republic" (Academia Dominicana de la Historia, 2011) was also helpful, as is "Dominican National Identity and Return Migration," *Occasional Papers of the Center for Latin American Studies*, No. 1 (Gainesville: University of Florida, 1982).

The rebellion on Diego Columbus and Melchor de Castro's sugar plantation is mentioned in the writings of Moya Pons and other books. I cited Eduardo Galeano's *Open Veins of Latin America* (Monthly Review Press; Twenty-fifth Anniversary Edition, 1997), page 83.

I learned about the passing of Law 391 in September 1943 in an awesome read by Silvio Torres-Saillant titled "The Tribulations of Blackness: Stages in Dominican Racial Identity," from *Latin American Perspectives* 25:3 (May 1998).

I emphasized the word "perceived" because when Trujillo's was in power, it would have made sense that what his goons were witnessing wasn't a pure African spiritual expression but a mixture of African and Indigenous religious practices. African and Indigenous peoples lived together in runaway slave communities, so the fusion, like our own racial makeup, is a natural consequence of this mixing.

Ginetta E. B. Candelario wrote an excellent book called *Black Behind the Ears: Dominican Racial Identity from Museums to Beauty Shops* (Duke University Press Books, 2007). It's a good point of departure to discuss racial identity in our community. I found the chapter titled "It Is Said That Haiti Is Getting Blacker and Blacker: Traveling Narratives of Dominican Identity" particularly useful when referring to how Dominicans were painted as white in relation to Haitians by American statesmen, journalists, and travel writers.

There are least thirty-two hundred Taíno words in the Dominican and Caribbean Spanish lexicon. Emiliano Tejera's book *Palabras Indígenas de la Isla de Santo Domingo* (Editora del Caribe, 1951), Dr. Cayetano Coll y Toste's *Prehistoria de Puerto Rico* (CreateSpace, 2011), Nicolás Fort y Roldan's *Cuba Indígena* (R. Moreno and R. Rojas, 1881), and Manuel Álvarez Nazario's *El Influjo Indígena en el Español de Puerto Rico* (Editorial Universitaria, Universidad de Puerto Rico, 1977) are several dictionaries and sources detailing Taíno retention in our Spanish-based Creole. Some American English words influenced by the Taíno language are: barbecue (*barbacoa*), hammock (*hamaca*), tobacco (*tabaku*), guava (*guayaba*), potato (*batata*), and savannah (*sabana*), to name just a few.

Speaking of *pajonasos*—or untrained, wild, and worse, not fried straight—hair: Kimberly Eison Simmons is the president of the Association of Black Anthropologists and associate professor of anthropology and African-American studies at

University of South Carolina. I dig her accessible and balanced book *Reconstructing Racial Identity and the African Past in the Dominican Republic* (University Press of Florida, 2011), especially for the clear parallels she draws between Black-American and Dominican culture and the differences between "denying" and "hiding" one's blackness on pages 2 through 4.

CHAPTER EIGHTEEN: BECOMING LATINA

CNN originally reported on the elderly woman in Azle, Texas, titled "Racist Sign Targets Hispanics" in 2009. It's available online at: http://cnn.com/video/data/2.0/video/us/2009/07/24/hispanics.keep.out.WFAA.html.

To read more about the resurgence of the antigovernment "patriot" movement, visit http://www.splcenter.org/get-informed/intelligence-files/ideology/patriot-movement, and for the weird wild world of the sovereign citizens' movement, check out http://www.splcenter.org/get-informed/intelligence-files/ideology/sovereign-citizens-movement.

Every Tuesday afternoon in the museum's rotunda, Jorge Estevez gives these spirited talks about Taíno artifacts and history. If you find yourself in New York City, it's a worthwhile trek to the National Museum of the American Indian, on Bowling Green, to check him out. Visit http://nmai.si.edu for more information. Tell him I sent you. Estevez is quoted in an interesting article by Robert M. Poole titled "What Became of the Taíno?," published in *Smithsonian* magazine (October 2011; available online at: http://www.smithsonianmag.com/people-places/What-Became-of-the-Taino.html).

Amy Green wrote a wonderful article titled "Some US Hispanics Trace Their Jewish Past" for the *Christian Science Monitor,* about a Latina who discovers her Sephardic Jewish roots through ancestral DNA testing (December 2008; available online at: http://www.csmonitor.com/USA/Society/2008/1229/p03s05-ussc.html).

Rav DovBer Pinson is a world-renowned scholar, author of more than a dozen books and booklets, a Kabbalist, and a master of both the revealed and hidden aspects of Torah. I'm forever grateful to him for fitting me into his crazy-busy schedule for the interview from which his section is sourced. His book *Jewish Wisdom on the Afterlife: The Mysteries, The Myths, and the Meaning* (Q&A Books, 2006) is required reading to learn more about *gilgul neshamot.* Rav DovBer Pinson heads the IYYUN Center: www.iyyun.com.

INDEX

CPSIA information can be obtained
at www.ICGtesting.com
Printed in the USA
JSHW030157250723
45345JS00012B/48